MISUNDERESTIMATED

ALSO BY BILL SAMMON

Fighting Back: The War on Terrorism from Inside the Bush White House

At Any Cost: How Al Gore Tried to Steal the Election

MISUNDERESTIMATED

THE PRESIDENT BATTLES TERRORISM, JOHN KERRY, AND THE BUSH HATERS

BILL SAMMON

1☉ ReganBooks
Celebrating Ten Bestselling Years
An Imprint of HarperCollins*Publishers*

HarperCollins books may be purchased for educational, business, or sales promotional use. For information please write: Special Markets Department, HarperCollins Publishers Inc., 10 East 53rd Street, New York, NY 10022.

FIRST EDITION

Designed by Erin Benach

Printed on acid-free paper

Library of Congress Cataloging-in-Publication Data

Sammon, Bill.
    Misunderestimated : the president battles terrorism, John Kerry, and the Bush haters / Bill Sammon.—1st ed.
    p. cm.
    Includes index.
    ISBN 0-06-072383-1
    1. Bush, George W. (George Walker), 1946—Public opinion.   2. Bush, George W. (George Walker), 1946—Military leadership.   3. Bush, George W. (George Walker), 1946—Relations with journalists.   4. United States—Politics and government—2001—   5. United States—Foreign relations—2001—   6. War on Terrorism, 2001—   7. Public opinion—United States.   8. Press and politics—United States.   I. Title.

E903.3.S36 2004
973.931'092—dc22

                                                                          2004046706

04   05   06   07   08   WBC/QW   10   9   8   7   6   5   4   3   2   1

For those who served

"They misunderestimated me."

—George W. Bush, November 6, 2000

CONTENTS

1
RISE OF THE BUSH HATERS

GEORGE W. BUSH STARED out the window of his limousine at the largest protest of his presidency. A thousand angry demonstrators—maybe more—were rampaging through the streets of Portland, Oregon, utterly overwhelming the meager contingent of police trying to restore order. The motorcade was headed directly into a melee so chaotic that the Secret Service could no longer guarantee the president's safety. Indeed, three minutes before Bush's limousine was supposed to make its final approach to the hotel, police lost control of Taylor Street altogether. They radioed the Secret Service, frantically directing the motorcade to a secondary route. Furious, the agents swung the president south and tried another approach. But the sophisticated protesters, using scouts with cell phones, got wind of Plan B. They rushed to head off Bush before he could penetrate the barricades surrounding the Hilton. Street cops joined in the footrace, hoping to prevent a calamity at Sixth Avenue. The president suddenly understood why his father had nicknamed this city "Little Beirut."

More than anything, the younger Bush was struck by the virulence of the demonstrators. Although he was accustomed to encountering protests in almost every city he visited, most were perfunctory, half-hearted affairs, largely overshadowed by crowds of exuberant support-ers. One almost felt sorry for the protesters, as if they were committing some unfortunate social gaffe. But these Portland protest-ers were different. They were seething with, well, *hatred*—there was no other word for it. Bush could see it in their contorted faces as they lunged toward the limousine, shrieking at the top of their lungs and extending their middle fingers. They jabbed placards that bore the most vulgar epithets imaginable. An attractive young woman with dark hair and sunglasses was brandishing a large sign that read BUSH: BASTARD CHILD OF THE SUPREME COURT. When she lifted it over her head with both arms, her sleeveless white T-shirt rode up to expose a swath of bare midriff above her low-slung jeans. The "belly shirt" was emblazoned with big black letters that spelled out the words F--- BUSH. The protestors seemed to take delight in such in-your-face vulgarity. One of them held a large photograph that had been doctored to depict a gun barrel pressed against the president's temple. Another waved a sign declaring, BUSH: WANTED, DEAD OR ALIVE, with an X over the word "alive." It was hard to avoid the conclusion that at least some of the protesters would have welcomed an assassination attempt. So much for reasoned political discourse. Meanwhile, a man hoisted an enormous placard that bizarrely proclaimed: IMPEACH THE COURT-APPOINTED JUNTA AND THE FASCIST, EGOMANIACAL, BLOOD-SWILLING BEAST! Bush had seen signs in other cities calling him an idiot, a liar, even "commander in thief," but never "a blood-swilling beast." This was getting downright ugly.

The president began to have second thoughts about the venue for tonight's event, a fund-raiser for Oregon senator Gordon Smith. Why did it have to be held in the heart of the city, where the protesters were obviously harder to control? In fact, Portland police had warned the

Secret Service and the White House advance team to expect trouble. They cautioned that the centrally located Hilton would be exceedingly difficult to defend against the hordes of protesters who were certain to descend on downtown. They recommended that the fund-raiser be moved a few blocks north, to the Benson Hotel, where access would be easier to control. When White House officials refused to budge from the Hilton, police asked them to at least reconsider their plans to keep the president there overnight. It would be much safer to get him out of the central city, perhaps to the outlying home of a wealthy supporter. Yet the president's handlers had dismissed the local cops as excitable yokels with overactive imaginations. They insisted on bringing Bush to the Hilton and keeping him there overnight. And now those same handlers were shocked by the size and severity of the protest. The unthinkable had happened—*the motorcade route had been lost!*

The president's limousine was now on the secondary route, making its final approach to the Hilton. But protesters had already arrived from the original route and were spoiling for a fight. Worse yet, there were hardly any cops to hold them back.

"That's him!" shouted one of ringleaders.

Several hooligans rushed the line of security vehicles that preceded Bush's limousine—two police motorcycles, a white police cruiser, and a black Chevy Suburban full of Secret Service agents. They brazenly darted across the street between these speeding vehicles. One man, dressed all in black, sprinted directly in front of the president's limousine, coming within a few feet of the leader of the free world. The rest of the mob pressed in from both sides of the street and let out a rolling *"Booooooooooooo!"* as the president passed. Although Sixth Avenue was a major bus thoroughfare, the local transit authority had closed it off with an abundance of orange traffic cones. Bush's limousine barreled right over the rubber cones, which thumped angrily against the undercarriage. Further slowing the motorcade were the protesters themselves, who continued to pour into the street and gesticulate with their vitriolic placards.

9/11, read one. YOU LET IT HAPPEN, SHRUB.

BUSH KNEW, shrieked another, quoting the infamous newspaper headline Senator Hillary Rodham Clinton had brandished on the floor of the U.S. Senate three months earlier.

Of all the insults hurled at Bush that day, he considered these the most profane. To suggest that he, the commander in chief, was somehow responsible for the deaths of 3,000 innocent civilians in New York, Washington, and Pennsylvania—the biggest mass murder in the history of the United States—was nothing short of monstrous. Everyone knew the attacks were perpetrated by Osama bin Laden and his al Qaeda terrorist network. Virtually the entire civilized world had united behind America's swift and righteous routing of Afghanistan's repressive Taliban regime, which sheltered al Qaeda. And yet these protesters were now blaming the whole thing on Bush.

The president could see that not all the placards were ad hominem attacks. Some, like the sign that admonished CREATE JOBS, NOT BOMBS, addressed the lackluster performance of the economy. Fair enough. The unemployment rate had risen from 4.1 to 5.8 percent since Bush took office. The federal budget had gone from a surplus of $124 billion to a deficit of at least $165 billion. And the stock market had recently sunk even lower than it had in the immediate aftermath of September 11. During a dozen business days in July alone, the Dow Jones Industrial Average lost a staggering 1,677 points—more than a sixth of its value. Although 1,255 of those points had been recovered in the ensuing month, the market remained deeply shaken. Not that these protesters were exactly rooting for the stock market. For crying out loud, some were carrying banners that counseled: COMPOST CAPITALISM.

The Secret Service was really sweating bullets now. There weren't enough police along the secondary route to cordon off the crowd. Wild-eyed protesters were approaching the motorcade from all directions; some coming within a few feet of the leader of the free world.

F--- YOU, MOTHERF---ER! declared one sign, with a picture of Bush's face. Another read CHRISTIAN FASCISM, with a swastika in place of the letter "S" in each word. A third urged motorists to HONK IF YOU HATE BUSH. Such extravagant mean-spiritedness! Such gleeful derision! All raining down on the commander in chief as his limousine clumped awkwardly over the orange traffic cones.

Although most of the protesters looked too young to remember much about politics from a decade earlier, they seemed determined to remind Bush of his father's presidency. One man had duct-taped a sign to his chest with the salutation, WELCOME TO LITTLE BEIRUT. A woman in frizzy pigtails and a black tank top waved a bright yellow sign that said: HEY! AVENGE YOUR FATHER ON YOUR OWN TIME! It was a reference, of course, to Iraq. Eleven years earlier, President George H.W. Bush had driven the Iraqi army out of Kuwait, only to stop short of ousting Saddam Hussein from Baghdad. "He cut and run early," his son told me in a series of interviews in the Oval Office. That act of presidential restraint was not, alas, reciprocated. In 1993, Saddam tried to have the elder Bush assassinated during a visit to Kuwait.

Now the younger Bush was mulling whether to rid the world of this brutal dictator once and for all. The thought had been growing for nearly a year.

"The world changed for me on September 11, to the point where every threat then had to be reexamined," Bush told me. "My presidency changed. I went from a peace president to a war president."

In the immediate aftermath of the attacks, some of Bush's advisers, including Deputy Defense Secretary Paul Wolfowitz, had urged him to strike both Osama bin Laden and Saddam simultaneously.

"I said no, let's do something well first. Let's first focus on achieving our objective in Afghanistan. We must destroy the al Qaeda bases and remove the Taliban," Bush told me. "My theory is that in order to do hard jobs, you must stay focused. You don't want to try to do too many things at one time."

But after destroying the Taliban, the president didn't want to lose momentum. As far as he was concerned, Afghanistan was merely one battle in an epic war that had begun on September 11. He viewed Iraq, Iran, and North Korea as the next batch of threats, branding them as an "axis of evil" during his State of the Union address in January 2002.

"Eventually, obviously, Afghanistan settled down," he said. "Iraq started getting into focus as we began to think about other theaters in the world. Where were we vulnerable? Where could we be hurt?"

Bush was particularly worried about Saddam's well-documented efforts to develop chemical, biological, and nuclear weapons. He fretted that terrorists would obtain such weapons from "this madman who hated America." But the old Cold War strategies of containment and deterrence seemed of little use in confronting this new threat.

"Deterrence—the promise of massive retaliation against nations—means nothing against shadowy terrorist networks with no nation or citizens to defend," Bush had said in a seminal speech at West Point on June 1. "Containment is not possible when unbalanced dictators with weapons of mass destruction can deliver those weapons on missiles or secretly provide them to terrorist allies." He added: "The war on terror will not be won on the defensive. We must take the battle to the enemy, disrupt his plans, and confront the worst threats before they emerge. In the world we have entered, the only path to safety is the path of action. And this nation will act."

This muscular new foreign policy, dubbed "preemption," was spelled out in the National Security Strategy drafted that summer by the president's most trusted foreign policy aide, National Security Adviser Condoleezza Rice. By articulating this profound change in U.S. foreign policy at West Point, Bush was laying the foundation for war against Iraq.

"Our security will require all Americans to be forward-looking and resolute, to be ready for preemptive action when necessary to defend our liberty and to defend our lives," he told the cheering cadets.

The president's preparations for war didn't end at West Point. By late summer, he had quietly given tentative approval to a preliminary battle plan that included such specifics as deploying troops to Turkey for a northern front against Iraq.

Speaking of battlefields, that's exactly what Portland looked like from the window of Bush's limousine. One of the protesters actually hurled a rock that bounced off the windshield of a car in the presidential motorcade. The vehicle, which was behind Bush's limousine, was packed with his most trusted advisers—counselor Karen Hughes, chief political strategist Karl Rove, and White House Press Secretary Ari Fleischer. The aides were startled by the noise and stunned by the security breach. None of them had experienced anything like this. As the motorcade struggled down the home stretch, one particularly audacious protester lunged forward and pounded his fist on the "package"—White House parlance for the presidential limousine. The Secret Service couldn't believe it. This was an even more grievous breach of security than a rock striking the presidential motorcade. Granted, the limousine was heavily armored. But if protesters managed to somehow stop and surround the package, all bets were off. Agents would have no choice but to use lethal force in order to protect the president. And to think the Portland police had warned them about just such a meltdown.

Instead of reproaching themselves for not heeding that warning, though, the Secret Service officials turned their wrath against the cops. As soon as the motorcade finally limped inside the bicycle-rack barricades and disgorged the president into the Hilton, the agents vented their anger at Assistant Portland Police Chief Greg Clark, who was in charge of security for the fund-raiser. *How could you lose the motorcade route? How could you let a protester get close enough to lay a hand on the package? What if he had been carrying a plastic explosive like C4?*

"The Secret Service agents got pretty upset with me," said Clark, who rode in the presidential motorcade. "But they were warned. Oh, they were warned in spades. We knew things were gonna go south and we told everybody, including the Secret Service and the White House staff, that this was gonna be a bad deal. We had previous interaction with the protesters, so we knew we were gonna go to war with them. But I just don't think the White House handlers chose to take us seriously. I'll bet they'll believe it in the future."

Bush was escorted to the twenty-second floor of the Hilton to freshen up before his meetings. Stepping from the elevator, he entered a hallway with a door at either end. One was labeled "Governor's Suite" and the other "Presidential Suite." Bush headed for the latter, unaware that the signs had been switched just before his arrival. The White House advance team had scouted both rooms and chosen the Governor's Suite for security reasons. But they didn't want the president to think he would be staying in the hotel's second-best room. So they arranged for a maintenance worker to unscrew the signs and reverse them, perpetrating a small fraud on the most powerful person in the world.

At length, the president emerged from his fraudulent suite and headed down to a first-floor banquet room to meet with a handful of business leaders. He went around the table, asking each person for ideas on how best to stimulate the economy, which was particularly sluggish in the Pacific Northwest. Bush listened politely as each leader responded, although it was obvious that everyone was distracted by the persistent noise of the protesters. The police had erected the barricades just 100 feet from the hotel in hopes that the demonstrators would be less disruptive if they could at least see the building where Bush was staying. But the strategy was backfiring. Emboldened by their proximity to such power, the protesters turned up the volume accordingly. They chanted, sang, and hollered at the top of their lungs. There was even an organized drum line. Half a dozen skilled drummers were outfitted with snare and bass drums of the sort used by college marching bands. In the center of each drum skin was a picture of the president's face, surrounded by the words BEAT BACK BUSH'S WAR. The drummers slammed their mallets directly into the presidential visage, thwacking away in perfect unison and sending up a terrific racket. The drumbeat could be clearly heard through the windows of the conference room, although neither Bush nor any of the business leaders mentioned it during their meeting.

Afterward, the president retreated to the relative serenity of his suite to prepare for the upcoming fund-raiser. And yet even from the twenty-second floor he could see the protesters on the streets below. There were now perhaps 1,500 of them, and they seemed even angrier than when Bush had first arrived. Indeed, the sight of the president slipping into the hotel had energized the demonstrators, who ended up taking out their frustration on anyone who happened to have the singular misfortune of venturing too close to the Portland Hilton on August 22, 2002. Some poor commuter trying to drive home after work suddenly found his sport utility vehicle surrounded by the raging mob. Appalled by this bystander's mode of transportation—a gas-guzzling SUV, the very symbol of America's wretched excess—the protesters began rocking it from side to side. Fearful that he would be tipped over, the terrified motorist threw it in reverse and began backing up through the crowd.

Meanwhile, the same police officers who had failed to secure the primary and secondary motorcade routes were now needed inside the perimeter to help bolster the barricades. But in order to hold back the crowd from the inside, they first had to wade through it from the outside. Demonstrators interpreted this movement as retreat, which only excited them more. They began hurling bottles, boards, and crumpled traffic cones at the cops. Some officers had to endure the indignity of being pelted by vegetables. *What kind of protesters packed their own produce?* The police tried to move through the crowd in a methodical fashion, hoping this would convey authoritativeness. But it was no use. Far from being intimidated, the protesters began taunting and even shoving the cops. Suddenly the only thing that mattered to the officers was to reach the safety of the barricades. To hell with dignity; they could nurse their wounded pride later. Right now their all-consuming imperative could be summed up in one word: *Retreat!*

Things only got worse, however, when the reinforcements finally straggled through the perimeter. Officers were getting intelligence reports that agitators were attempting to rally hardcore groups of protesters to break through the barricades. Sure enough, pockets of demonstrators were probing for weak spots in the 360-degree perimeter. They prowled in a counterclockwise direction, forcing police to match their movements from inside the barricades. The most concerted foray came at Fifth and Taylor, where the Secret Service had erected a checkpoint. The crowd was defiantly pushing against the bicycle racks, despite police orders to back away. While the frontline protesters were going toe-to-toe with police in riot gear, backbenchers were taking advantage of the confusion by chucking projectiles overhead. An orange cone sailed deep inside the barricades and landed on a cop. The Secret Service became increasingly alarmed. If the protesters managed to breach the perimeter, the situation would become grave. It was only 100 feet to the Hilton, where the president himself was staying. If even a small number of protesters made a desperate dash for the hotel entrance, Secret Service agents and police would almost certainly be forced to draw their weapons and fire.

The barricades were little more than a fragile line of demarcation between two starkly contrasting worlds. On one side stood the police, decked out in ominous black riot gear from head to toe. They had the unmistakable aura of futuristic storm-troopers. On the other side were the protesters, trying hard to look like hippies from the 1960s. They were a colorful mass of T-shirts and jeans, do-rags and dreadlocks.

The storm troopers used bullhorns to bark dispersal orders at the hippies. But after fifteen minutes, no one had budged an inch. The cops tried pushing the protesters back from the barricades. Instead of retreating, the demonstrators locked arms and advanced. A female police officer was knocked to the street, badly injuring her wrist. Her colleagues responded by donning rubber gloves and breaking out the pepper spray. The stuff came in red canisters shaped like miniature fire extinguishers. Police pointed the canisters at the crowd and pushed down on the black plastic levers, unleashing great streams of the burning, noxious fluid. The canisters were only about the size of one-liter bottles, but they packed a tremendous punch. The liquid stayed in a narrow trajectory for six or eight feet, then fanned out gradually into a spray that found its way directly into the eyes and noses of protesters. Journalists who were too close to the action also got a snootful of the stuff. The afflicted clawed at their eyes or belatedly pulled bandannas over their noses as they fell back, temporarily blinded by the overpowering chemical.

Meanwhile, wealthy Republicans were beginning to show up for the Smith fund-raiser, only to find that police had failed to clear a corridor for them. The impeccably dressed guests were forced to run a gauntlet of jostling, jeering, spitting protesters. Kevin Mannix, the Republican candidate for governor in Oregon, tried to lead his wife, Susanna, through the roiling crowd. Since the streets were jammed, the candidate and his wife had snake their way single-file through a narrow opening on the sidewalk as protesters along the curb screamed obscenities at them. Suddenly, a bearded demonstrator with dark hair stepped directly in front of Mannix, blocking his path. Mannix moved to the right in an attempt to skirt the man, who merely shifted to block him again. Mannix went left, but the man mirrored his movement like a bully in a schoolyard taunt. The protester remained silent, an expression of pure menace plastered across his face.

"Look," Mannix warned, "I am coming through here."

He headed to his right again, but the man shifted once more. Exasperated, Mannix—a widely recognizable gubernatorial candidate—

grabbed hold of the protester and shoved him aside, leading his wife deeper into the scrum.

In fact, all over downtown Portland tiny groups of Republicans were bunching together for protection as they waded fearfully into the mob for the perilous trek to the hotel. Frank Dulcich, the president and CEO of Pacific Seafood Group, was worried about the safety of his seventy-five-year-old father, Dominic, as well as an acquaintance's wife. The woman's red dress, though tasteful, seemed to incite the crowd even more than the men's business suits.

"Slut!" shrieked on protester.

"Whore!" wailed another.

"Fascists!" hollered a third.

Dulcich, who had lived in Portland most of his life, suddenly experienced an emotion that was utterly foreign to him—civic embarrassment. Upstanding citizens—including many who had no connection to the GOP fund-raiser—were being cursed, spat upon, and jostled simply for wearing business clothes. It was appalling.

Suddenly Dulcich noticed that his face was wet. An unidentifiable liquid was dripping off his cheeks onto his collar and suit coat. In an instant he turned and saw the culprit—a man with an empty cup and mocking grin, standing between two masked figures. Reflexively, Dulcich flew at his tormentor, shoving him hard.

"This is bullshit," Dulcich seethed. "If you want to debate politics, let's debate politics. But what you're doing is just totally uncalled for."

The two masked men stepped forward, as four or five more encircled Dulcich from behind. They had no way of knowing that this CEO was also a black belt.

"If you guys wanna get physical, I don't mind," Dulcich allowed. "I can handle myself. But let's take this incident and move it away from everything, 'cause I don't wanna get arrested."

"Hey, that's cool," mumbled one of the protesters from behind his mask.

Suddenly the entire crowd surged forward, pushing Dulcich to within twenty feet of the barricades. The next thing he knew, the masked men were gone. But so were his father and the Republican woman. Dulcich frantically searched the crowd, even climbing a light post for a glimpse of his dad's white hair or the woman's red dress. But they were nowhere to be found. Gripped by fear and panic, the CEO of the fifth largest seafood company in the nation leapt to the sidewalk and began zigzagging through the mob, desperately trying to find the people he was supposed to be protecting.

Dulcich's father was not the only seventy-five-year-old Republican who became separated from a loved one in the confusion. Donald Tykeson, a balding grandfather with multiple sclerosis, was trying to make his way to the Hilton in a motorized wheelchair when he realized his wife was no longer behind him. Clad in a light gray suit, the mild-mannered millionaire headed directly into the heart of the melee. He was stopped by a man wearing a baseball cap and a cloth mask over his face. Only the eyes and nose of the protester were visible.

"Where *you* goin'?" demanded the thirtyish man.

"I'm going to the reception," Tykeson replied. "To see the president."

"Well," the man taunted, "I'm not gonna let you pass."

Tykeson couldn't very well get into a fistfight with this swaggering six-footer. "I really need to go," Tykeson said in the most reasonable voice he could muster. "It shouldn't be a bother to you."

He started forward with his wheelchair, but the protester quickly moved to block him. Tykeson again tried to reason with the thug.

"You know, if you were in my shoes and I were in yours, I'd let you pass," the old-timer offered.

But this oaf was a monolith, utterly immovable. Tykeson tried in vain to appeal to his sense of fairness. He pointed out that many of the demonstrators were accusing Bush and Attorney General John

Ashcroft of curbing civil rights. Surely the protester didn't want to take away Tykeson's right to free assembly.

"If you believe in these ideas," he pleaded, "then I should be allowed to pass."

It was like talking to a wall. Tykeson was beginning to worry whether his wife was being similarly harassed. Ultimately, it took the intervention of another demonstrator to convince the bully to stop tormenting the crippled grandfather in the wheelchair.

Trying not to appear rattled, Tykeson pushed deeper into the crowd. He puttered through the perilous streets between police and protesters as streams of obscenities and pepper spray arced directly above his balding head. He breathed in some of the pepper spray, which seemed to drop like a rock straight to the bottom of his lungs. Suddenly he understood the chemical's debilitating effectiveness. To think he was shelling out $2,000 for the privilege of being bullied and pepper-sprayed on the teeming streets of Little Beirut!

At least Tykeson made it through the barricades on his own; that was more than some donors could claim. A number of them simply became stranded in the mob.

"How in the world am I supposed to get over there?" said one donor, pointing helplessly across the mob toward the Hilton. A cop in riot gear shrugged. He already had his hands full.

Some donors frantically called the Hilton on their cell phones. The hotel's director of security, positioned inside the barricades, searched the crowd for frightened faces and then directed police to go out and rescue these disheveled and deeply shaken Republicans.

By the time the president came back downstairs to give his speech at the fund-raiser, a full-fledged riot was going on outside. In addition to the incessant drumming, people were pounding lustily on the plate glass windows of downtown businesses that had been forced to close early because of the mayhem. The din could be heard in the ballroom as Bush stood backstage, preparing to address the shell-shocked donors. The noise evidently rattled one of the president's aides, who prematurely pushed the button on a sound system that began blaring "Hail to the Chief." Bush shot a disapproving look at the aide, who fumbled with the machine for a moment before cutting off the music. When the proper moment finally arrived, the anthem was restarted and the president emerged to take the lectern.

"It's great to be back in this beautiful state," he managed, as if unable to think of anything nice to say about Portland itself. "I am honored to end my day here in Oregon by urging the people of this state—the good people of this state—to send this good man, Gordon Smith, back to the United States Senate."

After all, that's why Bush was here, wasn't it? To try and get Republicans like Smith elected in November. The midterm election was less than eleven weeks away and by all historical precedents, Bush's party was supposed to take a shellacking. The last president in this position—Bill Clinton—lost both the House and Senate to the opposition in his first midterm. It was the most devastating wipeout in half a century. Nine Senate seats! Fifty-four House seats! The GOP's gains were so spectacular that they called it the Republican Revolution of 1994. The ascension of Newt Gingrich as Speaker of the House had made it infinitely more difficult for Clinton to enact his agenda.

Bush could only imagine what his first midterm would come to be called. The Republican Rollback? The Democratic Comeback? He was already being blamed for losing control of the Senate in May 2001, when Senator James Jeffords of Vermont deserted the GOP. That had given control to Democrats just four months into the Bush presidency. If history was any yardstick, the GOP would lose even more Senate seats in 2002 and fail to stop Democrats from gaining the six seats they needed to retake the House. Ever since World War II, presidents had lost an average of two to three Senate seats and a whopping twenty-four House seats in their first midterms. No president during that period had actually gained seats in the House. The last president to actually pick up seats in both houses of Congress during a midterm was Franklin Roosevelt, way back in 1934. Political pros weren't exactly counting on George W. Bush to become the first president in sixty-eight years to pull off that feat.

Nonetheless, Bush had resolved months earlier to campaign ferociously for the GOP. He was in the midst of visiting dozens of states and raising over $100 million for House and Senate candidates, not to mention gubernatorial hopefuls. He even inserted himself directly into Republican primaries, a dicey move for any sitting president. Bush's go-for-broke strategy was called "arrogant at best, foolhardy at worst," by *Time* magazine, which expressed astonishment that the president would put all his political capital "on the line like a Vegas gambler." The *New York Times* warned: "Bush has now irrevocably tied his prestige to the outcome of these elections and runs the risk of a bad outcome being interpreted as a judgment by voters on his policies." The *Washington Post* summed up the conventional wisdom by noting that there was "nothing smart about a president going into several dozen extremely close House, Senate, and gubernatorial races to campaign with potential losers. A sophisticated politician would know better than to risk it. He could be blamed for bad outcomes." Indeed, Bush was well aware that he would look foolish if he squandered his prestige on losing candidates. The press would have a field day. But he figured the alternative was even worse. A Democratic Congress would be all too eager to kill the Republican president's agenda. Better to avoid that fate, regardless of risk. So Bush barnstormed the nation like a man possessed.

"Turn out the vote," he implored the Smith supporters. "Go to your places of worship, go to your community centers, and remind the people of this state that you've got a good, honorable, decent man in Gordon Smith.

"And I want the message to go to friend and foe alike: We're in this deal for the long haul," Bush added, transitioning unapologetically to the war on terror. "See, this is our freedom at stake. History has called this nation into action. History has put the spotlight on the great beacon of freedom. And we're not going to blink. We're going to be a steady, patient, determined nation."

Bush was indeed determined to make this election about the war. That's why he went from talking about a "good, honorable, decent" candidate in one breath to a "steady, patient, determined" nation in the next. Instead of letting the disparate races around the country devolve into the sort of local politics that usually determined winners and losers, the president was striving to nationalize the election. In the process, he was making the contest into a referendum on himself. But there was a potential down side. If the Republicans took a trouncing in the midterms, Bush would get the blame.

"We cannot let terrorists get the upper hand, and we won't," he thundered, warming to his theme of moral clarity. He vowed—in his fractured but forceful stump syntax—that America would achieve peace only by making clear "the difference between good and the difference between evil."

The donors applauded, evidently beginning to forget the trauma they had endured to get there. Outside, though, the protesters were still trying mightily to break through the barricades. The badly outnumbered police were struggling to hold them back. Reinforcements arrived periodically, careful to enter the barricades at places where the crowd was relatively thin. But one group of eager patrolmen—a dozen cops in three cruisers—made the mistake of driving directly into the thick of things. Worse yet, they came in "code three," which meant they had their lights flashing and sirens wailing. This agitated the protesters, who surrounded the little caravan, slowing it to a crawl. As the lead car inched forward, demonstrators crowded in from all sides, including the front. There was an entire wall of bearded, dreadlocked protesters who actually refused to get out of the way of a moving police car. One carried a drum and drumsticks. Another wore goggles to protect his eyes from pepper spray. Several of them bent down and grasped the protective steel tubing that had been fitted around the cruiser's front grill. They leaned forward until their torsos were splayed across the hood, grunting as they tried to stop the car's glacial movement. The man in the goggles kept slamming a water bottle on the hood, making a loud noise as he inched backward before the advancing cruiser. *THWOCK! THWOCK! THWOCK!*

At the same time, a woman in a red shirt approached the driver's side and laid her protest placard across the windshield. The large white square of cardboard, mounted on a stick, completely blocked the driver's view. The cop behind the wheel tried to peer out the center of the windshield. But just then, a bearded man ran up from the passenger's side, slapped his hands on the fender and catapulted himself directly onto the center of the hood with a tremendous thud. He crouched down and hooked one hand into the space between the windshield and the hood. The startled cops found themselves eyeball-to-eyeball with a lunatic. He wore a big baggy cap, a white T-shirt, and a backpack. His face was blocking the center of the windshield, leaving the passenger side with the only unobstructed view. But in the next instant a woman hurried over and laid a section of brown cardboard across that part of the glass. It wasn't large enough to completely obscure the cops' vision, so she pressed her bangled wrist on the glass as well. All the while, the man in the goggles kept slamming that infernal water bottle onto the hood. *THWOCK! THWOCK! THWOCK!*

"DON'T HIT IT!" yelled one of the cops. Although the cruiser's windows were rolled up tight, the livid officer's voice could be heard above the din of the sirens and the roar of the crowd.

"Don't hit it!" echoed a second cop in a much calmer tone.

Unfazed, the goggled protester kept assaulting the hood, which was still occupied by the maniac with the baggy cap. *THWOCK! THWOCK! THWOCK!*

"DON'T HIT THE CAR!" hollered the first officer, astonished by the sheer insolence of these protesters.

By now the caravan had inched to within sight of the barricades. A line of riot police in the street was stunned to observe fellow officers being overrun by protesters. They knew that if the mob succeeded in stopping the cruisers, all hell would break loose. The cars would be tipped over, and the lives of the officers inside would be in danger. Demonstrators had already slashed the tires of several state troopers' cruisers. The riot police cocked their big black shotguns, took careful aim, and blew the protesters clean off the hood with nonlethal "sting balls." In addition to inflicting painful red welts, the balls broke apart on impact, releasing a potent chili pepper extract that inflamed the skin and burned the eyes, nose, mouth, and any other mucous membrane with which it came in contact. The sound of a woman hysterically screaming cut through the din of the melee as the protesters scrambled away from the cruisers. To make sure they kept moving, police fired a volley of rubber bullets after them.

"God *damn* it!" wailed one man, doubled over from the pain of being hit by a projectile.

"Serves ya right!" hollered a cop.

"You f---ing assholes!" the injured protester spat.

As the three cruisers finally pierced the perimeter, the demonstrators took up a chant that belied their actions: "PEACEFUL PROTEST! PEACEFUL PROTEST! PEACEFUL PROTEST!" After awhile they took up a second chant: "BUSH IS A TERRORIST! BUSH IS A TERRORIST! BUSH IS A TERRORIST!"

The chants could be heard inside the Hilton, where the president and his entourage were not the only guests. Also staying at the hotel were hundreds of homosexual men who were in Portland for the Gay Softball World Series. Returning from the day's games, these members of the North American Gay Amateur Athletic Alliance (NAGAA) were mortified to encounter violent protesters encircling the Hilton. One group of players made the mistake of trying to drive a car into the hotel's parking garage. The protesters swarmed the vehicle and rocked it from side to side. The players were terrified. Other team members—some of whom were wearing red satin shorts—tried to enter on foot, only to be manhandled like the Republican donors. Some made it through safely, but only after taking a circuitous, time-consuming detour. Gay columnist Marc Acito and his partner almost missed the gay talent show.

"Pretty Boy Floyd and I had to wander four blocks out of our way to get into the hotel," Acito explained. "But we just followed the crowds of tough-looking women and well-groomed men through the barricades."

The irony of gay softball players spending the night in the same hotel as a conservative president who considered homosexuality a sin was not lost on Acito, who said it proved "that the gods indeed have a sense of humor." Another gay writer, Byron Beck, agreed.

"Instead of spending the night in the White House curled up with First Lady Laura and a bowl of pretzels, Bush was stuck in a building with a battalion of 2,500 bat-wielding homos in the mood for love and other games," Beck observed. "This bizarre twist of timing essentially turned our very own Hilton Hotel into the most well-guarded gay bar on the entire planet. While I don't know about the hot and hunky Secret Service dudes (who seemed to be oh-so 'comfortable' in this sexed-up environment), the home-run homos who got stuck in this building weren't about to let the most queer-unfriendly of presidents spoil any of their fun. They were here to party!"

Some NAGAA members noticed that in addition to giving a speech at the $2,000-a-plate Smith fund-raiser, Bush was posing for photos with high rollers who were willing to part with much larger sums.

"Those who paid $25,000 a couple to have their picture taken with George W. got even more for their money when some of the players from Manhattan made a point of sucking face in the lobby," Acito observed.

Also in the lobby was a large canvas banner welcoming the gay players. Before Bush walked in, his underlings rolled the banner up, refurling it only after he was safely out of sight. Soon the gay softball players filed into the Grand Ballroom, which NAGAA had booked months in advance. When White House officials subsequently chose the Hilton for the Bush visit, they asked NAGAA to relinquish the Grand Ballroom for the Smith fund-raiser. But the players refused, relegating Bush—who was already staying in the second-best suite—to the second-best ballroom.

"The 'Twisted Talent Night' has always been a highlight of the annual Gay Softball World Series," explained Beck. "Basically an alcohol-fueled drag show, it's a chance for queer ball players to take off their gloves and pick up a few drinks."

Acito described the mood at the show as "cheerfully subversive." The emcee, dressed in drag, twice called out Bush's room number. At one point a woman known as Brownie took the stage while carrying what appeared to be tubes of caulk.

"Those lesbians, always ready to remodel," cracked Tim Bias, a softball official who was evicted by the Secret Service from the Mount St. Helen's Suite because it was directly beneath Bush's room.

"While Brownie proceeded to sing the paint off the walls, her team filled the room and, on cue, confetti shot out of the tubes, showering us all," Acito observed. "The effect was magical."

Beck added: "My fondest memory of the night will be that I was in the same building as the president when a drag queen from Los Angeles pretended to shove a plunger up her ass. How can you top that?"

The emcee decided to have a little fun at the expense of the president's daughters, Barbara and Jenna, who had been cited previously for underaged drinking.

"Are the Bush twins here?" the drag queen shouted. "No? Good. Otherwise we'd run out of booze."

The crowd roared its approval, although not everyone was having a good time. Some NAGAA members were still traumatized from their encounter with the mob, which continued to clash with police just outside. A few of the players who had been attacked by the protesters ended up commiserating with Fleischer, whose car in the presidential motorcade had been struck by a rock.

"People who say they're for peace and engage in violence are hard to understand," Fleischer told the White House press corps, which was also staying in the Hilton. He decried the protesters as "a left-wing fringe group," blaming them for "violence not only directed at the president and his traveling party, but others who were staying at the hotel who had absolutely nothing to do with politics. There was a softball team there who got attacked. And I talked to one of the people there whose car was attacked."

Fleischer's complaint left the press deeply conflicted. On one hand, reporters were always on the lookout for stories about gays being victimized. On the other, these attackers were left-wing Bush haters, not right-wing homophobes. Even more perplexing to the press was the fact that the person speaking out in defense of the gay victims was not some fashionable liberal icon. It was the buttoned-down spokesman for President Bush, a conservative Republican who opposed gay marriage. The image of Ari Fleischer commiserating with gay softball players about the violence of anti-Bush protesters simply did not fit the well-established media template for this sort of thing. To be sure, if a right-wing group had attacked a gaggle of gay softball players at an appearance by a Democratic president, the media would have immediately turned it into a cause célèbre about hate crimes. Journalists would have seized the story with all the gusto of the Rodney King coverage. The *New York Times,* in particular, would have had a field day. As *Times* reporter Richard Berke, who is gay, explained: "Literally three-quarters of the people deciding what's on the front page are not-so-closeted homosexuals." But because the assailants in this particular case were liberals, the *Times* and the rest of the press decided to pooh-pooh the antigay violence as a forgettable anomaly that did not merit coverage. The only media outlet in the traveling White House press corps to bother writing about this mistreatment of homosexuals was the *Washington Times*.

By this point Bush had gone to bed. Even during times of turmoil, the president liked to fall asleep by ten o'clock each evening so that he could get up by five the next morning. By contrast, the protesters preferred to party through the night and sleep late into the day. They were nowhere to be found when Bush departed the Hilton early Friday morning. Still, as he gazed through the window of his unmolested limousine on the way to the airport, the president could not forget the hatred on the faces of the protesters. The sheer intensity of their rage was something brand new to him.

Up until now, criticism of Bush had been divided into two distinct phases. There was the pre-September 11 phase, when liberal Democrats dismissed Bush as a weak one-termer, an illegitimate pretender who had stolen the election from Al Gore. In fact, they were so confident they would be able to vanquish the hapless president that they sometimes had trouble taking him seriously.

Then came the post-September 11 phase, when even Bush's most ardent critics lauded his decisive leadership and swift retaliation against the Taliban. Understandably, this rally-around-the-president effect faded over time. After a few months, liberal Democrats in Washington were once again routinely challenging Bush—if for no other reason than to chip away at his immense popularity and alarming re-electability. Still, such criticism remained mostly respectful as the nation prepared to mark the first anniversary of the terrorist attacks.

There was nothing respectful, however, about the Portland protesters. Their vituperative chants and poisonous placards went well beyond the bounds of civilized political debate. These people had brandished signs advocating the assassination of the sitting president of the United States. They had labeled him a terrorist and blamed him for September 11. They had stalked his motorcade, assailed his limousine, and stoned a car containing his advisers. Wild-eyed and ranting, these thugs had bullied innocent commuters, unsuspecting hotel guests, and a wheelchair-bound grandfather with multiple sclerosis. Their violent fervor had caught the Portland police flat-footed and even blindsided the Secret Service.

No, this harrowing spectacle was unlike anything Bush had witnessed in his nineteen months as president. It marked the beginning of a new phase of virulent dissent, one that would have been impossible to imagine in the immediate aftermath of September 11. Like many trends that started on the West Coast before gradually rolling across the rest of the country, this alien strain of acid partisanship would soon spread from the fringes of Portland's protest community to the highest levels of respectable Democratic politics in the nation's capital. It would color the looming debate over whether to wage war against Iraq. It would dominate the midterm elections, and perhaps even Bush's own bid for a second term.

The president didn't know it as he gazed out the window of his limousine, but he had just caught a glimpse of the Next Big Thing in politics: the rise of the Bush haters.

2

"SOMETHING OF A CHURCHILL SCHOLAR"

GEORGE GALLOWAY WAS SO far underground his ears were popping. He no longer knew whether he was still in Baghdad, having been hustled in and out of six different cars, all with curtained windows, and driven around for more than an hour before being spirited into a mysterious building with an elevator that descended at a high rate of speed to this tastefully lit room arranged with fresh flowers and, over in the corner, Saddam Hussein.

What a scoop Galloway would be able to bring home to the *Mail on Sunday*, the British newspaper for which he planned to write a column. As a Member of Parliament and one of Saddam's most outspoken defenders, perhaps Galloway could finally bring back firsthand reportage showing there was no need for Britain and the United States to rush into war against Iraq. And yet Galloway, a dapper dresser known as "Gorgeous George," was tempted to make the column as much about himself as the threat of war. In fact, when Saddam opened their August 2002 meeting by flattering Galloway on his physical appearance, the narcissistic MP saw a detail he could work into the column, which of course would be read by *tout le monde*. What a stroke of luck for Gorgeous George. Even Saddam had noticed his weight loss. The piece would practically write itself.

His first words are in clear English: "You've lost a stone since I last saw you," he says, which was unexpected on two counts: first, he would usually use kilos and, second, he was uncannily accurate. In fact it was 16 pounds—he was just two pounds out.

Thus would Gorgeous George Galloway impart to the world that he had lost not just fourteen pounds, as Saddam suggested, but a full sixteen. And why stop there? Although he would have just 1,800 words to convince Britain and the United States to call off their looming war, surely Galloway could spare a few *bon mots* to linger on the subject of his own weight loss. After all, Saddam was giving him the perfect opening. The dictator was offering him candy from a large tin marked Quality Street, an upscale British company whose products had evidently slipped through the Anglo-American embargo.

He offered me the tin. "No thanks," I said.
"It's Quality Street," he insisted, in English. Then, in Arabic: "Choose your personal favourite."
"I don't want to put that stone back on again," I said.

Such disciplined self-denial! Such cool-headed familiarity with—to use Galloway's own phrase—"the most demonized man on the planet." And to think these intimate exchanges would be pored over by government officials at the highest levels on both sides of the Atlantic. Surely the svelte MP could be forgiven for devoting a few more sentences to Saddam's impeccably tailored business suit, his flawless manners, the shy way he glanced downward when the backbencher from Scotland, Gorgeous George Galloway, approached with outstretched hand.

> He has a gentle handshake and is surprisingly diffident. With the aid of some classily-deployed hair and moustache dye, a strict health regimen, no drinking and a "suspended" Havana cigar habit, Hussein looks little older than when I met him nine years ago and, if anything, fitter.

That's the angle! Galloway would humanize Saddam Hussein. He would put a gentle, approachable face on this misunderstood man who was universally caricatured as some sort of wild-eyed monster. Looking at Saddam now, in his sartorial splendor and "classily-deployed hair and moustache dye," it was hard to believe he had come from such humble beginnings. Of course, it would be even harder to explain all that in an 1,800-word column. There was so much Gorgeous George would have to leave out. . . .

Born in a mud hut on the Tigris River in 1937, Saddam Hussein began life as a nobody with nothing. No electricity, no plumbing, no shoes. His father either died or disappeared around the time Saddam came squalling into the world via al-Ouja, a village so poor it didn't even have a school. Saddam's mother, a Sunni Muslim peasant, couldn't make enough money telling fortunes to raise her son. So she sent him to live with her brother in Tikrit, a down-at-the-heels textile town five miles to the north that was best known as the birthplace of Saladin, the sultan who captured Jerusalem during the Crusades. Saddam didn't know it at the time, but he was destined to become the most famous Tikriti in eight hundred years.

The most important person in young Saddam's life was his Jew-hating, Nazi-loving uncle—Khairallah Tulfah, an Army officer who wanted nothing more than to drive the British out of Iraq. Khairallah never forgot how Britain had reneged on its promise of self-determination to Arabs who helped defeat the Turks in World War I. Instead of letting Iraqis rule their newly created country, Britain installed a puppet monarchy. Most Iraqis, having endured four centuries of subjugation by the Ottomans, resigned themselves to being similarly subjugated by the British.

Well, not if Khairallah could help it. In 1941, emboldened by Hitler's conquests in Europe, a group of Arab nationalists, including Khairallah, attacked a British air base near Baghdad. The group evidently harbored some romantic notion that Hitler would send in reinforcements, but the Nazis never materialized and the revolt was crushed. Its ringleaders were hanged; the smaller fish, like Khairallah, were stripped of their military commissions and jailed. This forced Saddam to return to live with his mother, who had since taken up with a new man and was in the process of producing four new children. As Saddam grew, his mother regaled him with stories of how his heroic uncle had fought valiantly against the British.

So it was a happy day indeed when Khairallah was released from prison and Saddam returned to live with him in Tikrit. It was 1946 and the boy was finally able to enroll in an elementary school, where he quickly gained a reputation as a bully. At one point he avoided expulsion only by threatening to kill the principal. After managing to graduate in 1955, Saddam moved with his uncle to the sprawling metropolis of Baghdad. Failing to gain admission to the prestigious Baghdad Military Academy, Saddam enrolled in his seedy neighborhood's local high school.

All the while, Saddam was deeply influenced by his uncle's fervent nationalism. Now that the Nazis had been vanquished, the uncle was drawn to the fledgling Baath Party, which sought the overthrow of Iraq's imperialist government and the creation of a pan-Arab state. This led Saddam himself to join the Baath Party in 1957, while still a high school student. Through his uncle, he got to know one of the party leaders, a former Iraqi general from Tikrit named Ahmad Hassan al-Bakr, who would eventually become Saddam's most important mentor.

On July 14, 1958, Iraqi army units massacred the pro-British monarchy. Although the Baath Party was not involved in the coup, Baathists supported the establishment of the new government, headed by General Abdul Karim Qassem. Within months, however, Qassem broke his promise to join Egyptian President Nasser's proposed pan-Arab state. He even cozied up to the communists, whom the Baathists reviled as shills for Soviet imperialism. It looked as though the dream of Arab nationalism would be dashed yet again.

By this time, Saddam Hussein was a strapping twenty-one-year-old who found Baghdad's tumultuous political scene invigorating. Working as a bus conductor by day and assassin by night, he committed his first murder in October 1958. His uncle handed him a pistol and dispatched him to Tikrit to settle a petty score. The dutiful nephew ambushed his unsuspecting victim as the man walked home along a dark and deserted street. Saddam simply stepped out of the shadows and shot the man in the head. He and his uncle were jailed for six months in Tikrit, although the charges were eventually dropped for lack of witnesses. Saddam moved back to Baghdad, and soon found himself involved in a plot to overthrow the government, which of course the Baath Party no longer supported.

Saddam was one of four assassins who tried to kill the president of Iraq on October 7, 1959. They were supposed to ambush Qassem as he was driven home from work in Baghdad, but Saddam panicked and began firing his machine gun prematurely, prompting Qassem's security detail to return fire. The ensuing firefight killed Qassem's driver and one of the assassins. Qassem himself was shot twice, but survived. Saddam's leg was grazed by a bullet, possibly fired by one of his fellow assassins. But he managed to escape and soon fled to Damascus. After a few months the fugitive moved on to Cairo, where he would spend the next three years in exile.

While in Egypt, Saddam completed his high school education and enrolled in the University of Cairo's law school. Reading books about Josef Stalin, he became enamored of the Soviet dictator's ruthless methods of repression. Still, he retained his distaste for communism, especially as he became more deeply involved in Baathist politics. Perhaps that is why Saddam was reportedly contacted during this period by the CIA, which had become alarmed by Qassem's overtures to the Soviets.

Indeed, the CIA supported the Baathist coup that finally ousted Qassem in February 1963. The bloody insurrection was led by Saddam's communist-hating mentor, General Bakr. The new government's president, Abdul Salam Arif, named Bakr his prime minister. Believing it was finally safe to leave Cairo, Saddam hurried home to Baghdad, where his old mentor gave him a relatively low-level job in the government's farm bureau. But Saddam soon found a path for advancement, helping to hunt down hundreds of communists in a blood-soaked purge. He also took pains to ingratiate himself with Bakr, who rewarded Saddam with a position on the Baath Party's intelligence committee. That allowed the rising star to personally conduct interrogations of communists as they were tortured to death.

The fun was put on hold, however, in November 1963, when the military wing of the new government decided to oust the civilian Baathist Party. Bakr desperately tried to reconcile the rival factions by calling an eleventh-hour peace conference, at which Saddam served as his personal bodyguard. In the end, though, the new president sided with the military and expelled the Baathist civilians. Bakr was jailed and Saddam went underground, where he began to hatch yet another round of presidential assassination plots. The government's security forces caught up with the would-be assassin just outside Baghdad in

October 1964. After a brief firefight, Saddam ran out of bullets and was arrested. He spent the next two years in prison, but reportedly avoided the torture and harsh conditions that befell his fellow Baathists by ratting them out to the Arif government. This probably explains why Saddam managed to easily "escape" the prison on July 23, 1966, and resume Baath Party activities. He also resumed his education, enrolling at Baghdad University law school. He was perhaps the only student who came to class with his own phalanx of armed guards.

By now Saddam's reputation as a sadistic gangster was well established. In 1967 he pistol-whipped a man nearly to death on a bridge in central Baghdad, stopping to brag about it at a coffee shop afterward. He was the Baath Party's main enforcer, unafraid to use violence to achieve his goals. Even fellow Baathists grew wary of Saddam's aggressive brutality and shadowy links to foreign intelligence services.

Also sprung from prison was Bakr, who spent the next two years rising to the top of Iraq's Baath Party, taking Saddam with him. Determined never again to lose a fight with the Iraqi military, Saddam used his knowledge of Stalinesque tyranny to develop a civilian security apparatus that would make the party a formidable force. He and a group of other civilians, led by Bakr, made their move against the government on July 17, 1968. They were aided by a band of sympathizers in the military who were generous enough to bring a few tanks to the coup. Dressed in the stolen uniform of an Army lieutenant, Saddam rode atop one of these tanks to the Presidential Palace, where the government was overthrown in a coup d'etat. Bakr became president and Saddam became head of security. One of Saddam's first official acts was to oust the military sympathizers who had helped carry out the coup. He pulled a gun on one high-ranking officer and accompanied him to a plane waiting to whisk him into exile in Morocco. Saddam later had him assassinated anyway, just to be on the safe side.

This time the revolution stuck. The Baath Party set the tone for the new government on January 27, 1969, when nine Iraqi Jews and five others were hanged as spies for Israel in Baghdad's Liberation Square. Bakr declared a national holiday, busing in 100,000 citizens for the festivities. He and Saddam drove around the square in an open convertible, having a merry old time. The United Nations protested, but Saddam ignored the world body and discovered he could get away with it.

At first, most of the revolutionaries regarded Saddam as little more than an enforcer, certainly not someone who would one day be running the country. They were starry-eyed idealists, the intellectual champions of a glorious revolution that they believed was destined to transform the Arab world. Saddam, by contrast, was considered an unsophisticated peasant who was driven by brutality more than ideology. He spoke with a thick provincial accent and frequently mangled his syntax. His prospects for advancement in the new government seemed limited.

In short, Saddam's colleagues underestimated him. They badly misjudged his staying power, his ruthless determination to murder his way to the top. Before long, Saddam was vice president of what had become a Stalinist dictatorship that ruled through terror and purges, torture and show trials. Saddam mercilessly hunted down Jews, Kurds, Shiites, ethnic Iranians, communists, and even fellow Baathists who were suspected of insufficient party fervor.

Saddam saw traitors everywhere. He was forever liquidating political rivals, both real and imagined, and seemed to grow more paranoid as his power increased. Over the years he set up numerous security organizations and pitted them against one another in a never-ending quest to protect himself against assassination. He frequently claimed to uncover plots in the various security agencies and branches of the military, which gave him the pretext to kill anyone he perceived as a threat to his power. He had a Machiavellian gift for undermining the reputations of powerful officials and then moving in for the kill at just the right moment. Saddam was pathologically averse to trusting any-one, even family members. One by one, he systematically eliminated his closest friends and relatives, including people who had gone to great lengths to advance his career. And he was psychotically jealous of anyone whose career seemed to be advancing faster than his own.

Saddam had a sadistic streak a mile wide. He favored firing squads, hangings, poison, bombs and mafia-style assassinations. His victims were beaten, whipped, burned, frozen, shocked, and sodomized. Fingers, arms, and legs were chopped off by specially designed machines. Genitals were zapped with electric wires. Toenails, fingernail, teeth, and facial hair were ripped out with pliers. Prisoners were hung upside down and dipped into vats of acid or boiling water. Some were thrown off the roofs of tall buildings. Men were made to watch as their wives and daughters were raped and then killed. Women were forced to listen to the wails of their sadistically starved babies. Ordinary Iraqis disappeared in the middle of the night, never to be seen again. Or their bodies simply showed up on the side of some lonely desert road.

To help him maintain this Kafkaesque reign of terror, Saddam established a vast network of commissars who functioned as government informers, spying on the entire nation. Phones were tapped. Mail was monitored. Contact with foreigners was strongly discouraged. An atmosphere of fear and dread gripped the government as well as the general population.

Since he had absolute control over the state-run newspapers, radio, and TV stations, Saddam propagandized his witch-hunts into glorious victories for the Iraqi people. Like Stalin and Hitler before him, Baghdad's new strongman was creating a cult of personality.

Dissidents who managed to escape Iraq were often hunted down by Saddam's assassins abroad, where they were poisoned to death or shot point-blank as they walked down public streets. One man and his wife were brutalized by an ax-wielding assassin as they slept in their London bedroom.

By contrast, when foreign terrorists like the notorious Palestinian Abu Nidal came to Iraq, Saddam provided them with shelter and support. He was unfazed by the U.S. State Department's decision to add Iraq to its list of nations that sponsored terrorism. In fact, Saddam publicly rolled out the red carpet to terrorists who wanted to use Iraq as a staging ground for attacks on Israel.

"Regarding the Palestinians, it's no secret: Iraq is open to them and they are free to train and plan here," he matter-of-factly told *Newsweek,* July 17, 1978.

By the early 1970s, Saddam had married his first cousin, Sajida, who eventually gave birth to two sons, Uday and Qusay, and three daughters. Rich beyond his wildest dreams, he now indulged his taste for tailored suits, expensive cars, Cuban cigars, and American cuisine. He took over a fancy Baghdad restaurant called the Hunting Club, dropping in for a drink at the end of each day with a huge entourage of bodyguards. He amassed large chunks of real estate by seizing the land and then paying off the occupants—or, in some cases, simply throwing them into the street. He built dozens of ostentatious palaces with bombproof underground bunkers and tunnels. He had servants, swimming pools, tennis courts. And yet he wanted more.

So Saddam resolved to take government control of Iraq's vast oil reserves, which were second in size only to those of Saudi Arabia. For half a century, Iraq's oil had been controlled by the Iraqi Petroleum Company (IPC), a consortium of foreign oil firms like Shell and Mobil. Saddam knew these powerful conglomerates would not leave Iraq without a fight and might even retaliate by organizing a worldwide boycott of Iraqi oil, which would cripple the nation's economy. So he swallowed his anti-communism and entered into a strategic alliance with the Soviet Union, which promised to buy any Iraqi oil surpluses if the going got tough. France also pledged not to join a boycott, as long as it got a piece of future oil development and a cut-rate price on Iraqi oil exports.

On June 1, 1972, Saddam felt sufficiently empowered to expel the oil companies and nationalize the oil industry. The United States and Britain were alarmed by this threat to their oil interests in the Middle East. They also noted with dismay that the Moscow-Baghdad pact gave the Soviets access to Iraqi air bases. Washington and London were furious with Paris for helping seal the deal, prompting Saddam to speak out in defense of his French friends.

"We will not tolerate any wrong inflicted on France," he told the French newspaper *Le Monde,* June 20, 1972. "Any attempt to harm French interests would be considered as an act of hostility against Iraq."

The nationalization of the oil industry had a profound impact on Iraqi society. By increasing oil production and funneling at least some of the profits into public infrastructure, Saddam dramatically raised the standard of living for millions of impoverished Iraqis. Oil was suddenly transforming a backward, Third World country into a gleaming, modern, secular state—albeit a brutal and repressive dictatorship. With the help of eager contractors from countries like France, Germany, and the USSR, Saddam built schools, factories, and an electrical grid that brought power for the first time to remote villages like his hometown of al-Ouja. All citizens were provided free education and health care. He embarked on a uniquely Saddamesque campaign to eradicate illiteracy by threatening to jail peasants who refused to sign up for courses on reading and writing. This earned him a literacy award from the Paris-based United Nations Educational, Scientific and Cultural Organization (UNESCO).

But prosperity was not accompanied by peace. In late 1974, Saddam's forces battled separatist Kurds in northern Iraq, who enlisted the support of neighboring Iran. The Kurds were skilled mountain guerillas who by early 1975 had killed tens of thousands of Iraqi soldiers. Saddam realized the only way he could extricate himself from the debacle was to convince Iran to back off. So he held his nose and struck a deal with his mortal enemy, the Shah of Iran. In March, Saddam agreed to give Iran control of a disputed river to the Persian Gulf. In return, the Shah withdrew his support for the Kurds. Within a matter of days, Saddam crushed the Kurdish insurgents.

The ordeal convinced Saddam to embark on an even more aggressive military spending spree. He negotiated directly with French Prime Minister Jacques Chirac to buy scores of fighter jets, attack helicopters, and surface-to-air missiles. France became second only to the Soviet Union in arms exports to Iraq. But Saddam decided that if he wanted Iraq to become the preeminent Arab power, he would need to supplement conventional arms with biological and chemical weapons. He had already paved the way for a biological weapons program in November 1974 by dispatching an underling to Paris to sign a contract for a bacteriological lab. Meanwhile, East Germany assisted with the development of a chemical weapons program, which Saddam attempted to disguise. He claimed a $40 million nerve gas factory was a harmless "fertilizer plant." In time he had several of these facilities churning out deadly nerve agents like VX and anthrax.

But Saddam's grandest ambition was to become the first Arab state to develop a nuclear bomb, thereby establishing a strategic counterweight to Israel, which was already a member of the nuclear club. So he went to Paris, where Chirac gave him a personal tour of France's nuclear research center. The Frenchman, whose devotion to Baghdad had earned him the nickname "Jacques Iraq," agreed to sell Saddam several nuclear reactors that would be capable of turning uranium into weapons-grade plutonium. France was the only Western nation not to challenge the laughable claim by Iraq—a nation sitting on a sea of oil—that it needed the nuclear reactors to produce electricity. Not even Saddam pretended that was true.

In fact, when the $3 billion deal was inked in late 1975—after Saddam and Chirac had visited each other in their respective capitals—the Iraqi dictator told a Lebanese magazine: "The agreement with France is the first concrete step toward production of the Arab atomic bomb." The Franco-Iraqi Nuclear Cooperation Treaty was bad for Jews in more ways than one. The agreement stipulated that "all persons of Jewish race" be excluded from the deal, both in Iraq and France. Paris had no compunction about signing an obviously anti-Semitic treaty, because in addition to the nuclear reactors France was given contracts to build massive public works projects in Iraq, including a new airport and subway.

Meanwhile, Saddam was able to get Iraq elected to the International Atomic Energy Agency's (IAEA) board of governors, which essentially gave him a spy inside the world's nuclear club. He even finagled a nuclear inspector's job for one of his henchmen, who used the position to funnel valuable technical information back to the regime.

The information helped Saddam establish an elaborate nuclear development program. But instead of clustering the various components of the ambitious effort under one roof, which would make them an easy target for Israel, Saddam spread them across a variety of secret locations. Still, Israeli intelligence agents were able to sabotage Iraq's two reactors in April 1979. The Mossad operatives detonated bombs that severely damaged the reactor cores. Later that year, Saddam gathered his nuclear scientists together to express his impatience.

"When will you deliver the plutonium for the bomb?" he demanded, according to one of the scientists, Khidhir Hamza.

Incredibly, Hamza's supervisor was still naive enough to believe the team's work would be used for peaceful purposes.

"Bomb? We can't make a bomb," he replied. "They are covered by the Nuclear Nonproliferation Treaty, and we will be held in violation of our treaty obligations."

"Treaties," Saddam shot back, "are a matter for us to deal with. You, as a scientist, should not be troubled by these things. You should be doing your job and not have these kinds of excuses."

The supervisor was taken away, subjected to a show trial, tortured beyond recognition, and sentenced to life in prison. His job was given to the reluctant Hamza, who later defected and recounted the scene in his book, *Saddam's Bombmaker.*

Such were the lengths to which Saddam would go in order to consolidate his power base, which by now included both the civilian security apparatus and the military forces. As Saddam's power grew, Bakr's diminished until he was little more than a figurehead. Two decades older than Saddam, the increasingly frail president was plagued by health problems that made his energetic underling—who routinely worked sixteen hours a day—look ever more robust. Saddam was now running virtually every aspect of the government, micromanaging especially those agencies that had the misfortune of catching his attention at any given moment.

On July 17, 1979, exactly eleven years after the Baathist coup that brought Bakr to power, Saddam finally elbowed his old mentor aside and seized the presidency. He decided that his first sweeping gesture as Iraq's maximum leader would be to eliminate scores of real and perceived enemies in the Baath Party's leadership, but he needed someone to blame for the imminent bloodbath. He coerced a high-ranking government official into denouncing the men Saddam wanted to kill. This was accomplished by sacking the official and then torturing him in one of Saddam's dungeons. At length, the man's wife and daughters were brought into the room and he was told they would be raped in front of him unless he confessed to a "plot" against Saddam. He was ordered to name as coconspirators the men Saddam had secretly marked for death. The hapless official complied.

Armed with the list, Saddam set about the task of carrying out the most dramatic and cold-blooded purge of his career. He gathered the Baath Party's top one thousand officials in a Baghdad conference center and stunned them by announcing the discovery of the so-called plot against him. He explained that the conspirators were among the attendees, then watched with macabre satisfaction as terror gripped the audience.

"The people whose names I am going to read out should repeat the party slogan and leave the hall," Saddam said calmly.

Puffing on a Cuban cigar, the dictator produced the trumped-up list. One by one, the names were read and the men were dragged out by Saddam's guards. Sixty-six Iraqis—including some of the government's highest officials and the dictator's closest confidants—trembled with fear as they were blindfolded. Saddam personally handed out pistols to party officials whose names had not been called so they could help the dictator execute their terrified colleagues. Perversely, Saddam had the whole thing filmed, from the chilling denunciations to the graphic executions. Copies of the film were sent to other Baath Party officials around the country as an unsubtle warning never to cross the new president. Saddam then embarked on an even more sweeping purge of the party, army, and general population. Hundreds were killed, thousands were tortured, and countless others were thrown into prison. A palpable sense of dread gripped the nation's thirteen million inhabitants. The consolidation of Saddam's terrible power over Iraq was now utterly complete.

But Saddam still felt threatened by forces outside Iraq's borders—especially Iran, its much larger neighbor to the east. He watched with alarm as his arch enemy, the Shah, was deposed by radical Islamic revolutionaries and replaced by someone even worse—Ayatollah Khomeni. Iran's newfound Islamic fundamentalism was anathema to Saddam, a dedicated secularist. Worse yet, Khomeni seemed eager to export the religious revolution to his Shiite Muslim brothers in southern Iraq, who comprised 60 percent of the nation's population. These Iraqi Shiites had already staged riots, which Saddam's forces brutally crushed.

Meanwhile, Iran renewed its cooperation with Kurdish agitators in northern Iraq. Saddam, a member of the Sunni Muslim minority in central Iraq, was suddenly worried about being attacked simultaneously from the north, south, and east. He came to the conclusion that he would have to strike Iran preemptively to avoid being overrun. He decided that Iran's support for the Kurds was sufficient justification for initiating a major war. After all, Tehran had agreed five years earlier to abandon the Kurds in return for Saddam ceding control of the disputed river into the Persian Gulf. Now that Iran was reneging on the deal, Saddam figured he was entitled to the waterway.

On September 22, 1980, Iraq attacked Iran. Having used Iraq's oil revenues to nearly double the size of his military in recent years, Saddam assumed the war would be quick and easy. He was wrong on both counts. The megalomaniacal dictator, whose military experience amounted to having been rejected by the Baghdad Military Academy, now insisted on micromanaging the war—much to the chagrin of his generals. Within two years, 100,000 Iraqi soldiers were dead and thousands more imprisoned inside Iran. Iraq's oil production equipment was severely damaged, effectively cutting off the nation's prosperity. The strain on Saddam was obvious by March 1982, when he fatally shot his health minister at a cabinet meeting. In the months that followed he launched yet another purge of the military, killing hundreds of top officers who had the temerity to make suggestions that contradicted Saddam's battlefield strategy. On at least one occasion Saddam matter-of-factly murdered an officer by shooting him in the head. The dictator's mood was so dark that he even decided to liquidate former president Bakr, who had been living in forced retirement for three years.

"Bakr was killed by a team of doctors who worked for Saddam's security apparatus and were sent to treat him when rumors began to circulate that Bakr was preparing a comeback," journalist Con Coughlin revealed in his book *Saddam: King of Terror.* "The team sent by

Saddam injected Bakr with a large dose of insulin, which caused him to go into a coma. He never regained consciousness, and Saddam's doctors stayed by his side until they were sure he was dead. In this way Saddam repaid the generosity, encouragement, and support of the mentor and kinsman who had been the most important influence on his life and career."

Meanwhile, the conflict with Iraq degenerated into trench warfare, with neither side able to make much progress. Saddam abandoned any hope of regaining control of the disputed waterway. He simply wanted the war to end. Although he tried several times to enact cease-fires, the Iranians seemed determined to fight Iraq to the death. This alarmed Washington, which did not want Iran exporting its Islamic fanaticism. Although the United States remained officially neutral in the Iran-Iraq war, it unofficially backed Iraq.

As a gesture of support, in 1982 the State Department took Iraq off its list of countries supporting terrorism. The CIA began supplying Iraq with satellite photos of Iranian troop movements. This allowed Saddam to retaliate swiftly against Kurds who helped Iranian forces seize the Iraqi border town of Haj Omran. Saddam's forces captured and executed 8,000 Kurdish men and boys, some as young as twelve, in 1983. Meanwhile, President Reagan authorized the sale of scores of civilian helicopters that Iraq converted into military use against Iran. It was part of an effort to normalize relations between the two countries, severed in 1967 because of Iraq's role in the Arabs' Six Day War against Israel. In December 1983, Reagan dispatched his Middle East envoy, Donald Rumsfeld, to Baghdad to deliver a personal letter from the American president.

"The city was at war," Rumsfeld later recalled on NBC's *Meet the Press*. "They were being shelled, and there were bunkers around buildings.

"We came in and he was a wartime leader trying to prevail in a war that he had started," he said of Saddam. "He's tough. He's a survivor.

And I don't think anybody could live as he does—with his picture in every room in every building on every street corner—and not begin to believe you were something you weren't."

Even with behind-the-scenes help from the United States, Saddam came to the conclusion he could not defeat Iran with conventional weapons alone. He did not yet have a nuclear weapon, thanks to another Israeli attack in 1981 that severely damaged a reactor one month before it was scheduled to go operational. Although the French expressed outraged and promised to rebuild it, Saddam couldn't wait that long. In late 1981, with the help of West German companies, he began building a trio of chemical weapons plants that churned out artillery shells packed with nerve gas, mustard gas, sarin, and tabun. By 1984 Saddam was ready to use them.

But first the dictator wanted to test them on human guinea pigs. He decided to use some of the Iraqi Shiites he had been jailing since the start of the war in an effort to quell unrest in southern Iraq. Scores of these prisoners were taken to chemical weapons plants and subjected to grisly experiments. Hundreds more were actually trucked to the front lines, placed in trenches, and made to suffer horrible deaths from chemical agents dropped on them from airplanes.

Satisfied by the deadly results, Saddam resolved to unleash these weapons of mass destruction on the foreign enemy. In early 1984, Iraqi helicopters dumped mustard gas and nerve gas on Iranian troops. The victims perished so gruesomely that Saddam repeated the attacks several more times over the next few years.

By 1987, the success of chemical weapons against Iranians in the east and Shiites in the south emboldened Saddam to try them against Kurds in the north. Incensed that Iran had resumed its support for Kurdish separatists, Saddam sent his cousin, the man who would come to be known as "Chemical Ali," to crush the insurgency.

"I will kill them all with chemical weapons!" Ali Hassan Al-Majid bragged at a Baath Party meeting, an audiotape of which was later disseminated by Human Rights Watch. "Who is going to say anything? The international community? F--- them!"

Thus began the Anfal military campaign of 1988, in which at least 50,000 Kurds were massacred. Ali wiped out scores of Kurdish villages in an attempt to "ethnically cleanse" great swaths of Iraqi Kurdistan. In one attack alone, Ali's forces killed 5,000 men, women, and children, and grotesquely maimed thousands more by dumping nerve and mustard gases on the Kurdish town of Halabja. The gases had been developed with the help of Germans who took their cue from Hitler's gassing of Jews in the Holocaust. Saddam Hussein's reign of terror over his countrymen had escalated into unadulterated genocide.

His larger war against Iran was less successful. Year after year, the exhausting and bloody battle of attrition continued. By the time it finally ended in stalemate in the summer of 1988, a million Muslims had been killed and the economies of both nations had been decimated. Saddam hadn't even regained control of the disputed waterway to the Persian Gulf—his reason for going to war in the first place. But that didn't stop him from declaring victory and commissioning his own version of Paris's Arc de Triomphe—an enormous sculpture of two crossed swords over a boulevard in central Baghdad.

With the war against Iran behind him, Saddam redoubled his development of weapons of mass destruction. In late 1988, he gassed scores of Kurdish villages with chemical agents, killing thousands and driving huge numbers of refugees to the Turkish border. He also embarked on another round of purges, mostly against military officers who resented him for having bungled the war against Iran. His victims' bodies were unceremoniously dumped into scores of mass graves that now dotted the Iraqi countryside.

All the while, Saddam was becoming more reclusive and paranoid. He expanded his network of underground tunnels and bunkers. Terrified of assassination, he began moving from palace to palace, never sleeping in the same place for more than a few nights. He employed numerous body doubles, some of whom actually made public appearances on his behalf. He also employed fortune-tellers, perhaps to remind him of his mother, who had died in 1983. When he moved from one location to another in his presidential motorcade, he sent four or five decoy motorcades in various directions to confuse would-be assassins. Not even the president of the United States did that.

Saddam was every bit as devious in cheating on his wife, Sajida. Whenever a pretty young woman caught his eye, the dictator would instruct his food taster to procure her for a tryst at a house in Baghdad or one of the presidential palaces. Most of these women were cast aside after one-night stands. But Saddam became seriously involved with a tall blonde who was already married to the chairman of Iraqi Airways. When Sajida learned of the affair, she flew into a rage and implored her son Uday to intervene. Uday responded by going after Saddam's food taster. With shocking brutality, Uday clubbed the man to death at a party being thrown for the wife of Egyptian President Hosni Mubarak. The resulting scandal infuriated Saddam, who publicly denounced his son and punished Sajida by killing her brother. Sajida vowed never again to speak to her husband. That was fine with Saddam, who divorced her and married his mistress.

The moral bankruptcy of Saddam's personal life was matched only by the financial bankruptcy of his country. The ten-year war with Iran had left Iraq flat broke. Saddam owed billions to Gulf states for loans they had extended during the fighting. But instead of repaying these loans, he now demanded they be forgiven. Furthermore, he called on his neighbors to pony up tens of billions more for Iraqi reconstruction. The Gulf states refused and—adding insult to injury—drove down the price of Iraqi oil by exceeding their own production quotas, which had been set by the Organization of Petroleum Exporting Countries (OPEC).

The move incensed Saddam, who became particularly belligerent toward Kuwait. Like many Iraqis, Saddam regarded Kuwait as Iraq's "nineteenth province"; he was still bitter that the British had split it from Iraq after World War I. Although Kuwait was tiny compared with Iraq, its coastline on the Persian Gulf was many times longer, making it strategically valuable for the export of oil. Saddam, who now controlled the world's fourth largest army, was spoiling for a fight. On July 18, 1990, he issued an ultimatum to Kuwait: forgive all loans, help fund Iraqi reconstruction, and stabilize oil prices—or face Saddam's wrath. In an attempt to avoid war, Kuwait reluctantly capitulated to all demands. But Saddam had already made up his mind to invade. One week after issuing his ultimatum, he summoned U.S. Ambassador April Glaspie to the presidential palace. Strongly hinting of his intention to wage war against Kuwait, Saddam threatened America with terrorist attacks if it interfered.

"If you use pressure, we will deploy pressure and force," he warned Glaspie. "We cannot come all the way to you in the United States, but individual Arabs may reach you."

According to a transcript of the meeting, Glaspie replied: "We have no opinion on Arab-Arab conflicts like your border disagreement with Kuwait." She would later deny tacitly giving Saddam a green light to wage war, telling the *New York Times* she did not believe "that the Iraqis were going to take all of Kuwait."

But all of Kuwait was precisely what Saddam wanted. On August 2, 1990, he sent 100,000 troops and 300 tanks across the border, easily overrunning the Kuwaiti army and seizing control of the entire nation in a matter of hours. In an effort to prevent military interference from outside forces, Saddam detained all foreign workers and their children in both Kuwait and Iraq for use as human shields. Condemnation by the international community was swift and severe, with the loudest protests coming from the United States and Britain. When France and the Soviet Union called for a nonmilitary solution, Saddam expressed his gratitude by releasing hundreds of French and Russian human shields. Saddam also offered free oil supplies to Soviet President Mikhail Gorbachev's dying regime. The Iraqi dictator figured he would need a few friends if he was to get away with the first formal annexation of a sovereign state since World War II.

And he might have pulled it off if he hadn't become greedy. But shortly after invading Kuwait, Saddam deployed numerous tanks and troops to the Saudi border, prompting the royal family to make a frantic appeal to the U.S. for protection. President George H. W. Bush was suddenly facing the very real possibility that Saddam would take over the entire Gulf, along with more than half the world's oil reserves. Having already summoned Glaspie back to Washington, Bush instructed her second-in-command, Joseph Wilson, to find out whether Saddam planned to invade Saudi Arabia.

"We will not attack those who do not attack us," Saddam assured the U.S. charge d'affaires in Baghdad on August 6. "We will not harm those who do not harm us."

Unconvinced, Bush took action the next day. Declaring that "appeasement does not work," he began a massive deployment of U.S. forces to Saudi soil. Saddam responded by installing Chemical Ali as governor of Kuwait. The dictator's cousin began terrorizing Kuwaitis in makeshift torture chambers.

For nearly four months, Bush assembled an international coalition that deployed hundreds of thousands of troops to Saudi Arabia. On November 29, the U.N. Security Council passed a resolution authorizing the use of force if Iraq did not unconditionally withdraw from Kuwait by January 15, 2001. Saddam, who had been ignoring the world body's demands for more than two decades, dug in his heels.

The day after the deadline expired, U.S.-led forces began a punishing aerial attack that Saddam dubbed "the mother of all battles." Allied planes relentlessly pounded targets in Iraq and Kuwait with impunity. Saddam's aging anti-aircraft guns proved impotent against

America's radar-dodging warplanes and sophisticated "smart bombs." The desperate dictator concluded that his only chance was to draw the allies into a ground war so he could inflict casualties that the West would consider unacceptable.

To that end, Iraq attacked Israel on January 18 with five Scud missiles, three of which landed in Tel Aviv. Remarkably, Bush persuaded Israel not to retaliate. Grasping for another tactic, Saddam set fire to oil fields in Kuwait and pumped massive amounts of crude into the Persian Gulf, creating an ecological disaster. When this too failed to provoke a ground war, Saddam paraded a handful of captured allied pilots before TV cameras. He even publicly threatened to arm his missiles with biological, chemical, and nuclear weapons.

"I pray to God I will not be forced to use these weapons," he warned CNN's Peter Arnett. "But I will not hesitate to do so should the need arise."

But it was all a bluff. Allied air strikes had already decimated Saddam's weapons of mass destruction facilities. As January gave way to February, the dictator knew he could not withstand the merciless air assault much longer. Increasingly desperate to provoke a ground war, Saddam sent some of his forces across the Kuwaiti border to capture a town a dozen miles into Saudi Arabia. But his troops were quickly driven out. Meanwhile, air strikes continued to pulverize Iraq's infrastructure, which had already fallen into disrepair because of the long and grueling war with Iran.

Bush's final ultimatum to Saddam was chillingly straightforward: Begin withdrawing from Kuwait by noon on February 22, or face what the dictator had long sought but could no longer survive—a devastating ground war. Instead of complying, Saddam torched more oil wells and began mass executions of Kuwaiti prisoners. So on February 24, General Norman Schwarzkopf unleashed the long-awaited ground offensive. Saddam responded the next day by firing a Scud into an American barracks in Dhahran, Saudi Arabia, killing twenty-eight GIs and injuring ninety-eight others. But it was the last gasp of a losing campaign. Schwarzkopf's ground offensive quickly turned into a rout. Terrified Iraqi soldiers surrendered by the tens of thousands as they hightailed it out of Kuwait. The remnants of Saddam's vaunted Republican Guard were actually surrendering to bewildered American journalists along what became known as Iraq's "highway of death."

After one hundred hours, Bush pulled the plug on the Gulf War. It was a decision that would be second-guessed by innumerable critics, prompting administration officials like Defense Secretary Dick Cheney to defend the president's restraint.

"If we'd gone to Baghdad and got rid of Saddam Hussein— assuming we could have found him—we'd have had to put a lot of forces in and run him to ground some place," Cheney told the BBC. "He would not have been easy to capture.

"Then you've got to put a new government in his place," he added. "And then you're faced with the question of, what kind of government are you going to establish in Iraq? Is it going to be a Kurdish government or a Shiite government or a Sunni government? How many forces are you going to have to leave there to keep it propped up? How many casualties are you going to take through the course of this operation?"

Besides, Bush and most other experts figured Saddam wouldn't last another year in power. The dictator's adventure in Kuwait had proven disastrous. Iraq was in ruins; 150,000 of its citizens were dead. There was no electricity or running water in Baghdad or other major cities. The Iraqi economy, which had been so vibrant a dozen years earlier, lay in tatters after two major wars. Kurds in the north and Shiites in the south rose up in rebellion after Bush publicly urged them to "take matters into their own hands and force Saddam Hussein, the dictator, to step aside." Saddam was able to crush the revolts, but only because Bush, fearing a takeover by Islamic fundamentalists, refrained from aiding the rebels. That allowed Saddam to execute Shiites by the hundreds and drive Kurds out of their villages by the hundreds of thousands, creating a massive humanitarian crisis.

Racked by guilt, the allies belatedly took action to protect the insurgents. Establishing a "no-fly zone" to bar Saddam's forces from operating aircraft north of the 36th parallel, they airlifted food and medicine to Kurdish refugees in Operation Provide Comfort. Some ten thousand American, British, and French troops set up shop in northern Iraq to supervise the humanitarian assistance. Another no-fly zone was later established in the south to protect the Shiites.

Meanwhile, the U.N. Security Council passed a resolution imposing tough economic sanctions against Iraq, including a ban on the sale of oil. The resolution also demanded that Iraq come clean on its weapons of mass destruction programs once and for all. Iraqi Foreign Minister Tariq Aziz accepted the terms, although Saddam had no intention of honoring them. He put his eldest son, Qusay, in charge of hiding the weapons programs from U.N. inspectors.

It didn't take long for the inspectors to realize that the Iraqis were cheating. In June 1991 chief inspector David Kay and his team showed up unexpectedly at a military base, prompting panicked Iraqis to flee out the back gate with giant magnets that were used for enriching uranium. The inspectors raced to rear of the base and filmed the magnets being driven away as Iraqis fired shots over their heads.

Three months later, Kay and his team found a cache of documents detailing Iraq's efforts to develop nuclear weapons. Alarmed by the ramifications of the discovery, Iraqi forces barred the inspectors from leaving a Baghdad parking lot. The standoff dragged on for days, ending only after Kay agreed to let Iraqis "inventory" the documents, which resulted in much sensitive information being scrubbed from the files before they were returned to the inspectors. The cat-and-mouse campaign of organized deception would drag on for years.

In November 1992, Saddam celebrated Bill Clinton's victory over

President Bush by appearing on a balcony and firing his rifle into the sky. As if to taunt the lame duck president one last time, Saddam sent anti-aircraft guns into the no-fly zones less than a month before the end of Bush's term. The president responded by attacking the guns with U.S. warplanes just six days before leaving office. Saddam repaid the favor by trying to assassinate Bush during a visit to Kuwait in April 1993. A car jammed with explosives was set to go off as Bush's motorcade passed through Kuwait City. After the plot was uncovered, President Clinton retaliated by firing dozens of missiles at Baghdad. But as the years wore on, Clinton put Iraq on the back burner of American foreign policy.

Although the economic sanctions had little effect on Saddam and his henchmen, they proved crippling to ordinary Iraqis. Disease and hunger were rampant. Cancers and birth defects skyrocketed, a result of the chemical and biological weapons caches that had been blown up during the war. The bombed-out electrical grid worked only a couple of hours a day and the public still had no clean drinking water. When the U.N. allowed a limited amount of oil to be sold to fund the purchase of desperately needed food and medicine for ordinary Iraqis, Saddam traded these items for cash on the black market in order to rebuild his decimated military. He and his inner circle illegally exported additional oil reserves, using the proceeds to build more lavish palaces and buy more fleets of luxury cars. Uday alone amassed hundreds of millions of dollars through such illicit commerce.

All the while, Saddam kept uncovering plots to oust him. He killed or imprisoned hundreds of suspects, including several top army generals. One on occasion, Saddam sat in an office and calmly watched two vicious dogs tear a general to shreds. Such purges alarmed the dictator's sons-in-laws, Hussein Kamel and Saddam Kamel, who defected to Jordan in August 1995 with their wives. Hussein Kamel, who had been in charge of procuring Iraq's weapons of mass destruction, gave the CIA an earful about Saddam's operation, which caused the dictator no end of headaches with the U.N. inspectors back in Iraq. Temporarily concealing his rage, Saddam telephoned the brothers and offered them pardons if they returned. They foolishly agreed and in early 1996 showed up at the Iraqi border. Saddam unceremoniously stripped them of their military ranks, forced them to sign papers divorcing his daughters, and sent them to a villa outside Baghdad. The dictator then dispatched Chemical Ali, now head of Iraq's special forces, to the villa along with three busloads of spectators—the doomed men's friends and relatives. Ali and his troops then opened fire on the men, who also happened to be his own cousins. Uday and Qusay watched from a bulletproof car as the battle raged for hours. Finally their brothers-in-law were dead, along with several family members inside the villa.

By this time the U.S. presence in Iraq had dwindled to a mere handful of soldiers who shared a tiny base camp with British and French counterparts in northern Iraq. The CIA had spent years cultivating the Iraqi National Congress (INC), an opposition network consisting of Kurds and other Iraqis. But all that work was destroyed in August 1996, when Saddam's forces crossed north of the 36th parallel to help one group of Kurds defeat a rival Kurdish faction. The Americans fled across the Turkish border hastily, leaving behind Humvees, pickup trucks, and loaded weapons. After pushing the targeted Kurds into Iran, Saddam's forces embarked on a search-and-destroy mission against the INC. The CIA saved the lives of more than six thousand helpful Iraqis by hustling them into Turkey and then loading them on planes for Guam. The Iraqis were given U.S. citizenship and kept under wraps on the remote island until after the presidential election, when this little-known but embarrassing chapter in America's foreign policy would no longer pose a political problem. Clinton fired a few more cruise missiles at Iraq, but it was more of an afterthought than a sustained foreign policy initiative. For all practical purposes, the U.S. effort to undermine Saddam's regime was over.

In case anyone missed the point, Saddam expelled all American weapons inspectors the following year. Tariq Aziz announced that not even U.S. employees of the U.N. inspections regime would be allowed inside Iraq. Saddam's emasculation of the Clinton Administration was complete.

It wasn't until 1998, when his presidency was threatened by the Monica Lewinsky scandal, that Clinton began to see the political benefits of getting tough on Iraq. A month after the scandal broke, Clinton went to the Pentagon to deliver a major foreign policy address on the threat posed by Saddam's weapons of mass destruction.

"If we fail to respond today, Saddam and all those who would follow in his footsteps will be emboldened tomorrow," he said. "Some day, some way, I guarantee you, he'll use the arsenal."

Sensing an opening, the Republican-controlled Congress overwhelmingly passed the Iraq Liberation Act, which stated: "It should be the policy of the United States to support efforts to remove the regime headed by Saddam Hussein from power in Iraq." Clinton had little choice but to sign it, which he did on Halloween. Six weeks later, on the eve of congressional debate over his impeachment, the beleaguered president decided to play the Iraq card one last time. Citing Saddam's long-standing refusal to cooperate with weapons inspectors, Clinton abruptly ordered hundreds of missile strikes against Iraq. Congress postponed the impeachment debate amid grumblings that the attack had been politically timed. (Clinton had already been accused of "wagging the dog" for firing missiles at Sudan and Afghanistan in August, on the day Lewinsky testified against him before a federal grand jury. On both occasions, the bombings temporarily knocked the Lewinsky scandal from atop the headlines.) After the Iraq bombing, Saddam announced a permanent ban on all weapons inspections—both U.S. and U.N.

Thus, for the next four years, the international community was kept in the dark about Saddam's programs to develop weapons of mass destruction. Iraq largely disappeared from the radar screen of U.S. foreign policy, except for occasional skirmishes between Saddam's anti-aircraft guns and allied warplanes patrolling the no-fly zones. When Bush's son became president in 2001, the new commander in chief talked of replacing the "Swiss cheese" economic sanctions with targeted measures that the White House dubbed "smart sanctions."

Still, few Americans paid much attention to Iraq—until the terrorist attacks of September 11, 2001, which Iraq's government openly praised. After President George W. Bush dispatched the Taliban, Washington began buzzing about the possibility of Saddam providing weapons of mass destruction to al Qaeda or some other terrorist network for use against the United States or its allies. While Bush himself remained coy, his administration did nothing to dampen growing speculation throughout the first half of 2002 that the United States and Great Britain were planning a preemptive strike against Iraq. In June, the Pentagon quietly stepped up patrols in the no-fly zones, provoking fire from anti-aircraft installations that the warplanes easily destroyed. Few Americans noticed this development, but Saddam certainly did. As far as he was concerned, Bush was already softening up Iraq for the coming war. In addition to destroying the anti-aircraft guns, the allied warplanes were also cutting fiber optic communication lines that would be needed in the coming conflict. The normally reclusive dictator became so alarmed that he resolved to reach out to London and Washington. Having long ago destroyed all normal diplomatic channels, Saddam was reduced to summoning one of the few Western politicians who seemed to support him: British MP George Galloway, who now joined the dictator in his underground lair.

Alas, Galloway decided there would be insufficient space in his self-referential column to recount Saddam's blood-drenched biography. Instead, the left-wing MP would play up the "human" side of the dictator—and work himself into the text whenever possible.

The man radiates power—there's a nervousness and over-eagerness among those around him—but also a zen-like calm.

"Ahlen wasahlen," he says, taking my hand in his. "Welcome, welcome."

Having intimated to the world that he was fluent in Arabic, Galloway indulged himself with a few more words about the ruthless dictator's gentle disposition.

Along with the civilian suit, Saddam had donned his most civil manners. No insult fell from his lips, nor threats.

Finally settling down to the task at hand—making Saddam's case against war—Galloway parroted the genocidal maniac's denials about weapons of mass destruction. He also decided to devote some of his 1,800 words to exploring the possibility that British Prime Minister Tony Blair might rein in the warmongering American president. And he concluded his *Mail on Sunday* column by passing along a defiant threat from the mass murderer himself, whom Galloway gushed was "something of a Churchill scholar."

"If they come, we are ready," Saddam told me. "We will fight them on the streets, from the rooftops, from house to house. We will never surrender.

"That is what Churchill promised the invaders threatening England.

"And that is what we can promise the Crusaders if they come here."

3

A MILESTONE AND A MISSION

ONE YEAR LATER, THERE was still a bare spot in the meadow. It was something of a mystery, since knee-high grass had overgrown the rest of the crash site, obscuring the massive scar on the earth. Just this one spot, perhaps ten yards across, remained barren. The jetliner had plowed in at a 45-degree angle, burrowing up a lot of earth that finally came to rest at the spot in question. It seemed like the right place to lay the wreath on this first anniversary of the crash.

President Bush stood on the unmarked patch of dirt and bowed his head. He worried that the nation was already beginning to forget the significance of Flight 93. Granted, an entire generation of Americans would always remember the story of those brave passengers, including Todd Beamer, who declared "Let's roll!" and overpowered the hijackers before the 757 slammed into this remote field in Shanksville, Pennsylvania. But for a while it had been more than just an heroic story. For much of that first year after the terrorist attacks, Flight 93 had symbolized nothing less than a transformation of America's collective consciousness. A generation raised on self-gratification suddenly was reminded of the virtue of sacrifice. Bush called Flight 93 "the most significant example of serving something greater than yourself." It was, perhaps, understandable that Bush had been especially moved by the heroism of the passengers. After all, they had prevented the plane from reaching Washington, where the hijackers had planned to crash it into the White House or the Capitol. Bush was not about to forget anyone who made the ultimate sacrifice in order to stop a sixty-three-ton airplane from slamming into his own house. Most Americans, of course, didn't have such acutely personal feelings about Flight 93. But that didn't mean they should forget its significance.

Bush lifted his gaze as the strains of Taps began to waft over the field, expertly played by two U.S. Air Force buglers—one in the woods, the second echoing his notes from a nearby hill. When they finished, the president turned away from the wreath and walked through the tall grass across the gently rolling landscape. It was his first visit to this desolate place, a former strip mine that had long ago been covered with dirt and overgrown with vegetation. In the distance, he could see two enormous drag line cranes abandoned decades earlier, when cheap steel imports undercut the market for strip-mined coal around these parts. They stood on the horizon next to piles of rusting scrap metal, which first-time visitors often mistook for wreckage of the plane. Truth be told, there wasn't much left of the plane, which disintegrated into about a billion tiny pieces. Most of it telescoped on impact, although the front of the fuselage broke off and bounced into the woods at the edge of this massive meadow. The resulting fire burned back the tree line, which used to come right up to the utility poles separating forest from field. Someone suggested cutting down the charred trunks and burying them elsewhere in a sort of proxy funeral, since there were no actual bodies that could be laid to rest. Indeed, 92 percent of the human remains had been incinerated on impact. But the local coroner, a lanky, bespectacled man named Wallace E. Miller, assured the victims' family members that this lonesome field, for better or worse, was now their loved ones' final resting place. He had the charred trees cut down and chipped into mulch that was now heaped in great piles near the bare spot. A young girl, presumably one of the victims' daughters, played on one of the piles as Bush walked over to greet more than five hundred other family members who had gathered to pay their respects at this unmarked cemetery.

"One of the things you've got to understand is that these people don't have any connection to this area," Miller told me at the edge of the field as Bush worked the crowd. "When we see jets out here, they're like a dot in the sky."

Leaning forward for emphasis, he added: "You're in the middle of nowhere—it's not a myth; it's reality. This is probably the remotest place there is between Cleveland and D.C. There's no doubt about it."

Yet on this day, the middle of nowhere was every bit as important as Washington and New York, which were also on Bush's itinerary. He had begun the somber anniversary in the nation's capital, emerging from the White House just as the sun was breaking over the tops of the trees. After attending a tearful service at St. John's Episcopal Church across from Lafayette Park, he and Laura joined White House employees on the South Lawn to observe a moment of silence at 8:46 A.M., the precise time of the first crash at the World Trade Center in New York.

Then it was off to the Pentagon for a solemn memorial in the shadow of the exterior wall that had been staved in a year earlier. Bush was greeted by the applause of 13,500 attendees in a makeshift stadium. He and Defense Secretary Donald Rumsfeld stood on a windswept stage with a group of young students clutching miniature American flags—classmates of the children who were among the passengers killed when Flight 77 plowed into the Pentagon. As a Marine sang the National Anthem, four soldiers on the roof directly behind Bush broke out the large American flag that had waved defiantly from the site of the wreckage immediately after the attack. Although the edge of the flag was weighted with a long pole, there was so much wind that the soldiers had trouble unfurling the giant banner. The pole clattered against the windows of the pristine wall, one of which was taped with a plaintive sign proclaiming, MARIAN WE MISS YOU. Then the entire flag, which was faded and streaked with dirt from its service a year earlier, blew completely back up on the roof, prompting good-natured laughter from the crowd. The soldiers struggled mightily with Old Glory, which utterly enveloped one of them. They finally managed to unfurl the flag just as the singing Marine hit the word "wave." The crowd applauded appreciatively as the anthem ended.

Then it was time for the Pledge of Allegiance. But just as the president put his hand over his heart, another gust of wind blew the flag back up on the roof. Everyone plowed ahead with the pledge anyway, and the soldiers on the roof finally decided to remove the flag from its overhang. Meanwhile, U.S. Solicitor Ted Olson, whose wife Barbara had been among the passengers killed in the attack, was ushered to the front row of the stadium. As he and the rest of the audience settled into their seats, Bush stepped to the lectern and began his brief speech with characteristic plainspokenness.

"One year ago, men and women and children were killed here because they were Americans," he said. "The memories of a great tragedy linger here. And for all who knew loss here, life is not the same.

"The one hundred and eighty-four whose lives were taken in this place—veterans and recruits, soldiers and civilians, husbands and wives, parents and children—left behind family and friends whose loss cannot be weighed. The murder of innocents cannot be explained—only endured. And though they died in tragedy, they did not die in vain. Their loss had moved a nation to action, in a cause to defend other innocent lives across the world."

As Bush spoke, the wind swayed a giant electronic billboard that was suspended overhead by a construction crane. The makeshift Jumbotron, which flashed full-color images of children's artwork, was tethered by cables that clanged noisily against metal scaffolding with every gust. As if to make the Secret Service even more nervous, several large canvas screens snapped and popped in the wind.

"In every turn of this war, we will always remember how it began, and who fell first—the thousands who went to work, boarded a plane, or reported to their posts," he said. "Today, the nation pays our respects to them. Here, and in Pennsylvania, and in New York, we honor each name—and each life."

Bush returned to his row, where he and Laura were given small American flags to wave as an Air Force soloist led the audience in singing "God Bless America." Then four jet fighters flew low and fast over the crowd, and it was time for the president to begin his pilgrimage to the next sorrowful site. But the tears he shed in Washington and Shanksville were just a warm-up for the most emotional stop of the day—New York City.

The air was cool and the water choppy as Bush stood at the bow of a fireboat that churned through the darkness of New York Harbor. To his right he could see the gaping hole in the Manhattan skyline where the World Trade Center had stood until one year and twelve hours earlier. To his left he could see the Statue of Liberty, illuminated by even more spotlights than usual. Straight ahead was Ellis Island, where the president eventually docked and disembarked. Having spent the last year coping with the immediate aftermath of the terrorist attacks and forcibly removing the Taliban regime from Afghanistan, Bush was eager to pivot into the next phase of the war against terrorism. But first he had to bring some semblance of closure to the current phase. He needed a fitting postscript for this wrenching chapter in American history. He decided to give one last speech devoted solely to September 11, summing up the sorrow and resolve that had consumed the nation for 365 days. It was a year in which Bush had learned to speak starkly and without embarrassment about epic themes—good and evil, love and hate, grief and righteousness. So it was without a hint of self-consciousness that he stood beneath a blackened New York sky—with the light from Lady Liberty shimmering off his shoulder—to address a televised audience that numbered in the tens of millions.

"Good evening. A long year has passed since enemies attacked our country. We've seen the images so many times they are seared on our souls, and remembering the horror, reliving the anguish, re-imagining the terror, is hard—and painful.

"For those who lost loved ones, it's been a year of sorrow, of empty places, of newborn children who will never know their fathers here on earth. For members of our military, it's been a year of sacrifice and service far from home. For all Americans, it has been a year of adjustment, of coming to terms with the difficult knowledge that our nation has determined enemies, and that we are not invulnerable to their attacks.

"Yet, in the events that have challenged us, we have also seen the character that will deliver us. We have seen the greatness of America in airline passengers who defied their hijackers and ran a plane into the ground to spare the lives of others. We've seen the greatness of America in rescuers who rushed up flights of stairs toward peril. And we continue to see the greatness of America in the care and compassion our citizens show to each other.

"September 11, 2001, will always be a fixed point in the life of America. The loss of so many lives left us to examine our own. Each of us was reminded that we are here only for a time, and these counted days should be filled with things that last and matter. Love for our families. Love for our neighbors, and for our country. Gratitude for life, and to the Giver of life.

"We resolved a year ago to honor every last person lost. We owe them remembrance and we owe them more. We owe them, and their children, and our own, the most enduring monument we can build: a world of liberty and security made possible by the way America leads, and by the way Americans lead our lives.

"The attack on our nation was also an attack on the ideals that make us a nation. Our deepest national conviction is that every life is precious, because every life is the gift of a Creator who intended us to live in liberty and equality. More than anything else, this separates us from the enemy we fight. We value every life; our enemies value none—not even the innocent, not even their own. And we seek the freedom and opportunity that give meaning and value to life.

"There is a line—in our time and in every time—between those who believe all men are created equal and those who believe that some men and women and children are expendable in the pursuit of power. There is a line—in our time and in every time—between the defenders of human liberty and those who seek to master the minds and souls of others. Our generation has now heard history's call, and we will answer it.

"America has entered a great struggle that tests our strength, and even more our resolve. Our nation is patient and steadfast. We continue to pursue the terrorists in cities and camps and caves across the earth. We are joined by a great coalition of nations to rid the world of terror. And we will not allow any terrorist or tyrant to threaten civilization with weapons of mass murder. Now and in the future, Americans will live as free people, not in fear, and never at the mercy of any foreign plot or power.

"This nation has defeated tyrants and liberated death camps, raised this lamp of liberty to every captive land. We have no intention of ignoring or appeasing history's latest gang of fanatics trying to murder their way to power. They are discovering, as others before them, the resolve of a great country and a great democracy. In the ruins of two towers, under a flag unfurled at the Pentagon, at the funerals of the lost, we have made a sacred promise to ourselves and to the world: We will not relent until justice is done and our nation is secure. What our enemies have begun, we will finish.

"I believe there is a reason that history has matched this nation with this time. America strives to be tolerant and just. We respect the faith of Islam, even as we fight those whose actions defile that faith. We fight, not to impose our will, but to defend ourselves and extend the blessings of freedom.

"We cannot know all that lies ahead. Yet we do know that God has placed us together in this moment, to grieve together, to stand together, to serve each other and our country. And the duty we have been given—defending America and our freedom—is also a privilege we share.

"We're prepared for this journey. And our prayer tonight is that God will see us through, and keep us worthy.

"Tomorrow is September the twelfth. A milestone is passed, and a mission goes on. Be confident. Our country is strong. And our cause is even larger than our country. Ours is the cause of human dignity—freedom guided by conscience and guarded by peace. This ideal of America is the hope of all mankind.

"That hope drew millions to this harbor. That hope still lights our way. And the light shines in the darkness. And the darkness will not overcome it.

"May God bless America."

The president had purposely avoided mentioning Iraq, although everyone knew that his vow not to allow any "tyrant to threaten civilization with weapons of mass murder" was directed squarely at Saddam Hussein. Bush figured there would be plenty of time for speeches devoted to Saddam, starting with a major address to the United Nations General Assembly the very next morning.

He hoped the U.N. speech would silence his critics, who for weeks had been accusing him of failing to "make his case" against Iraq. The criticism had been especially intense during the president's August vacation, a monthlong hiatus at his beloved Prairie Chapel Ranch in Crawford, Texas. Hardly a day went by when Democrats and journalists weren't expressing alarm about Iraq, especially after the Pentagon began leaking preliminary war plans that had been drawn up at Bush's direction.

"It was the summer of '02 that you began to see the planning functions begin to emerge," the president told me in an interview. "You plan and look at options and look at opportunities, conforming the military plan to the best intelligence you've got and your best view of the enemy.

"It started at low levels," he recalled. "And it started to bubble up, started hitting the surface. And it was there, that hot August of '02, that we began to have to fend off questions about: Is America getting ready to attack?"

He added: "In this town, many times the options being presented to the president end up in the papers—getting ahead of the reality."

To complicate matters, a number of elder statesmen from former Republican administrations had decided to offer the young president advice through newspaper op-ed columns. The most critical of these was written by Brent Scowcroft, who had served as national security adviser to the first President Bush.

"An attack on Iraq at this time would seriously jeopardize, if not destroy, the global counterterrorist campaign we have undertaken," Scowcroft warned in the *Wall Street Journal.*

This view was not shared by Henry Kissinger, who argued forcefully "for bringing matters to a head with Iraq." Richard Nixon's former secretary of state explicitly endorsed the Bush doctrine of striking enemies before they could strike America.

"The case for removing Iraq's capacity of mass destruction is extremely strong," Kissinger wrote in the *Los Angeles Times*. "The imminence of proliferation of weapons of mass destruction, the huge dangers it involves, the rejection of a viable inspection system, the demonstrated hostility of Saddam combine to produce an imperative for preemptive action."

Although Kissinger clearly disagreed with Scowcroft, the *New York Times* insisted that they both opposed Bush's march toward war. The paper ran a news article lumping their op-eds together as evidence that prominent Republicans "have begun to break ranks with President Bush over his administration's high-profile planning for war with Iraq, saying the administration has neither adequately prepared for military action nor made the case that it is needed. These senior Republicans include former Secretary of State Henry A. Kissinger and Brent Scowcroft."

The article was co-authored by *Times* reporter Todd Purdum, the husband of Dee Dee Myers, former press secretary to President Clinton. It was widely viewed as yet more evidence that *New York Times* Executive Editor Howell Raines was using the paper's news columns to crusade openly against war. Before September 2001, critics noted, Raines had run the *Times*'s liberal editorial page, where he had endorsed Bush's opponent, Vice President Al Gore, in the 2000 election. Since moving to the paper's ostensibly objective news pages, Raines—who once famously remarked that "the Reagan years oppressed me"—had been accused by conservatives and liberals alike of using those pages to make the case against war with Iraq.

"Not since William Randolph Hearst famously cabled his correspondent in Cuba, 'You furnish the pictures and I'll furnish the war,' has a newspaper so blatantly devoted its front pages to editorializing about a coming American war as has Howell Raines's *New York*

Times," thundered conservative columnist Charles Krauthammer in the *Washington Post* in August. "That's partisan journalism, and that's what Raines's *Times* does for a living."

Days later, liberal media critic Cynthia Cotts of the *Village Voice* chimed in with a column headlined "Howellin' Wolf: 'Times' Hounds Bush Over War Plan."

"No one denies the *Times* is flying in the face of Bush's war plans," Cotts wrote. "The *Times* has shown no signs of backing down from its casus non-belli."

Despite such bipartisan criticism of Raines's anti-war bias, he refused to publish a correction on the Kissinger mischaracterization. After three weeks of intense criticism, he grudgingly ran an "editor's note" that admitted the "article listed Mr. Kissinger incorrectly among Republicans who were warning outright against a war." But the lengthy note went on to argue that Kissinger didn't really want war after all.

Meanwhile, a third op-ed was written by James Baker III, the elder Bush's secretary of state and the man who helped the younger Bush win the Florida recount wars in the 2000 presidential election. Baker came right out and said that an attack on Iraq was the only way to get rid of Saddam. At the same time, he cautioned against unilateralism.

"Although the United States could certainly succeed, we should try our best not to have to go it alone," he wrote in the *New York Times* on Aug. 25.

Baker had a suggestion for building international support: Bush should ask the United Nations Security Council to pass a resolution "requiring that Iraq submit to intrusive inspections anytime, anywhere, with no exceptions, and authorizing all necessary means to enforce it."

The president, as it happened, agreed with Baker's advice. But he was determined to wait until the right moment before requesting such a resolution. Despite the growing calls for him to "make his case,"

Bush did not believe August was the appropriate time to kick off a rhetorical offensive against Saddam. The U.N., Congress, and much of America—not to mention the president himself—were all on vacation until September. Besides, Bush wanted to commemorate the first anniversary of the terrorist attacks before starting to beat the war drums. So all through August and into of September, he let the pressure build for him to make the case. Although he allowed Vice President Dick Cheney to test-market the case with a speech to the Veterans of Foreign Wars on August 26, Bush himself stayed mum. His detractors misinterpreted this silence as weakness, which only emboldened them to redouble their criticism. They scored short-term political points by gleefully characterizing the White House as "on the defensive." As part of this "defensiveness," White House Chief of Staff Andy Card pointed out that lots of major initiatives were routinely withheld until September.

"From a marketing point of view," the former auto executive told Elisabeth Bumiller of the *New York Times,* "you don't introduce new products in August."

This was widely interpreted as evidence that Bush was planning to politicize the Iraq issue—a misimpression Card blamed on Bumiller.

"Her quote was accurate, but the context wasn't exactly," he told me. "I wasn't talking about the war. It was a collection of things."

In the long run, however, Bush's decision to stay mum about Iraq would pay enormous political dividends. It allowed for the emergence of a national consensus that the president should forcefully and persuasively lay out his case for war—which of course was what he wanted to do all along. In short, Bush created a demand for his own argument. A few shrewd Democrats tried to warn their party about the dangerous timing of this development. With the midterm elections less than two months away, they desperately wanted to shift the national debate away from national security—which would presumably help the GOP—and onto the sluggish economy, which would pre-

sumably help the Democrats. Yet most liberals couldn't resist the urge
to pillory Bush on Iraq. In addition to demanding that he make his
case, they kept imploring him not to "go it alone" against Saddam.
They relished portraying him as a rogue Texas cowboy whose unbri-
dled unilateralism was isolating America and alienating allies. Some
even publicly predicted that Bush would recklessly attempt to wage
war without first seeking the blessing of Congress.

The president had little choice but to answer his critics by schedul-
ing a major speech at—of all places—the United Nations. He figured
that would quell the carping about "unilateralism."

"The case must be presented to the world," Bush told me. "And
the best place to present a case to the world is at the very body that has
been rejected by Saddam Hussein year after year after year.

"I had a twofold purpose going to the United Nations," he added.
"One was to begin to make the case. But the other was to say to the
United Nations: We want you to be effective. And Saddam Hussein
has made you ineffective on this issue because he has totally ignored
what you said. Now, why don't we work together to deal with this
threat?"

Bush hoped the detailed, methodical indictment he was preparing
against Saddam would put an end to complaints about his failure to
make the case against Iraq. Those complaints were lodged even in the
final minutes before he took the stage to address the General Assembly
on September 12. He was preceded by U.N. Secretary General Kofi
Annan, who gave a speech lauding the "restraints" of multilateralism
over the "political convenience" of unilateralism.

"There is no substitute for the unique legitimacy provided by the
United Nations," Annan tut-tutted.

When it was finally time for Bush to speak, he made clear that
while he welcomed the support of the international community, he
was willing to go it alone if necessary. "The purposes of the United
States should not be doubted," the president warned. "We must stand

up for our security, and for the permanent rights and the hopes of mankind. By heritage and by choice, the United States of America will make that stand."

Bush reminded the U.N. Security Council that for years Saddam had been flouting its resolutions on everything from human rights to weapons inspections. "He agreed to prove he is complying with every one of those obligations," the president said. "He has proven instead only his contempt for the United Nations."

Far from supplicating the international community, Bush was attempting to shame it. "Iraq has answered a decade of U.N. demands with a decade of defiance," he lectured the world's leaders. "Are Security Council resolutions to be honored and enforced, or cast aside without consequence? Will the United Nations serve the purpose of its founding, or will it be irrelevant?"

Stopping just short of calling the U.N. spineless, Bush nonetheless rubbed the organization's nose in Saddam's defiance.

"The conduct of the Iraqi regime is a threat to the authority of the United Nations," he challenged. "All the world now faces a test, and the United Nations a difficult and defining moment."

In a particularly stinging rebuke, Bush likened the U.N. to a toothless debating society. "We created the United Nations Security Council so that, unlike the League of Nations, our deliberations would be more than talk, our resolutions would be more than wishes," he scolded.

Switching gears, the president added insult to injury by patronizing an organization that was more accustomed to being scorned by conservative Republicans such as Bush. "We want the United Nations to be effective and respectful and successful," the president condescended. "We want the resolutions of the world's most important multilateral body to be enforced. And right now those resolutions are being unilaterally subverted by the Iraqi regime."

Mindful of Baker's advice, Bush also pledged to work with the

U.N. on whatever new resolutions might be necessary to end Saddam's tyranny. But he insisted that this time, the resolutions would actually mean something.

"The Security Council resolutions will be enforced, the just demands of peace and security will be met—or action will be unavoidable," the president vowed. "And a regime that has lost its legitimacy will also lose its power."

The speech carried unmistakable echoes of Bush's address to a joint session of Congress one year earlier, when he made the case for war against Afghanistan. In both speeches, the president spelled out specific conditions that the offending leader must fulfill to avert attack. In Saddam's case, Bush made three major demands: that he end support for terrorism; stop persecuting Iraqi civilians; and abandon his development of weapons of mass destruction. This last demand was the one Bush emphasized the most.

"Our greatest fear is that terrorists will find a shortcut to their mad ambitions when an outlaw regime supplies them with the technologies to kill on a massive scale," the president said. "In one place, in one regime, we find all these dangers, in their most lethal and aggressive forms—exactly the kind of aggressive threat the United Nations was born to confront."

Unlike George Galloway, who couldn't find room in his 1,800-word column to recount Saddam's blood-soaked biography, Bush managed to squeeze the whole sordid tale into a mere 1,300 words—which took up about half his twenty-five-minute address. The speech would have taken longer, but the president was interrupted by applause only once—when he announced the United States was ending its nineteen-year boycott of UNESCO, the U.N. educational organization that had given Saddam a literacy award for jailing truant students.

As for the oft-repeated complaint that Bush hadn't made his case against the butcher of Baghdad, the president pointed out that "by his deceptions, and by his cruelties, Saddam Hussein has made the case against himself."

Bush concluded his indictment of Saddam with an ominous warning to those who might be tempted to appease the dictator.

"Saddam Hussein's regime is a grave and gathering danger," he said. "To suggest otherwise is to hope against the evidence. To assume this regime's good faith is to bet the lives of millions and the peace of the world in a reckless gamble.

"And this is a risk we must not take."

After the speech, Bush dispatched a senior administration official to answer questions from the White House press corps, which had accompanied him to New York. Before long, the discussion turned to whether Saddam would actually comply with any resolutions the president might succeed in extracting from the U.N.

"Perhaps he will surprise us," the administration official said unconvincingly.

"You don't really believe that, do you?" asked Mark Knoller of CBS News.

"No," the official replied. "I don't."

4

MIDTERM MELTDOWN

EXACTLY ONE WEEK BEFORE the midterm elections, Karl Rove received an urgent phone call from White House Political Director Ken Mehlman.

"Are you watching TV?" Mehlman asked incredulously.

"No," Rove replied. "Should I be?"

At Mehlman's urging, Rove turned on the memorial service for Senator Paul Wellstone, the liberal Minnesota Democrat who had been killed in a plane crash four days earlier. The tragedy had thrown the white-knuckled contest for control of the Senate into absolute chaos. Before the crash, Wellstone had been expected to narrowly lose his seat to Rove's handpicked candidate, Republican Norm Coleman. Yet just twenty-four hours after the disaster, GOP polls showed Coleman trailing Wellstone's likely replacement, former Vice President Walter Mondale. Astonishingly, Mondale's lead over Coleman widened the next day to 52–39, according to a poll by Paul Harstad of Minnesota's Democratic-Farmer-Labor Party.

Rove could see exactly what was happening. Coleman's campaign was being swamped by the same wave of public sympathy that had drowned Republican John Ashcroft of Missouri in the 2000 Senate race. Back then, a plane crash had killed Ashcroft's opponent, Democratic Governor Mel Carnahan, twenty-two days before the election. Ashcroft immediately suspended his campaign out of a sense of decency. But then the acting governor, Democrat Roger Wilson, announced that if Missourians would elect Carnahan posthumously, Wilson would appoint his widow, Jean, to fill the vacant Senate seat. Although she was a political neophyte, Jean Carnahan soared in the polls. Ashcroft eventually began to close the gap, but it was too late. He became the first U.S. senator to lose an election to a dead man.

The same thing was happening all over again, only this time the tragedy had occurred eleven days before the election instead of twenty-two. Coleman, the former mayor of St. Paul, immediately suspended his campaign and refused to even discuss politics. But that merely allowed Democrats to pound him without opposition. One of his harshest critics was Harry Reid of Nevada, the Senate's second-ranking Democrat, who savaged Coleman two days after Wellstone's death.

"He stood for everything that Paul was against," railed the majority whip on CNN's *Late Edition*. "If I were in Minnesota, I would certainly want a Walter Mondale over a Coleman, I'll tell you that."

Reid went on to ridicule the notion that Coleman was conducting a "principled race."

"One of my responsibilities is to look at Senate races all over the country and how they're going and what's happening," he said. "The most negative, derogatory campaign to take place anyplace in the country was conducted by Mayor Coleman."

Reid claimed this view had been shared by Wellstone and his wife, Sheila, who was also killed in the crash. "I've spoken to the Wellstone family, both Sheila and I've talked to Paul, and I know how they felt about Coleman and his campaign," he said. "His was the most negative campaign in America."

Over at Fox News Channel that same day, conservatives resigned themselves to the inevitability of a Mondale victory.

"I suppose he'll be favored over Norm Coleman and Democrats will probably hold that seat," lamented commentator Bill Kristol on *Fox News Sunday*.

"I can almost guarantee that Walter Mondale will be the new senator," added anchorman Brit Hume, already warming to the idea. "This is a very high-quality individual, a very honorable man, wonderful sense of humor, extraordinary decency and integrity, a man of the highest caliber. Minnesota will be lucky to have him."

The next day, Judy Woodruff of CNN's *Inside Politics* went to Minnesota to interview Coleman, who still refused to talk politics. It was the day of Wellstone's funeral and the day before the public memorial service.

"We still have to bury the dead," Coleman said. "If I ruled the world, Judy, we'd all still be on our knees and saying some prayers."

Coleman refused to criticize Wellstone or Mondale, calling each a "great man." He seemed unfazed by the very real possibility that he would be responsible for his own party failing to regain control of the Senate.

"It's just an election," he shrugged. "We've got to deal with the loss of lives now. Let us do that. Let us do that."

"Norm Coleman, thank you very much for talking with us—we appreciate it," said Woodruff. But in her very next breath she suggested she didn't really believe what Coleman had said. "Up next, I will ask the No. 2 Democrat in the Senate, Harry Reid of Nevada, if some Republicans in Minnesota are going on the attack even before Paul Wellstone is buried."

After a commercial break, Woodruff allowed Reid to resume the rant he had begun on CNN a day earlier. The senator was particularly contemptuous of Coleman's claim that he had put his campaign on hold. "Judy, Mr. Coleman is campaigning and that's why he's on your program," he said. "Couldn't they wait until he's buried before they do their campaigning?"

Reid did not mention that he himself had openly campaigned for Mondale, and trashed Coleman a day earlier on that very network— clearly a campaign activity. Nor did he mention Democrat Paul Harstad's 52–39 poll the previous evening. Yet he accused Republicans of taking their own polls while rescue workers were still "gathering the bodies out of the woods in Minnesota."

"This is really about as much as I have seen before, Judy," Reid complained. "I mean, couldn't they keep their polls quiet until after the man is buried? I just think this is so—this is classless."

With Coleman refusing to defend himself against such attacks and the wave of public sympathy for Democrats expected to crest at the televised memorial service scheduled for the next day, Woodruff was pessimistic about the Republican's prospects.

"Norm Coleman clearly in a tough spot politically," she told viewers in that verbless syntax peculiar to TV journalists. "Houdini couldn't get out of this box."

Coleman was not the only Republican candidate who went from likely winner to likely loser in the eleventh hour of the campaign. GOP challenger Doug Forrester was thirteen points ahead of New Jersey Senator Robert Torricelli just five weeks before the election when the scandal-plagued Democrat abruptly quit the race.

"I will not be responsible for the loss of the Democratic majority in the United States Senate," a tearful Torricelli said at a news conference.

But the state deadline for changing the name of a candidate on the ballot had passed more than two weeks earlier. Forrester, who had spent months transforming himself from underdog into the odds-on favorite, denounced the Democrats for their "desperate attempt to retain power."

"The laws of the state of New Jersey do not include a 'we-think-we're-going-to-lose-so-we-get-to-pick-someone-new' clause," he said at his own news conference.

But the Democrats—borrowing a page from Al Gore's playbook in the Florida recount wars—filed a lawsuit. Sure enough, the Democrat-dominated New Jersey Supreme Court ruled that Torricelli could be replaced by former Senator Frank Lautenberg, a Mondalesque warhorse who immediately pulled ahead of Forrester in the polls.

"Mulligans are bad in golf and they're even worse in politics," a senior White House official grumbled to me in the West Wing.

With Democrats controlling the Senate by a single vote, Republicans had been counting on wins in both New Jersey and Minnesota to have a fighting chance at regaining the majority. But now that weak Democratic candidates had been replaced by strong in both races, the GOP's hopes were fading.

Still, there were signs that Democrats were beginning to overplay their hand. For starters, Vice President Dick Cheney was supposed to represent the White House at the Wellstone memorial. But Democratic organizers claimed that Wellstone's sons, David and Mark, did not want the vice president to attend. They hadn't forgotten how Cheney personally intervened to make their father's race more difficult: In the spring of 2001, Wellstone was looking forward to facing a less formidable GOP opponent—Tim Pawlenty, majority leader of the Minnesota House. But two hours before Pawlenty was to announce his candidacy at a press conference, he received an extraordinary phone call from Cheney, who urged him to step aside. The vice president made clear that he and Bush and the rest of the White House political team planned to throw their considerable clout behind Coleman, a better known and more electable candidate. For the good of the party, Cheney intoned, Pawlenty should immediately abort his Senate candidacy. Pawlenty reluctantly acquiesced, deciding to run for governor instead. The White House then vigorously backed Coleman, who proceeded to make Wellstone's life miserable.

"These last few weeks, few months—they weren't easy," Mark Wellstone acknowledged wearily. "They were not easy."

So he and David were not about to let Cheney share the limelight of their father's memorial service, Democrats said. Besides, the vice president was already planning to come to Minnesota later in the week to campaign for Coleman. He would be followed by First Lady Laura Bush and even the president himself. Why give the White House any more free publicity?

When the snub became public, Democrats blamed it on the vice president's security detail, claiming that they had merely wanted to save mourners the trouble of being subjected to intrusive Secret Service protocols. That explanation collapsed, however, when it was revealed that the list of invitees included former President Clinton, who brought along his own Secret Service detail.

Clinton was given a hero's welcome when he entered Williams Arena at the University of Minnesota, which was packed with more than 20,000 Democrats and a handful of Republicans. TV cameras flashed the former president's face on an enormous cubic Jumbotron suspended over the center of the cavernous arena, which prompted wild applause from the crowd. Other Democrats were also cheered, including Senator Hillary Rodham Clinton; former Vice President Al Gore; the Reverend Jesse Jackson; Democratic Senator Ted Kennedy; and Senate Majority Leader Tom Daschle. The loudest and most sustained cheer, however, was reserved for Wellstone's replacement on the ballot, Walter Mondale.

By contrast, when Senate Majority Leader Trent Lott's face was flashed on the Jumbotron moments later, the Republican was roundly booed. So were two major figures in Minnesota politics—former GOP Senator Rod Grams and Governor Jesse Ventura, a political independent.

In the short term, these partisan outbursts were quickly forgotten as various speakers rose to deliver eloquent eulogies to Wellstone, his wife, and the six other people killed in the crash. One after another, the victims' friends and family members gave speeches that focused on the personal, not political, aspects of the tragedy.

But then Wellstone campaign treasurer Rick Kahn took the stage. Instead of reflecting on his thirty-three-year friendship with Wellstone, Kahn boldly leapt across the line of decorum by imploring the crowd to elect Mondale. Never mind that the broadcast was being carried live on Minnesota's TV and radio stations, which were not supposed to air unpaid campaign commercials. Kahn whipped the crowd into a partisan frenzy by exhorting Democrats to "stand up for all the people" Wellstone had championed. Thousands of Democrats leapt to their feet and roared their approval. When Mondale's smiling face was flashed again on the Jumbotron, the place went ballistic.

"If Paul Wellstone's legacy comes to an end, then our spirits will be crushed and we will drown in a river of tears," Kahn warned. "We are begging you: Do not let that happen. We are begging you to help us win this Senate election for Paul Wellstone."

Despite the crowd's enthusiastic response, Democratic staffers for Mondale and Wellstone sensed that Kahn had veered into dangerous territory. They began cutting nervous glances at each other. But Kahn was just getting warmed up.

"WE'RE GONNA ORGANIZE! WE'RE GONNA ORGANIZE! WE'RE GONNA ORGANIZE!" he thundered, making a chopping motion with his right arm to punctuate each repetition. "WE'RE GONNA ORGANIZE! WE'RE GONNA ORGANIZE! WE'RE GONNA ORGANIZE!"

Bill and Hillary Clinton looked at each other and grinned.

The arena was really rocking now. People had no intention of sitting down anytime soon.

But there were audible gasps when Kahn began demanding that

Republicans switch allegiances and start campaigning for Mondale. He called out the names of five GOP senators in attendance and unabashedly beseeched them to heed the voice of Wellstone's tortured ghost.

"Can you not hear your friend calling you one last time to step forward on his behalf?" Kahn implored.

He then singled out Representative Jim Ramstad of Minnesota's 3rd District and put him on the spot in front of 20,000 people, not to mention a national C-SPAN audience, which by now included a mesmerized Karl Rove.

"You know that Paul loved you," Kahn said. "He needs you now. I am begging you: Please let the people of this state hear your voice on his behalf to keep his legacy alive. And help us win this election for Paul Wellstone!"

Appalled, Governor Ventura and his wife walked out in protest. Senator Lott also departed the building.

Kahn's fire-and-brimstone speech was followed by a relatively sober eulogy from Wellstone's eldest son, David. Still, when the thirty-seven-year-old spoke wistfully about "the win that was gonna happen Tuesday," the crowd whooped excitedly.

"That's what was gonna happen; it was moving that way," he added. "Let's not worry. It's gonna be all right. We know what we gotta do. We know what we have to do and let's do it."

Both David and his thirty-year-old brother, Mark, who gave the next speech, described their parents and sister, who also died in the crash, in tender, heartfelt terms that moved many to tears. But the poignancy was obliterated when Mark ended his speech with a defiant call to arms. With thirty-four TV cameras trained on his every move, the mournful son suddenly morphed into an enraged partisan.

"WE WILL WIN! WE WILL WIN! WE WILL WIN!" he screamed, stabbing his finger in the air with a ferocity that shook his long curly hair. "WE WILL WIN! WE WILL WIN! WE WILL WIN! WE WILL WIN! WE WILL WIN! WE WILL WIN!"

The once-solemn memorial was now a shameless, foot-stomping, rafter-rattling political rally. The audience was positively delirious by the time Mark turned the stage over to the final speaker of the evening, Senator Tom Harkin.

The Iowa Democrat's voice rose dramatically as he spoke of Wellstone's beloved campaign bus, which had been painted green and fitted with a rear platform so that the candidate could wave to supporters.

"And now we must continue Paul's journey for justice in America," Harkin said. "Tonight I ask you all: Will you stand up and join together and board that bus? SAY YES!"

He raised his right fist in defiance as the crowd answered: "YES!" Harkin was getting so worked up that he stripped off his suit jacket.

"For Paul Wellstone, will you stand up and keep fighting for social and economic justice? SAY YES!" he exhorted, this time punching his left fist into the air.

"YES!" came the reply.

"For Paul!" Harkin cried. "For Paul, will you stand up and keep fighting for better wages for those who mop our floors and clean our bathrooms, for those who take care of our elderly, take care of our sick, teach our kids and help our homeless? SAY YES!"

"YES!"

Now Harkin was gesticulating like a revivalist preacher, expertly inciting the crowd with populist fervor.

"For Sheila!" he shouted. "For Sheila, will you stand up and keep fighting for our families, so women and children will be safe from domestic abuse? SAY YES!"

"YES!"

"For Paul, will you stand up and keep fighting for cleaner air and cleaner water, for a cleaner environment for our children and our future? SAY YES!"

"YES!"

"For Paul, will you stand up and keep fighting, for peace and understanding, and to stop the exploitation of women and children around the world? SAY YES!"

"YES!" hollered Bill Clinton as he pumped his fist twice in approval. He and Hillary and Mondale were grinning with delight at Harkin's outburst.

"For Paul! For Paul, will you stand up and keep fighting to end discrimination based on race, gender, religion, ethnicity, or sexual orientation? SAY YES!"

"YES!"

The crowd was convulsing in paroxysms of partisan fervor. Although Harkin never mentioned the GOP, his implication was clear: Republicans like Coleman could not be trusted to carry on Wellstone's fight for the downtrodden.

"NOW! NOW! NOW! NOW!" commanded Harkin as he neared his feverish crescendo. "Let's all get on that bus together, that green bus, that bus of hope, and let's keep it moving to a better America! Keep standing up! Keep fighting! Keep saying YES! To justice, to hope, for people!

"FOR PAUL! FOR PAUL! FOR PAUL!" he cried, spinning 360 degrees to face the various sections of the audience. "FOR PAUL! FOR PAUL! FOR PAUL! FOR PAUL!"

The place was going wild. The liberal *Minneapolis Star Tribune* would later compare the "chanting and ranting" of Harkin and Kahn to "Nazi or totalitarian rallies."

Although the TV cameras did not show him, Coleman was also in attendance. He spent those three hours watching quietly from the shadows, where a steady string of embarrassed Democrats approached him to apologize for their wretched excess.

Indeed, the state's Democrats were forced to issue a statement admitting they "may have crossed the line." Even before the rally was over, Minnesota TV stations and newspapers were deluged with angry phone calls from mortified viewers.

Rove, having watched the entire spectacle from his home in Washington, was utterly flabbergasted. "It's like watching a slow-moving car wreck," he told me. "And then they reran it on C-SPAN and I watched it from start to finish again. I mean, the angry treasurer saying 'he loved you' to the Republican congressman. And the booing. The whole thing was unseemly."

Rove hadn't seen this level of acid partisanship since the Florida debacle two years earlier. Back then, Gore and his team had engaged in scorched-earth political warfare—even organizing a campaign to throw out military ballots—in their desperate quest to overturn the election. Now it was time for another election, and the hard-edged stridency had returned. The same nastiness he'd seen during Bush's Portland visit, Rove mused, had raised its head again. He should have seen it coming.

The trend line of the Democrats' frustration was easy enough to trace. Having spent August demanding that Bush "make his case" against Iraq, they spent September regretting their demand. Suddenly it was politically acceptable for the president to talk up national security—his strong suit—right before an election, and the Democrats, who had demanded the discussion, were in no position to complain. Bush had merely called their bluff.

"We were doing exactly what they wanted us to do," Rove told me. "The fact of the matter was, we were taking them at their word."

Even before the president's big speech to the United Nations, the White House had quietly planted the seeds of a public relations offensive aimed at selling the war. It started the day after Labor Day, when Bush summoned leaders of the reconvened Congress to the White House for a high-level briefing on Iraq. The next day, additional lawmakers were brought to the Pentagon for a similar presentation by Cheney, Defense Secretary Donald Rumsfeld, and CIA Director George Tenet. Some jittery Democrats sought assurances from the administration that there would be no war until after the election. Knowing it would be logistically impossible to prepare for war in such a short span anyway, Bush magnanimously promised not to spring an "October surprise." But if Democrats insisted on talking about Iraq in the run-up to the election, then by God Bush was going to oblige them.

By the time the president delivered his U.N. speech on September 12, the Iraq public relations offensive was taking on a life of its own. Bush made sure the story had legs by demanding the next day that the Security Council pass a resolution within "weeks, not months." This gave the world body the green light to deliberate for just under two months, effectively guaranteeing that the Iraq debate would come to a head right around the time of the election.

Having given the U.N. its marching orders for a resolution against Iraq, Bush now did the same to Congress. Again, he played the shame card.

"Democrats waiting for the U.N. to act?" he asked reporters with exaggerated incredulity. "It seems to me that if you're representing the United States, you ought to be making a decision on what's best for the United States."

Bush even imitated an imaginary Democrat trying to defend such a wait-and-see approach. "Vote for me, and, oh by the way, on a matter of national security, I think I'm going to wait for somebody else to act," he said derisively. "I think I'm going to wait for the United Nations to make a decision."

Democrats saw the handwriting on the wall and called for debate on the resolution to be postponed until after the election.

"I think we should give the president a little breathing room," counseled Senator Joseph Biden, chairman of the Foreign Relations Committee. "We should all just calm down a little bit."

But polls showed two-thirds of the public supporting Bush, who was calling for a firm expression of support from Congress. The president helpfully drafted a resolution and submitted it to lawmakers on September 19. He made clear that he wanted the measure passed before Congress adjourned in mid-October, which put the onus on lawmakers to spend the next month debating national security. Realizing it was no longer politically feasible to delay the vote until after the election, moderate Democrats instead called for speedy passage so they could change the subject to the economy. But liberal Democrats like Senator Edward Kennedy of Massachusetts insisted on giving long-winded floor speeches arguing against war, which guaranteed a protracted debate on national security down the midterm homestretch.

Only after all these timelines had been set into motion did the Democrats begin to suspect that they'd been outmaneuvered. It dawned on them too late that they were powerless to change the topic of the national conversation away from national security before the midterms.

"It's like playing a very bad gin rummy game where you play the wrong card every time," said Rove, who attributed the losing strategy to Senate Majority Leader Daschle. "It's like he was constantly thinking: What can I feed Bush? What can I discard that would be helpful?

"Every card he played, he played to our advantage," Rove marveled. "And we sat there going: Why is he doing this?"

Even when there was an occasional lull in the Iraq debate, some prominent Democrat would come forward and give a big speech on the subject, reigniting the entire controversy. On September 23, for example, Al Gore gave a major address accusing Bush of pandering to conservative Republicans by pushing for war. The former vice president, who was mulling another run for the White House, could afford to stir up the debate because he wouldn't be voting on the congressional resolution. But his former running mate, Connecticut Senator Joe Lieberman—who was also considering a presidential campaign—

had no such luxury. The day after the Gore speech, Lieberman made front-page headlines of his own by sharply disagreeing with Gore's contention that Bush was politicizing the war.

"I have never said that and I don't believe it," said Lieberman, who supported the idea of ousting Saddam. "I'm grateful President Bush wants to do this and I don't question his motives."

The Gore-Lieberman split illustrated a larger chasm within the Democratic Party. While most congressional Republicans were united behind Bush, Democrats were divided into three camps—antiwar liberals, pro-war moderates, and those who could not or would not make up their minds. Things got nasty when the liberal wing began accusing undecideds like Daschle of going soft on Bush. Like many in his caucus, Daschle was conflicted about whether to support the war, and had yet to take a strong public position one way or the other. He, too, was contemplating a run for president, which made him even more wary of staking out the wrong position. But the complaints from liberals mounted, and Daschle finally decided to placate his critics. On September 25, he went to the floor of the Senate for a major speech on Iraq. But instead of announcing his clear-cut support or opposition to war, Daschle contented himself with accusing Bush of politicizing the debate.

For evidence, Daschle relied on that morning's *Washington Post.* Reporter Dana Milbank had written a front-page story accusing the White House of talking up national security "to boost Republican candidates in the midterm elections." To support his thesis, Milbank cited Cheney's appearance two days earlier at a Kansas fund-raiser for Adam Taff, a Republican who was trying to unseat Democratic congressman Dennis Moore.

"Cheney said security would be bolstered if Taff were to defeat Rep. Dennis Moore," Milbank wrote. To prove his point, the reporter cited a headline in the *Topeka Capital-Journal:* "Cheney talks about Iraq at congressional fund-raiser/Electing Taff would aid war effort."

Milbank did not, however, quote what Cheney actually said about Taff at the fund-raiser, which was far less sinister.

"He'll be vital in helping us meet the key priorities for the nation—in terms of winning the war on terror, strengthening the economy and defending our homeland," Cheney told the donors. "President Bush and I are very grateful for the opportunity to serve our country. We thank you for your support, not just for our efforts, but for candidates like Adam Taff, who will make a fine partner for us in the work ahead."

By political standards it was an innocuous set of remarks, a far cry from politicization of the war. Yet Daschle decided to follow Milbank's lead, steering clear of actually quoting Cheney and contenting himself by quoting the *Post* quoting the *Capital-Journal.*

"I listen to reports of the vice president," Daschle said. "The headline written in the paper the next day about the speech he gave to that fund-raiser was, 'Cheney talks about war/Electing Taft would aid war effort.'"

Actually, the headline had Cheney talking about "Iraq," not "war," but Daschle was already moving on to Exhibit B in his indictment of the White House. He recalled a mysterious incident from three months earlier, when a Democratic Senate staffer obtained a White House computer diskette containing a confidential PowerPoint analysis of the upcoming midterms by Rove and Mehlman. The anonymous staffer, who gleefully leaked the disk to several newspapers, claimed to have found it in Lafayette Park, which Rove and Mehlman and an intern had traversed en route to a presentation to the party faithful in the Hay Adams Hotel across from the White House. One of the slides, labeled "Republican Strategy," recommended six campaign themes for GOP candidates:

- Focus on war and economy
- Promote compassion agenda—education, welfare, faith

- Highlight Democrats' obstructionism on judges, agenda
- Mobilize GOP base, reach out to Hispanics, unions, African Americans
- Strong teamwork between White House, political committees and members
- Maximize outside resources and create new forums

Despite the comprehensiveness of this wide-ranging strategy, Daschle managed to boil it down to three words—and they weren't "promote compassion agenda."

"We find a diskette discovered in Lafayette Park, a computer diskette that was lost," Daschle fumed. "Advice was given by Karl Rove, and the quote in the disk was 'focus on war.'"

Rove disputed Daschle's claim that Democrats just happened to "find" the diskette.

"It's never become clear to me exactly how they got the disk," he told me. "I don't accept the fact that the young lad dropped it into the middle of Lafayette Park. I don't believe that. I don't know how they got it."

Daschle, in his speech on the Senate floor, portrayed himself as having spent months refusing to believe the White House would ever politicize the war. But after reading Milbank's story that morning, for which he himself had been interviewed, Daschle announced that he'd changed his mind. In the article, he noted, Milbank quoted Bush as saying in a recent speech that "the Democratic-controlled Senate is 'not interested in the security of the American people.'"

Truth be told, the president had not singled out Democrats for criticism. In fact, he had gone out of his way in that speech to praise both parties.

"People are working hard in Washington to get it right," Bush said, "both Republicans and Democrats. See, this isn't a partisan issue."

Moreover, Bush had not even been talking about the war. Rather, he had been referring to the debate over creation of the new Homeland Security Department, the biggest reorganization of the federal government in over half a century. Bowing to labor unions, Democrats did not want Bush to have hiring and firing authority over employees of the new department. The dispute was holding up passage of a bill to establish the agency.

"The Senate is more interested in special interests in Washington and not interested in the security of the American people," the president said.

Although it was abundantly clear that Bush was talking about the Homeland Security bill, Daschle seized on this quote as evidence that the president was politicizing the war.

"Not interested in the security of the American people? You tell Senator Inouye he is not interested in the security of the American people," he said, referring to Democrat Daniel Inouye of Hawaii, who lost an arm during World War II. "You tell those who fought in Vietnam and in World War II they are not interested in the security of the American people. That is outrageous! Outrageous!"

Daschle, whose supporters had alerted TV news crews to have their cameras trained on him when he went to the floor, was positively seething. His voice lowered into a growl; he appeared to be struggling mightily to retain his composure.

"The president ought to apologize to Senator Inouye and every veteran who fought in every war who is a Democrat in the United States Senate. He ought to apologize to the American people. That is wrong! We ought not politicize this war! We ought not to politicize the rhetoric about war in life and death!"

As TV viewers watched in rapt fascination, Daschle implored Bush to haul himself out of the political gutter.

"Our founding fathers would be embarrassed by what they are seeing going on right now," he fairly spat. "Mr. President, it's not too late it end this politicization. It's not too late to forget the pollsters, forget the campaign fund-raisers, forget making accusations about how interested in national security Democrats are."

In one short burst of political theater, Daschle had mischaracterized the words of the president, the vice president, and Rove, who told me: "Daschle lost it." When a journalist questioned the veracity of Daschle's accusations later in the day, the Democrat shrugged and said he was merely citing what the media had reported. Never mind that the full text of the Bush and Cheney speeches, not to mention the Rove slide show, had been widely available to anyone with an Internet connection. The majority leader of the Senate simply professed ignorance of these source materials, and held himself blameless for any media misinterpretations he may have cited. The important thing for Daschle was that he had satisfied the liberal wing of his party by attacking Bush on the war.

Emboldened by this attack, a liberal Democratic congressman stood on Iraqi soil four days later and told millions of television viewers that President Bush would lie to the American people in order to justify war against Saddam.

"I think the president would mislead the American people," said Representative Jim McDermott on ABC's *This Week.*

By contrast, McDermott insisted Saddam's henchmen would be truthful with U.N. weapons inspectors. "They said they would allow us to go and look anywhere we wanted," the Washington Democrat said. "I think you have to take the Iraqis on their face value."

"Why should we take the Iraqis at their word?" asked host George Stephanopoulos, a former Clinton aide. "As the White House points out, they have a decade-long record of denying inspectors access and deceiving the U.N. inspectors."

The question was answered by Representative David Bonior, one of two other Democratic congressmen with McDermott in Baghdad. "Well, you know, we could go back and play the blame game here until, you know, the, the moon comes out, but that's not going to do us any good," said Bonior, who shared McDermott's penchant for bad-mouthing the United States while on enemy soil. "There is very little support for the United States, our position, in the international community right now, because we're trying to push and dictate."

Rather than "push and dictate," McDermott suggested a wait-and-see approach for both Congress and the United Nations.

"We don't have to pass a resolution in the Congress or in the Security Council right now," he said. "Things are moving forward."

Things were moving forward, all right, but not in the direction Democrats wanted. The public was livid over McDermott's stunt, which recalled Jane Fonda's infamous visit to Hanoi. House Minority Leader Richard Gephardt came under intense pressure to get his caucus under control. Sensing an opportunity, the White House quietly opened a direct line of negotiation with the Missouri Democrat over the congressional resolution authorizing war. Gephardt, who was contemplating his own presidential run, was receptive to the idea of out-maneuvering Daschle, a potential rival, on an issue that might figure prominently in the 2004 election. The administration, still smarting over Daschle's anti-Bush rant on the Senate floor, disinvited him to a White House meeting on the resolution. To complete Daschle's isolation, Senate Minority Leader Trent Lott, Mississippi Republican, discreetly enlisted yet another presidential hopeful, Senator Lieberman, to be the Democratic sponsor of the Senate version of the resolution. On October 2, realizing he was the odd man out, Daschle canceled a morning press conference and watched helplessly as Lieberman went to the Senate floor minutes later to announce that he would be leading a group of Democrats in support of the resolution authorizing Bush to wage war.

"It was a night-and-day difference between Gephardt—who was straightforward and 'I'm with you'—and Daschle, who was the nuanced, on-the-one-hand-this-on-the-other-hand-that guy," Rove said. "Daschle basically was saying very noncommittal things."

Thus, Daschle was the only congressional leader not present at a bipartisan show of support for the president in the Rose Garden the next day. The Senate majority leader's absence was glaringly obvious as Bush surrounded himself with Democrats and Republicans from both houses of Congress. With Gephardt and Lieberman at his side, Bush looked and sounded like a man who was about to get his way on the resolution.

"The issue is now before the United States Congress," he declared. "This debate will be closely watched by the American people, and this debate will be remembered in history."

He added: "As the vote nears, I urge all members of Congress to consider this resolution with the greatest of care. The choice between them could not be more consequential."

Nine days later, even Daschle came around to Bush's way of thinking. He was among a minority of congressional Democrats who voted yes on the resolution authorizing the president to wage war against Iraq. Not surprisingly, this group encompassed most of the presidential hopefuls, including Gephardt, Lieberman, Senator John Kerry of Massachusetts, and Senator John Edwards of North Carolina. Two other White House aspirants, Senator Bob Graham of Florida and Representative Dennis Kucinich of Ohio, were among the majority of congressional Democrats who voted no. The vote crystalized the deep divide within the Democratic Party—43 percent were hawks, 57 percent doves. By contrast, a whopping 97.4 percent of congressional Republicans voted for the resolution. For better or worse, the GOP was remarkably united behind President Bush.

"That was a difficult debate," Daschle acknowledged in a speech from the Senate floor on October 15.

It was the understatement of the season. With the midterm elections now just three weeks away, the beleaguered majority leader was desperate to pivot to an issue that was less divisive for his own party and more damaging to Republicans. So he seized on the stock market's tumble to five-year lows as proof of Bush's "poor economic leadership."

"This isn't just a bear market—it's a grizzly bear market," Daschle said. "The broad Standard and Poor's 500 stock index has now lost nearly half of its value. Since President Bush took office, Americans have seen the markets lose $5.7 trillion in value—that's $9.5 billion a day.

"Here's what that means to a person with $100,000 in a 401(k) invested in the S&P 500 when President Bush took office: the value of their investment has now decreased by $35,000," he added.

While these attacks were effective in driving down public approval of Bush's economic performance, they were not exactly boosting support for the Democratic alternative—tax hikes. Prominent Democrats wanted to repeal Bush's $1.35 trillion tax cut, which had been enacted in the summer of 2001. Daschle himself was on record saying the tax cut had hurt the economy. The clear implication was that Democrats wanted to raise taxes. But Daschle didn't dare put it that bluntly in his Senate speech three weeks before the midterms.

"Last week, it became even more clear that this administration's focus is not on the economy," he said. "The White House announced that the president will be hitting the campaign trail for fourteen straight days before the November 5th election. President Bush should cancel that political trip. He needs to spend less time trying to save the jobs of Republican politicians, and more time trying to save the jobs of average Americans."

Not everyone in Daschle's party wanted Bush to stop campaigning. Others egged him on, confident the president would drag down the GOP. "Several Democrats argued that Mr. Bush was taking a chance in leaving the White House to campaign, noting that President Bill Clinton did much the same thing in 1994, when the Democrats lost," the *New York Times* reported on October 23. "Mr. Clinton's chief of staff at the time, John Podesta, said he now believed that Mr. Clinton might have had a more positive influence on voters had he stayed above the partisan fray and remained in the presidential setting of the White House." Even on the issue of Bush's go-for-broke campaign strategy, Democrats were deeply divided.

Ironically, Clinton himself had no intention of staying above the fray this time either. He and Hillary, and Al Gore, were campaigning just as frenetically as Bush, turning the midterm elections into as much of a referendum on the old Clinton-Gore platform as one on Bush-Cheney. Clinton was on a tear through twenty states, including Hawaii. His wife was also crisscrossing the country, at one point telling Democratic supporters of Missouri Senator Jean Carnahan that Bush had been "selected," not elected. Gore kept up his own busy schedule, which included a rally for Maryland Governor Kathleen Kennedy Townsend.

"I am Al Gore," he deadpanned. "I used to be the next president."

Although his defeat in 2000 had been a painful repudiation of the Clinton-Gore legacy, Gore and his old boss had been able to defer blame by claiming Bush's victory was illegitimate. But they knew that if their party lost again in 2002, they could no longer plausibly deny the public's rejection of their way of governing. To make sure this did not happen, Clinton arranged for his best friend, fund-raiser Terry McAuliffe, to be installed as chairman of the Democratic National Committee, which was charged with orchestrating the Democratic strategy for the midterm elections.

Now, just days before the midterms, McAuliffe's party was widely perceived as antiwar and pro-tax. Worse yet, McAuliffe was still fixating on the recount wars of 2000. He told reporters and editors of the *New York Times* on October 23 that his number one goal was to defeat Florida Governor Jeb Bush, whom McAuliffe blamed for his brother's ascension to the presidency. As the *Times* explained, "The goal is not only to avenge Al Gore's failure to capture the state in 2000, but also to set the stage for a Democratic presidential candidate in 2004."

McAuliffe couldn't have agreed more.

"To have a governor in a state in a presidential year—for money, message, mobilization—will help us tremendously," he enthused. "I cannot tell you the impact of us having the governor of Florida heading into the '04 presidential."

The DNC chief was so certain of victory that he became downright cocky. "There won't be anything as devastating to President Bush as his brother's losing in Florida," McAuliffe crowed. "Jeb is gone!"

But there were nearly two weeks remaining before the election, and Jeb's brother, the president, was campaigning as if his political life depended upon the outcome.

"The president had made a critical decision back in August that he's just gonna basically take all his political chips and toss them onto the table and bet big," Rove explained. Bush was determined not to repeat the failure of his father, whose record popularity in the wake of the Gulf War evaporated when it came time for reelection

"You've got to spend capital to earn capital," the president told me. "And if you don't spend it, it fritters away, it dissipates."

Still, even some of the Bush's closest advisers had second thoughts about betting the farm on the midterms.

"There was some consternation inside the White House," Rove acknowledged. "Would the president be looking too political? Would he be putting himself in harm's way?

"I mean, in most midterm elections the incumbent tries to stay hidden, because the results are going to turn out to be bad. And the more visible you are, the more you bear the blame for it.

"But the president said: Look, I came here to get something done. It's easier for me to get something done if we've got allies. And we've got a chance to affect these races. Let's be bold, put it out on the table and go."

Rove attributed Bush's gamble to the president's own political instincts. "He smelled that there were issues out there—national issues that would work to our advantage," he explained. "And that the Democrats had created—particularly in the Senate—a couple of very high-visibility issues and didn't understand how badly they'd mishandled them. Judges was one."

Thus, when Bush himself showed up in Minnesota to campaign for Norm Coleman two days before the election, he mercilessly castigated Senate Democrats for blocking his judicial nominees to the federal bench.

"They don't like the fact that I named good, honorable people," he told a crowd of nineteen thousand in a St. Paul hockey arena.

"Norm and I understand," he added. "I know I can count on his support when it comes to making sure the judiciary is strong and capable and not have any vacancies."

When the exuberant crowd broke into a chant of "USA! USA! USA!", the president was encouraged enough to start pushing some other political hot buttons. He excoriated Senate Democrats for holding up passage of his bill to establish the Homeland Security Department. Ignoring Daschle's meltdown on the Senate floor, the president once again accused Democrats of caving in to "special interests" on a bill that was crucial to national security.

"USA! USA! USA!" cheered the Minnesotans.

"I've never seen a crowd like that," Rove said. "The place was going wild."

Sitting near a couple in their thirties with two small children, Rove struck up a conversation with the husband, who described himself as a "totally apolitical" voter who had never before attended a campaign rally. So Rove asked why the man had decided to come to the Bush event.

"Paul Wellstone was a good guy," the man replied. "But I was really offended by how they tried to turn his memorial service into a political rally."

Rove had been hearing similar comments all over the country in the campaign's closing days. "It had an impact nationally—people felt it was unseemly," he told me. "It energized our base. You could just sense, in that final week, the recognition that we had a chance."

Bush sensed the same thing as he addressed the packed hockey arena.

"Even though your state is still in mourning, I'm here to remind people from all political parties that you have a duty to vote," he said. "Now, once you get in that voting booth, I've got a suggestion. The best candidate for the future of Minnesota is the next United States Senator, Norm Coleman.

"The best choice for governor of Minnesota," he added, "is Tim Pawlenty."

Now Bush was really in deep. If things went badly, he would get blamed for not only dragging Coleman to defeat, but also forcing Pawlenty into a losing gubernatorial bid. And yet the president seemed strangely confident.

"You watch," he told the Minnesotans, "and see what happens next Tuesday."

5

THE NO-GLOAT ZONE

THE DAY AFTER NORM COLEMAN won the Minnesota Senate race, President Bush went into hiding to preclude accusations of gloating. Not that gloating was even necessary. The president could not possibly top the language being thrown around by the press to describe the defeat of Democrats from one end of the country to the other.

"Debacle. Humiliation. Landslide," began one postmortem in Harvard's liberal magazine *Perspective,* which lamented "the Democrats' election-night disgrace."

Democratic bomb-thrower James Carville was so embarrassed that he actually covered his bald head with a trash can while analyzing election night returns on CNN.

"It was nothing short of astonishing," marveled Matthew Cooper of *Time.* "George W. Bush's relentless campaigning had paid off big time for his party."

Howard Fineman of *Newsweek* was even more succinct: "The Clinton era is finally, finally over."

Since there was no point in piling on, Bush kept a low profile the day after the election. He did not want Democrats to be able to accuse the GOP of arrogance, a charge that had been leveled after Republican gains in the midterm elections of 1994.

"The president thought that the most appropriate way to mark the day would be with a touch of graciousness," White House Press Secretary Ari Fleischer explained to reporters who were cynically demanding a Bush victory lap. "And so the president is not going to have any public statements today."

But even as Fleischer was demurring, Bush's political fortunes were multiplying. The United Nations Security Council was signaling it was finally ready to pass a resolution authorizing war against Iraq if Saddam Hussein did not disarm. Even France and Russia were coming around. It seemed that everywhere Bush turned—both overseas and at home—he was getting his way.

So when he finally emerged from seclusion on Thursday, November 7, to treat himself to a press conference in the Eisenhower Executive Office Building next to the White House, the president's biggest challenge was to avoid looking like the cat that ate the canary.

"I congratulate the men and women, Republicans and Democrats, who were elected this week to public office all across America," he said with a straight face.

What he didn't say, of course, was that a lot more Republicans had been elected than Democrats. In fact, Bush had become the first Republican president in a century to emerge from a midterm with net gains in both houses of Congress. While presidents since World War II had lost an average of two dozen House seats in their first midterms (Clinton had lost a staggering fifty-four), Bush didn't cede even the handful of seats that Democrats needed to regain the majority. Instead, he actually gained six seats. This extraordinary feat of presidential padding meant that House Republicans now outnumbered Democrats by a full two dozen.

Yet the epicenter of this political earthquake was in the Senate, not the House. Ever since FDR, presidents had been losing an average of two to three Senate seats in their first midterms. (Clinton had lost nine, and Democratic control in the process.) Going into the 2002 election, most pundits anticipated that Bush might be able to defy historical trends by clinging to his forty-nine seats, but they certainly never expected him to wrest control of the chamber away from Democrats. And yet the president ended up gaining two seats, leading Republicans from a forty-nine-seat minority to a fifty-one-seat majority. Senator Daschle, whose anti-Bush rant on the Senate floor had been widely viewed as an unseemly meltdown, would soon be losing his job as majority leader. Dick Gephardt, the Missouri Democrat who had fought so hard to become speaker of the House, was even stepping down as minority leader.

"I talked to Senator Daschle yesterday and said that, although the Republican Party now leads the Senate, I still want to work with him to get things done for the American people," Bush allowed. "I talked to Leader Gephardt as well."

But the GOP gains were not limited to the House and Senate. Republicans now controlled twenty-six governorships, including Minnesota's, compared with twenty-four for the Democrats. Although that represented a net loss of one governorship for the GOP, most experts had expected Democrats to pick up several states in the midterms. And Democratic control of California, the biggest state of all, looked tenuous at best.

In short, George W. Bush now presided over a nation in which the Republican Party dominated government at all levels. In addition to controlling the White House, the GOP now held majorities in the Senate, House of Representatives, governorships and—for the first time in nearly half a century—the state legislatures.

"Joint control of the White House and the Congress means that you have a chance for an extraordinary burst of center-right legislative initiatives," Rove told me. "Robust tax cuts, Medicare reform, re-orientation of the Defense Department—it gives the Republicans a chance to do very big things.

"But it also gives them a chance to constantly be advancing issues that are less visible, but nonetheless critical, like the partial-birth abortion ban or a science-based environmental policy," he added. "I mean, it gives us a chance to at least have a shot at getting these things considered and discussed and moved forward."

Although Bush was not on the ballot in the midterms, he had succeeded in making the contest a referendum on himself. Ponying up his political capital in what some Democrats and Republicans alike considered a reckless gamble, the president hit paydirt by both nationalizing the election and then, of course, winning it.

"But ironically, he wouldn't have been able to do it without the actions of the Democrats, particularly in the Senate," Rove explained. "The nationalization occurred because they opposed him on judges, they were vociferous in their opposition to tax cuts, and they made demands about Iraq—which he then answered.

"And on Homeland Security, it looked like they were playing games with security of the people of the United States, all to benefit a few of their allies," he added.

When Americans were asked to name one factor that most influenced their votes, they cited Bush's job performance more than anything else. Clearly, the public had forged a bond with the president in the wake of September 11. Voters also appreciated his unrelenting opposition to both terrorism and high taxes. At the same time, as Fineman suggested, they had unambiguously closed the door on the Clinton-Gore era. No longer could Democrats defer this reality by claiming to have been cheated in a bogus election. This time around, the scope and breadth of the president's victory was undeniable.

Bush ran "right over us," Clinton lamented, "by convincing people the Democrats can't be trusted with national security."

"We shouldn't whine about that," Clinton told the liberal magazine *American Prospect*. "Their job is to beat us. Our job is to beat them."

He added, "We can't win if people think we're too liberal."

Clinton also noted that in 2002, unlike in previous elections, Republicans did a better job of turning out the vote than Democrats. This was a direct result of the GOP's near-death experience in Florida two years earlier, after which Republicans resolved to end the Democratic Party's historical dominance of grassroots politics.

"We were really derelict," Clinton said, "in not being tougher in the last six, eight weeks of the election cycle."

Clinton's postmortem was more realistic than the media's, which held that Bush would misinterpret the election results as a green light to ram through a "far-right agenda." In fact, that was the subtext of the very first question at Bush's news conference.

Associated Press reporter Sandra Sobieraj, a former aide to liberal Democratic Representative Louise Slaughter of New York, asked, "Do you believe that Tuesday's election gave you personally a mandate?"

Bush knew that if he claimed a mandate, he would immediately be accused of hubris. Besides, the quickest way to lose a mandate was to brag about it. So the president sidestepped the "gloat trap" altogether by refusing to take any credit for the Republican sweep.

"Candidates win elections because they're good candidates, not because they may happen to have the president as a friend—or a foe, for that matter," he shrugged. "Races that were won were won because people were able to convince the voters they could trust their judgment, convince the voters they care deeply about their circumstances.

"I believe if there is a mandate in any election, at least in this one, it's that people want something to get done," he added. "They want people to work together in Washington, D.C. to pass meaningful legislation which will improve their lives."

But the press wasn't buying Bush's "aw-shucks" routine. Reporters were still on the lookout for signs that the president would be over-reaching, not gracious, in victory.

"Sir, in referring to the elections, you're being quite humble about the results and your role," protested CNN's John King. "But many conservative lawmakers and many more conservative groups are saying: Seize the moment."

"Well, I appreciate all the advice I'm getting," Bush demurred, prompting laughter from the press corps. "Listen, there's going to be a huge laundry list of things people want to get done, and my job is to set priorities and get them done."

He explained that his top priorities were national security and economic security. He felt no need to mention the fact that they were also potent political issues.

Unsatisfied, Elisabeth Bumiller of the *New York Times* suggested that Bush was already a tool of the right wing, essentially daring him to repudiate his GOP base.

"You just said you've reached out to Democrats," she said, referring to the president's phone calls to Daschle and Gephardt. "Does this mean that you will be governing more from the center and taking fewer cues from the conservative arm of your party?"

"I don't take cues from anybody," the president shot back. "I just do what I think is right. That's just the way I lead."

He added, "I will just tell people what I think about how to solve the problems we face. And I ran on a political philosophy. I'm not changing my political philosophy. I am who I am."

Realizing it was impossible to score points against the president on the GOP rout of 2002, NBC reporter Campbell Brown reached back to the debacle of 2000. Ignoring the fact that Bush had won every re-count in the Florida post-election struggle—and even the ballyhooed media recounts in the year that followed—Brown questioned the va-lidity of his first two years as president.

"You were very gracious earlier, giving credit in this last election to the individual candidates—but a lot of those candidates say they have you to thank," she flattered before plunging in the knife. "Given the fact that your own election for president was so close it had to be decided by the Supreme Court, do you now feel personally reassured that these midterm elections validated your presidency?"

"Thank you for that loaded question," Bush said, cracking up Brown's colleagues. "Look, sometimes you win them, and sometimes you lose elections. That's just the way it is."

"I really don't put this in personal terms. I know people in Washington like to do that. You know: 'George Bush won, George Bush lost.' That's the way they do it here," he added. "I appreciate you pointing out that some people have given me credit. The credit belongs to people in the field."

Significantly, the first of those people he singled out for credit was Coleman. "If you're really interested in what I think, I think the fact that Norm Coleman ran a very difficult race in difficult circumstances—and won—speaks volumes about Norm Coleman," Bush said.

It also spoke volumes about the Wellstone memorial-turned-rally. As Rove had suspected, the spectacle had backfired badly on Democrats not just in Minnesota, but across the nation.

"Voters were turned off in large numbers," lamented liberal *New York Times* columnist Bob Herbert. "It was a fiasco that extended beyond Minnesota. Not only did the Democrats lack a message, they seemed also to lack class."

Voters were particularly appalled at searing images of national Democrats like Bill and Hillary Clinton yukking it up amid the unseemly partisan spectacle. Even Terry McAuliffe acknowledged the blunder saying "I was at the memorial service. I went in hoping, envisioning it to be a memorial service. It did turn into a political rally."

Such humility was a far cry from McAuliffe's preelection prediction that "Jeb is gone!"—in part, no doubt, because Jeb ended up crushing his Democratic challenger by thirteen points. Furthermore, voters sent Jeb's secretary of state, Katherine Harris, to the House of Representatives. This was particularly demoralizing to the many Democrats who still blamed Harris and Jeb for the Florida recount debacle of 2000. Now these two Floridians were part of the historic GOP victory of 2002.

Although Bush refused to claim credit for that victory in public, he later acknowledged to me that his frenzied stumping had indeed tipped the scales in a number of races.

"When a president goes into a close election, it pretty much dominates the news," he explained. "And when you go in at a crucial time, it can help a candidate get the news necessary for his or her message to be listened to."

Naturally, Bush didn't mention any of this during his press conference. He was too busy enjoying his exchange with reporters, despite their needling questions. In fact, he was downright jocular by the time he called on me.

"Sammon," he said before adding his usual nickname: "Superstretch."

As I unfolded my six-foot-seven frame, Bush made an exaggerated upward motion with his head, as if craning to take in the full extent of my height. The president, whose claim to be six feet tall entailed rounding up half an inch, noticed with delight that the stage put the two of us on equal footing.

"Now you and I are eye-to-eye, right?" he said mischievously as the press chuckled. Then he raised himself up on his tiptoes and mugged for the other reporters.

"Thank you, Mr. President," I said. "Now that the 2004 presidential campaign has unofficially begun, can you tell us whether Vice President Cheney will be your running mate again? Or will you instead choose someone who might harbor greater presidential ambitions to perhaps succeed you one day?"

There had been rumors that Bush was planning to replace Cheney, perhaps with Secretary of State Colin Powell or National Security Adviser Condoleezza Rice.

"Well, first of all, I'm still recovering from the '02 elections," the president allowed as I sat down. "And we got plenty of time to deal with this issue. But should I decide to run, Vice President Cheney will be my running mate."

The president went on to praise Cheney for his friendship, counsel, and hard work during the campaign. Despite a history of heart disease, the vice president had traveled to more than seventy campaign events and raised more than $40 million for Republicans.

Before Bush could call on another reporter, I caught his eye with body language that signified I had another question.

"If I may follow," I began. "Last time you had—"

"Thank you for not standing up," Bush deadpanned, gesturing to the news crews at the back of the room. "You block the cameras."

Bush was enjoying his role as stand-up comic, so I decided to give him a taste of his own medicine. With exaggerated deliberation, I rose to my feet and turned around to smile at the White House's official camera crew, completely blocking their shot of the president.

"Last time you had to kind of convince him to take the job," I said of Cheney, after the laughter died down. "Have you talked to him this time, whether he is interested in serving another term?"

"I'm confident that he will serve another term," the president said, cutting off further discussion of the topic. He was still in a joking mood. "By the way, we're here in honor of Ari Fleischer," Bush said. "Since he's getting married this weekend, I thought it appropriate to leave the podium that he occupies empty, in honor of the fact that he's getting married. I hope you all have sent your gifts to him." Then he looked directly into the cameras and said, "Ari, I did what you asked me to do."

* * *

Bush was still smiling when he called on Helen Thomas, the liberal doyenne of the White House press corps, who had covered every American president since John F. Kennedy. Up until 2000, the fiercely pro-Arab Thomas had worked for United Press International, which was owned by a company controlled by the brother-in-law of King Fahd of Saudi Arabia. But she quit when the Saudis sold the ailing wire service to News World Communications, which also owned the *Washington Times*, a newspaper with a conservative editorial page. Thomas was then hired by Hearst Newspapers as a columnist, not a reporter, which allowed this pro-Palestinian daughter of Lebanese immigrants to express her leftist views more openly. Thomas was adamantly opposed to war against Iraq.

"Mr. President, what is the logic of your insistence on invading Iraq at some point, which may some day have nuclear weapons, and not laying a glove on North Korea, which may have them or may produce them?" Thomas began. "Both of which, of course, would be against international law. And I have a follow-up."

The press corps, which prided itself on posing sharply adversarial questions that stopped just short of blatant advocacy, chuckled nervously. Thomas had crossed the line of decorum, although Bush let her off the hook by starting his answer on a lighthearted note.

"Well, I may decide to let you have that follow-up or not," he teased, "depending on whether I like my answer.

"I am insistent upon one thing about Iraq, and that is that Saddam Hussein disarm," he added, turning serious. "Saddam Hussein said he would disarm. And he hasn't. And for the—"

"And you don't care about North Korea?" Thomas interrupted.

"Is that the follow-up?" Bush said, prompting more nervous laughter from the press. "Okay, that is the follow-up. I do care about North Korea. And as I said from the beginning of this new war in the twenty-first century, we'll deal with each threat differently. Each threat requires a different type of response."

After explaining his strategy of multilateral diplomacy with North Korea, Bush called on another reporter. But Thomas wasn't finished.

"Mr. President, can I have a follow-up?" she said.

"Of course you can," Bush replied. "Yes, it's fine. If the elections had gone a different way, I might not be so generous."

"You are leaving the impression that Iraqi lives, the human cost, doesn't mean anything," she began.

"Say that again?" Bush said incredulously.

"You are leaving the impression that you wouldn't mind if you go to war against Iraq," she backpedaled. "There are two other impressions around. One, that you have an obsession with going after Saddam Hussein at any cost. And also that you covet the oil fields."

"Some people have the right impressions and some people have the wrong impressions," Bush said.

Thomas tried to interject: "Can you—"

"Well, those are the wrong impressions," Bush snapped.

"Okay," Thomas said.

"I have a deep desire for peace," the president continued. "And freedom for the Iraqi people. See, I don't like a system where people are repressed through torture and murder in order to keep a dictator in place. It troubles me deeply.

"And so the Iraqi people must hear this loud and clear," he added. "This country never has any intention to conquer anybody."

In truth, there was no sign that the United States had any intention of seizing Iraq's oil, either, although that didn't stop the Left from making the accusation. This conspiracy theory actually gained a certain amount of currency because of Bush's stint as a Texas oilman years before he got into politics. Instead of dignifying that part of Thomas's rant with an answer, Bush called on Terry Moran of ABC News.

"There's a school of thought that says that going to war against Iraq would be a dangerous and misguided idea," Moran said, "because it would generate a tremendous amount of anger and hatred at the

United States, and out of that you'd essentially be creating many new terrorists who would want to kill Americans. What's wrong with that analysis?"

"Well, that's like saying we should not go after al Qaeda because we might irritate somebody and that would create a danger to Americans," Bush responded. "People say: 'Oh, we must leave Saddam alone; otherwise, if we did something against him, he might attack us.' Well, if we don't do something, he might attack us, and he might attack us with a more serious weapon. The man is a threat."

"Terry, listen, there's risk in all action we take. But the risk of inaction is not a choice, as far as I'm concerned," he added. "If he's not going to disarm, we'll disarm him, in order to make the world a more peaceful place. And some people aren't going to like that—I understand. But some people won't like it if he ends [up] with a nuclear weapon and uses it. We have an obligation to lead. And I intend to assume that obligation."

That meant securing an international resolution against Iraq, which the U.N. Security Council was expected to pass the next day. Sure enough, the member nations had met Bush's deadline of "weeks, not months." The high-profile diplomacy, which Bush derisively called "gnashing of teeth," had the effect of keeping Iraq in the headlines right through the election. So much for Democratic efforts to change the subject by disposing of the congressional resolution more than three weeks earlier.

Despite all these headlines, the press did not realize that the administration had originally considered drafting three separate resolutions.

"I'm not sure we've ever mentioned this to anybody," Rice told me. "We actually thought at one time of trying to get resolutions from the U.N.—after the president's speech—not just on WMD, but on terrorism and on human rights as well."

But she added: "We couldn't really get anybody else interested in it—in the world community—because there was a kind of sense that well, the WMD was what people considered most pressing. But we actually tried to do that."

Bush himself believed that halting Saddam's human rights abuses was every bit as important as disarming him of weapons of mass destruction.

"I tended to give the arguments equal weight," he told me. "I think that it was important to do both."

He added: "I think it's essential that the United States never turn a blind eye to torture, repression, brutality. I believe we owe it to people in the world to pay attention to those situations."

However, he acknowledged that resting his case for war primarily on human rights abuses would lead to cries of· "All you want to do is use the military." Thus, he concluded, "in making the case, I spent more time" on WMD.

Deputy Defense Secretary Paul Wolfowitz told *Vanity Fair* that Saddam's abysmal human rights record, by itself, "is a reason to help the Iraqis. But it's not a reason to put American kids' lives at risk."

As for using Saddam's terrorism links as a rationale for war, Wolfowitz observed that this argument "is the one about which there's the most disagreement within the bureaucracy." In part, that was because international outrage had faded over Saddam's continued sheltering of terrorists like Abu Abbas, mastermind of the 1985 Achille Lauro hijacking. During that infamous crime, Abbas ordered one of his fellow Palestinian terrorists to murder a sixty-nine-year-old handicapped American Jew named Leon Klinghoffer and dump him and his wheelchair into the sea.

"He created troubles," Abbus explained matter-of-factly to the *Boston Globe* in 1998. "He was handicapped, but he was inciting and provoking the other passengers. So, the decision was made to kill him."

By 2002, U.S. indictments against Abbas for piracy, hostage-taking, and conspiracy had expired, and Bush was not about to resurrect acts of terrorism from the Reagan era as justification for war—even with Abbas still living comfortably in Baghdad. Besides, the president had been unable to establish an ironclad link between Saddam and al Qaeda, the terrorist network that had perpetrated the September 11 atrocities. That would have been the only terrorism argument persuasive enough, on its own, to justify war.

"The truth is that for reasons that have a lot to do with the U.S. government bureaucracy, we settled on the one issue that everyone could agree on—which was weapons of mass destruction—as the core reason," Wolfowitz concluded.

Powell arrived at the same conclusion after taking his cue from Bush's U.N. address.

"I mean, the whole thrust of the president's speech—it talked to human rights and it talked to terrorism—but it rested on the foundation that this is a dangerous regime with weapons of mass destruction," he explained to me. "The inspectors were not going in to look for mass graves or evidence of terrorist attacks. They were going in to look for weapons of mass destruction. And so that's what the resolution rested on, even though it has tucked in it other pieces."

Powell also tucked in some language designed to make Saddam's life miserable upon passage of the resolution, which was known simply by its number, 1441. The document promised "serious consequences"—code for war—if Saddam was deemed in "material breach" of 1441 or, for that matter, numerous earlier resolutions the dictator had been flouting for years, including one that ordered Iraq to "end repression of its civilian population."

"We built a lot of ambushes or traps into 1441 for Saddam Hussein," Powell told me. "The big one was the initial one, where we said, you're in material breach now. That took a couple weeks to get that in there."

Indeed, some members of the Security Council wanted to forgive Saddam for thumbing his nose at earlier resolutions, and instead hold him accountable only to the new one. Powell disagreed, saying that

Saddam must immediately bring himself into compliance with earlier resolutions in order to avoid violating the new one.

"We can't say: Everything is okay now, and if he does anything in the future, it'll be bad," Powell told me. "That's what the French and a lot of others wanted—start him fresh, and if he doesn't come clean now he's in material breach. And we fought hard and said, nuh-uh, you can't wipe out twelve years' worth of bad behavior. He is in material breach now—ambush one."

To hedge his bet, Powell also made sure that 1441 included a demand that Saddam submit a detailed report to the U.N. disclosing the full extent of his weapons programs. Any omissions or falsehoods in that report would be considered further material breaches.

"If it's a false declaration, or anything else like that, *bang,* you go right to serious consequences. That took a couple weeks," Powell told me. "So we built another ambush."

Still, none of these ambushes would be enough to trigger all-out war. So Powell made weapons of mass destruction the centerpiece of 1441, relegating the issues of Saddam's human rights abuses and terror links to the status of secondary arguments.

Rice explained: "As the debate unfolded—I think in large part because 1441 got really focused on WMD—other things tended to fall away."

Meanwhile, France sought to vest all decision-making authority about war in Hans Blix and his team of U.N. weapons inspectors. Having benefitted for so many years from its close relationship with Saddam, Paris was now reluctant to see it destroyed by the warmongering Americans. Initially, France even demanded that the United States obtain not one, but two resolutions before pulling the trigger. Powell balked, but then compromised by agreeing at least to consult with the U.N. if Saddam violated the first resolution. But he made clear that the first resolution would be considered sufficient authority to proceed, if necessary.

"We believed that we came out of 1441 with all the authority necessary to act if there was continued material breaching of the various resolutions," Powell told me. "The French always would maintain that it required us to come back to the council for another action. They can't point to that anywhere in the resolution."

Powell insisted that France and every other member of the Security Council knew what they were getting into.

"If you ever got to 'serious consequences,'" Powell said, "the United States was gonna act.

"This is where we rest our case; there was no doubt in anyone's mind; the French could not dispute this," he added. "'That's what the debate was all about. But we got it."

Indeed, 1441 now had the support of not just the Security Council's five permanent, veto-wielding members—the U.S., France, Russia, China, and Britain—but also its ten nonpermanent members, with the possible exception of Syria. Although Bush acknowledged during his press conference that Saddam had been flouting such resolutions with impunity for years, he promised that era was about to end.

"This time we mean it—see, that's the difference, I guess—this time it's for real," the president vowed. "This time something happens."

To drive home his point, Bush mockingly alluded to an episode from the Gulf War that had become emblematic of Western gullibility. In 1991, CNN correspondent Peter Arnett parroted Saddam's claim that America had bombed a Baghdad "baby milk factory," which turned out to be a biological weapons plant.

"The status quo is unacceptable—you know, kind of send a few people in there and hope maybe he's nice to them and open up the baby milk factory—it's unacceptable," Bush said. "You must know that I am serious—so are a lot of other countries—serious about holding the man to account."

Finally, the president made it abundantly clear that while he would welcome the U.N.'s blessing the next day, he would never seek the world body's permission. To the eternal mortification of Democrats and the press, George W. Bush simply did not care that the international community might disapprove of America doing the right thing.

"I don't spend a lot of time taking polls around the world to tell me what I think is the right way to act; I've just got to know how I feel," he said. "I feel strongly about freedom. I feel strongly about liberty. And I feel strongly about the obligation to make the world a more peaceful place.

"And I take those responsibilities really seriously."

When the press conference ended, Bush bade the journalists farewell and headed for a door at the rear of the stage. Several reporters called out to ask him what he had given his wife for her birthday and to mark the couple's twenty-fifth wedding anniversary the previous week. Bush merely smiled and winked as he disappeared through the door. It was an innocuous gesture by a man who made a practice of keeping secret his gifts to his wife.

But the press, its sensibilities hopelessly mired in the gutter, let out a long and leering laugh.

6

"WHINING POOL"

THE GRASS WAS THE color of bleached driftwood, although recent rains had turned some patches gloriously verdant. President Bush reveled in the beauty of these meadows as he strode briskly down an old dirt track on his 1,600-acre spread in Crawford, Texas. It was not yet nine A.M. on the day after New Year's, but the hyperkinetic fifty-six-year-old had been up for hours. With early morning briefings by the CIA and Vice President Cheney behind him, Bush was engaging in one of his favorite pastimes—hiking across his beloved Prairie Chapel Ranch. Too bad he was accompanied by one of his least favorite groups of people: the White House press corps.

"Let's go," urged Bush, not wishing to slow down for the out-of-shape journalists. "I'll tell you what we'll do. We'll walk about three or four miles, and then we'll end up having coffee. Mrs. Bush wants to say hello to everybody."

This was not good news for Holly Rosencranz, a Bloomberg reporter who was six months pregnant. The president was walking so fast that even the longest-legged reporter in the group had to take big strides just to keep up. Holly, who was barely five feet tall, was practically running. As if to add insult to injury, the man who seemed determined to induce premature labor didn't even remember her name.

"Are you going to make it, Heidi?" said Bush, confusing her with another Bloomberg reporter, Heidi Przybyla.

"I'll be fine," puffed Holly, not bothering to correct the president.

"We've got a truck for you back there," said Bush, gesturing to a pickup that was trailing the presidential tour group.

"Don't worry about me," the reporter wheezed.

Bush shrugged and hurried on, as if to compensate for what he considered a late start to his morning walk. He and Laura had begun much earlier on New Year's Day.

"We go for a sunrise walk on the first day of the year," he explained. "So yesterday we popped out of bed about 7:20 A.M. and we started moving. We walked four miles." This astonished the journalists, most of whom had stayed up late to celebrate New Year's Eve and were consequently dead to the world at 7:20 the next morning.

"Do you ever sleep in?" one reporter asked.

"No," said Bush, whose early-to-bed, early-to-rise routine precluded him from ringing in the New Year. "I was probably asleep at 10 P.M.," he remarked matter-of-factly.

"Couldn't even see the ball drop on the East Coast," said an incredulous journalist. (New York is an hour ahead of Texas.)

"I was looking for that ball dropping in London," Bush shot back. (Britain is six hours ahead of Texas.)

Onward he raced, determined to demonstrate that his property encompassed more than the dreary flatlands that dominated the street entrance to Prairie Chapel Ranch.

"We brought some friends out here, and one of the guys said, 'I can't imagine why President Bush bought this place; this is some of the worst country in Texas.' But what he didn't realize is that the fingers of the Hill Country"—Bush spread his own fingers wide—"south of Austin extend up here."

"The topography on the map shows this is some unique country," he added. "You wouldn't ever envision this driving into the ranch."

The president then proudly launched into a dissertation on his property's diverse landscape.

"So what you'll see is three different parts of Texas. You'll see this: the central plains, flat," he said, gesturing in one direction before turning to another. "This is more rolling, where the rock is closer to the surface—oh, here comes Laura."

Before Bush could explain the third distinct topography of his ranch—which consisted of dramatic limestone canyons—he greeted his wife, who was walking Spot, their English springer spaniel.

"Hey, Spotty!" The president whistled to the aging animal, which was having trouble with its eyesight. Spot barked in recognition.

"Loyal dog," Bush murmured. "Great athlete."

The president's other dog, a Scottish terrier named Barney, had stubby legs that were already tuckered out from trying to keep up with his master. The pooch was hitching a ride on a six-wheeled vehicle, known as a "gator," that was bringing up the rear of the presidential entourage. Bush saw his wife's appearance as an opportunity to send both dogs home for a rest.

"Take Barney with you, okay? He's in the truck," the president said. "We'll see you back at the house."

Liberated from his plodding pets but not the panting press, Bush bounded across the landscape under a glorious blue sky. Despite the brilliant sunlight, temperatures remained stuck in the low forties, and the strong gusts of prairie wind prompted the president to don winter gloves. He also wore a beat-up pair of running shoes, faded blue jeans and a baseball cap. His medium-weight, navy blue windbreaker was embroidered with the words "George W. Bush, President" over the right breast and "United States of America" over the left. The "d" in

"United" was elongated like a flagpole, from which an image of Old Glory fluttered.

"We're going to go down into the canyons, so it won't be quite as cold," Bush said.

"Will we see the waterfall?" I asked.

"Absolutely," said Bush, remembering that the site had been bone dry when he took the press there in August 2001. "I went in there yesterday to make sure there was water."

He led the reporters into a canyon he called "the cathedral," which had been carved out of chalky soft limestone. A waterfall cascaded from a jutting shelf of stone into a clear pool at the bottom. The cathedral was Bush's pride and joy, the place he brought his favorite world leaders during ranch visits. "Jiang Zemin did not come down here," he observed, "but Vladimir Putin did."

Bush explained that when he first bought the ranch, the canyon was so choked with cedar trees he could barely get inside. But during frequent visits to the property, which he called the Western White House, he gradually chainsawed away enough brush to allow access by visitors.

"All right, retreat," Bush commanded after a while. "Watch those rocks, they're slick."

Despite the warning, several journalists stumbled along a narrow walkway on their way out of the canyon. Fortunately, the most treacherous stretch had recently been fitted with rope railings and wooden planking. It was one of many projects completed with the help of White House aides who accompanied the president on visits to Crawford.

"My typical day is, I will work from about 7 A.M. until 10 A.M., and then we'll come out and we'll cut cedar or fool around—you know, repair something," Bush explained. "And then we'll eat lunch about 12:30 P.M. And generally make phone calls then or answer mail or do whatever, and then get back out about 4 P.M. and fish. I love to fish."

The fishing was done in a seventeen-foot-deep man-made lake that covered eleven acres behind the president's house.

"I put six hundred black bass in there a few years ago—and about thirty thousand bait fish—and they're about two-and-a-half to three pounds now," he said. "A bad time to fish, because the fish are lethargic during the cold. We've got bluegill and shad and perch."

The president joked that although he stocked the fish himself, he still took credit for catching them. "The only time you don't get credit," he said, making a motion of a fish being hooked, "is when the Secret Service frogman puts it on for you—you see the snorkel."

Although Bush was showing no signs of slowing down, he glanced behind him and noticed that Holly was straining to keep up.

"You're doing great," he called to her.

"Oh, thanks," Holly panted. "Don't worry about me."

"The medical unit will be up here," Bush joshed.

Although scores of journalists had accompanied the president on his holiday trip to Crawford, only a dozen of us went along for this tour—as members of the White House press pool, a representative sampling of the larger media mob. Fewer than half the journalists in the pool were actually reporters—one newspaperman, one TV correspondent, and three wire service writers. The rest were technicians who manned the still cameras, video cameras, boom microphones, and other broadcast equipment. Thus, for the most part, there were only five people actually posing questions to Bush. And all five had mixed emotions about the opportunity.

On one hand, we felt fortunate to have such unprecedented access to the president, who hardly ever granted interviews and ran a White House that many considered secretive. The chance to spend several hours in informal conversation with the commander in chief was nothing short of extraordinary.

On the other hand, White House staffers warned us in advance that if we peppered the president with a lot of policy questions right out of the gate, he might cut the hike short.

This presented us with a dilemma. If we refrained from asking policy questions, we would enjoy unparalleled access to the president of the United States. But afterward, we would have to explain to our editors and the larger White House press corps that our hours with Bush had yielded no hard news. This was clearly an untenable journalistic position.

So the other reporters and I got together before the hike and collectively decided to withhold policy questions until the tail end of the journey. Once we were deep into the woods, we figured, it would be too late for Bush to curtail the hike.

That meant engaging the president in hours of small talk, all of which would be tape-recorded by a White House stenographer, transcribed, and posted on the White House website for the world to inspect. This created a bizarre conversational dynamic. Reporters wanted to chat up the president without looking like they were sucking up. Each instinctively felt compelled to compete with the others for the president's ear, even though they had few competitors and lots of time. NBC News correspondent David Gregory quickly established himself as the alpha male, staking out a position by Bush's side for much of the walk. On several occasions he dropped back to place calls on his cell phone, only to return after a few minutes and wedge himself between Bush and whichever reporter had the temerity to have taken Gregory's spot. The six-foot-five reporter, nicknamed "Little Stretch" by Bush, passed the time discussing such topics as his family members and electronic gadgets.

"Oh, look at this," Gregory said, pulling out his latest toy. "My wife just got me this little Palm Pilot here, and my organizer—it's got a camera in there."

"Oh, fantastic," Bush said. "I notice telephones have got that now."

When the president brought up the subject of secure videoconferencing on Air Force One, Gregory related that to his own work at NBC.

"Oh, yes," he said. "There is so much that we're starting to do now on computers, where you can edit stuff on laptops."

"Maybe they can enhance your face," cracked the president, who once publicly ridiculed Gregory for speaking French at a press conference. "Super enhancement."

Bush kept steering the conversation back to his favorite topic—the staggering diversity of flora and fauna bursting from every inch of the waterlogged flatlands, gently rolling hills and limestone canyons. He enthusiastically pointed out all manner of trees, including magnificent live oaks, which never shed their green leaves, and water-hogging cedars, which he frequently cleared and burned for the benefit of hardwoods. But he also had plenty to say about cottonwoods, sycamores, ashes, walnuts, pecans, hackberries, Chinaberries, lacy oaks, red cedars, and cedar elms.

"I am a tree man," he said as he passed a young thicket. "Those are little oaks and ashes. The sturdy will emerge."

Bush also glimpsed a white-tailed deer in the underbrush. He spoke of seeing gray fox and wild turkeys, although the only creatures he actually hunted on the ranch were doves. As for domestic animals, the president explained that "two hundred mother cows and six bulls" grazed the land as part of a lease arrangement with ranch foreman Kenneth Engelbrecht, whose parents sold Bush the property in 1999 for an estimated $1.3 million.

"Wow, look at the hawk," I said, pointing to one of two large raptors circling in the cool blue sky.

"Those are big buzzards," Bush said. "Turkey buzzards. They're hoping one of us drops."

The president also talked extensively about geological formations and underground aquifers, pausing here and there to point out springs that bubbled out of rocks and trickled into ravines.

"Let me show you something that's really pretty here," he enthused. "When the sun sets, the cliffs over here, which you'll see in a minute, just completely glow."

At various points in the journey, Bush veered off crude, rocky roads to point out particularly picturesque scenes. He ducked under trees to show off a pristine brook that dropped from flat rock to flat rock. He recalled cooling off in a swimming hole after a jog in the summer of 2000.

"The next day we killed a water moccasin—cottonmouth," Bush said. "That's the last time we jumped in there."

He was uncharacteristically stumped when I asked him to identify a brilliant green plant growing atop the water. But he pointed out a cardinal that flitted through the underbrush as we noisily approached.

At another point the president alarmed Secret Service agents by striding to the edge of a ninety-foot cliff, which had no railings, to point out the rain-swollen Rainey Creek below. He joked that it was safe because the wind was blowing the group away from the cliff, not toward it. But when I ventured too close to the edge, he cautioned: "Be careful up here, seriously."

At still another point, the president scurried up a hillside to point out an idyllic valley hidden over the crest.

"Can you envision me sitting here, on the rock, writing some poetry?" Bush mused.

"Writing the State of the Union," one wag deadpanned. "Longhand."

"Speaking of," began a journalist, sensing an opening for news.

"Yes, we're working on it," the president said.

"Anything you want to sneak preview?" I ventured.

"I think all you've got to do is call the White House staffers," Bush said sardonically. "They'll tell you, evidently. You know what I mean."

It was a barbed reference to recent press reports previewing the president's economic stimulus package, which he planned to discuss in his speech to a joint session of Congress at the end of the month. As Bush walked back down the hill, he remarked that he didn't blame the press for printing such leaks. In fact, he said he would seek the same sort of information if he were a journalist.

Truth be told, such leaks were exceedingly rare in this White House. Bush had made clear even before taking office that he expected his top advisers to be discreet. Although this annoyed the press, it was reassuring to political strategist Karl Rove.

"I almost didn't come here because I talked to friends who worked for 41 or Reagan or Nixon or Ford," Rove told me. "They said: Oh, it's a great job, you'll love it. But it'll also be the worst job you'll ever have, because there'll be backbiting and the internecine warfare is intense, and people will leak to the *Washington Post* or the *New York Times* to sort of win their part of the policy battle."

Rove took these concerns to the president-elect.

"I'm not up for that," he recalled telling Bush. "I'm too simple a person for that. And I'm not good at that kind of stuff."

"Look, you just gotta trust me," Bush replied, according to Rove. "I know from what I've seen that I can set the right tone."

Once he succeeded in quelling the fears of Rove and other advisers, Bush found they were remarkably frank during policy discussions. In fact, it was not uncommon for top aides to forcefully challenge the president on a variety of issues.

"Being liberated from worrying about how we each appear in the pages of the *Washington Post* or the *New York Times* or how we're gonna be portrayed on the national news means that you can have the most robust arguments about policy with people that you love and respect, and know that at the end of the day, regardless of how it's resolved, everybody's gonna salute and move on," Rove said. "You can speak your mind and not worry about having it coughed up in the newspaper in such a way to make you look foolish or stupid."

He added: "A president is best served if he can create an atmosphere in which people can express themselves in a strong and deliberate fashion. Roosevelt got that by playing everybody off of each other. Here, it's a much different tone.

"And it starts by the president saying: I'll define for you where we need to go. And none of us needs to be worried about how we're gonna be viewed in the short run. And by the time it really matters, we'll all be dead."

As Bush kept clambering over hill and dale, the cameramen tried to keep ahead of him, scrambling backward to capture head-on shots of the approaching president. One photographer stumbled and fell to the ground, somersaulting spectacularly in front of Bush.

"You all right?" the president said. "You okay?"

"Yes," said the photographer, springing to his feet as if nothing had happened.

"Medical gator!" Bush joked.

The president's brisk pace was now a major problem for the journalists, one of whom suggested putting the photographers in the bed of the pickup and moving the truck to the front of the pack.

"Mr. President, would you mind terribly if we would just let the truck pass so they can get some walking shots?" he asked.

"Not at all," said Bush, stopping to survey the journalists he had been leaving in the dust, including poor Holly.

"Heidi, what are you doing?" the president called merrily.

"I want to catch up to you," Holly panted.

More than a mile later, as Bush prepared to ascend a steep hill, he suggested that "Heidi" join the photographers in the pickup truck. At this point several other journalists pulled the president aside and gently corrected him. He responded by playfully pretending he had been calling her Holly all along and demanding, in mock indignation, how they could possibly accuse him of getting the name wrong.

"Holly, get in here," he commanded.

Later, he felt compelled to demonstrate he had not forgotten her name.

"Holly?" he said.

"Yes?"

"Quit calling me Jeb," Bush joked.

At length the president's house came into sight, and it became apparent the journey was ending.

"Sir, will you let us do a little bit of business before we go in the house?" asked NBC's David Gregory.

"Yes, what do I care? I don't watch TV," Bush said.

Nor did he spend a lot of time reading newspapers, preferring instead to be briefed each morning by aides who distilled the day's headlines down to their essence. Bush was constantly amazed that British Prime Minister Tony Blair took the time to agonize over articles written about him in the British press. Despite Bush's breezy banter with the White House press corps, he disapproved of the fourth estate's liberal bias and self-importance. In fact, when leading journalists first learned that the president wasn't personally poring over their articles, they were crestfallen.

"I hear you don't pay attention to the press," one of them said to the president at the ranch on another occasion.

"Not really," Bush replied.

"Why?" the reporter asked.

"Well, because sometimes your opinion matters to me and sometimes it doesn't," the president said.

"Well, how do you know what the people think?" the reporter persisted.

"People don't make up their mind based upon what you write," Bush replied.

Dismissing the press as an institution of questionable relevance had a liberating effect on the president, shielding him from the fickle winds of conventional wisdom. This sense of liberation was also enjoyed by top aides like Rice.

"Look, at some level you have to decide—and I think the president is very much like this—I'm just going to do what I'm going to do, and we'll let the chips fall where they may," she told me. "And ultimately, it doesn't matter because if we do the right things, then this will come out right, and history will be the judge."

This attitude could be maintained "with more self-assurance" during a period of historical consequence like the Bush presidency, she added.

"Either we are right or we're wrong about the future of the Middle East," Rice shrugged. "But it's not about to be decided by the time somebody writes their daily news cycle."

Andy Card, Bush's chief of staff, agreed. "It's comforting, because the president is not captured by tomorrow's newspaper," he said. "Heck, he understands the press may not even get it right. It's very liberating."

Rove was particularly wary of the press because it frequently caricatured him as the Svengali of the White House, a diabolical genius who pulled the strings of a puppet president. And yet there was a certain political utility in this characterization, because it allowed Rove to serve as Bush's lightning rod.

"The president has what he calls the better-you-than-me theory," Rove explained. "Look, this town runs on myths. It's a convenient myth."

He added: "This town is riven by currents of fad and fashion. What matters is achieving big goals. The president is very good at keeping people focused on: What is it that we're attempting to achieve here? And if you allow other people to start substituting things for his vision—which is essentially what happens when the press gets involved, unconsciously or intentionally—they start substituting other goals. And suddenly lots of bad things happen."

Besides, remaining focused on a vision spared Bush the dreary experience of plowing through the daily deluge of negative articles on his every word and act, not to mention enduring the televised political food fights.

"I don't watch the nightly newscasts on TV, nor do I watch the endless hours of people giving their opinion about things," he told me. "I don't read the editorial pages; I don't read the columnists."

Yet he regularly monitored the news pages of a handful of daily publications.

"I get the newspapers—the *New York Times*, the *Washington Times*, the *Washington Post*, and *USA Today*—those are the four papers delivered," he said. "I can scan a front page, and if there is a particular story of interest, I'll skim it."

The president prided himself on his ability to detect bias in ostensibly objective news stories.

"My antenna are finely attuned," he added. "I can figure out what so-called news pieces are going to be full of opinion, as opposed to news. So I'm keenly aware of what's in the papers, kind of the issue du jour. But I'm also aware of the facts."

Those facts were extracted from opinionated news stories each day and presented to Bush by half a dozen aides, including chief of staff Andy Card.

"Since I'm the first one to see him in the morning, I usually give him a quick overview and get a little reaction from him," Card told me. "Frequently I find that his reaction kind of reflects Laura Bush's take."

Indeed, Bush often cited articles that Laura had flagged for greater scrutiny, even when he had not personally slogged through those stories. Laura routinely delved more deeply into the news pages than her husband, who preferred other sections.

"He does not dwell on the newspaper, but he reads the sports page every day," Card said with a chuckle.

Even Card, one of the aides charged with briefing the president on the day's news, made a conscious effort to remain above the fickle winds of coverage.

"I really do not get lost in the newspaper every day," he said. "I'm sure there are people in the White House who dwell on that challenge—I try not to."

Bush believed that immersing himself in the voluminous, mostly left-leaning news coverage might cloud his thinking and even hinder his efforts to remain an optimistic leader.

"I like to have a clear outlook," he told me. "It can be a frustrating experience to pay attention to somebody's false opinion or somebody's characterization which simply isn't true."

While the president was not steeped in the minutiae of individual news articles, he was mindful of the media's collective power as a political force. So he made it his business to keep track of broad news trends, even if he didn't plow through all the details.

"I'm aware if there is yet another story about X, Y, Z in the newspaper," he said. "I'm aware if there is seven straight days of a certain news story being run. I'm aware if there is three days of something."

In fact, he regularly strategized with his spokesmen, including Dan Bartlett and Scott McClellan, about how to best manage the news.

"There's a lot of discussion about news on a daily basis here," Bush told me. "After all, a lot of times we're making the news."

He added: "I'm in constant touch with Dan and Scott about how to handle a particular story. I help fashion responses—'are you comfortable with us saying this about that?'—on a regular basis.

"I'm involved in this White House," he said. "People on the staff will tell you that I pay attention to what's going on here, because a decision-maker has got to be aware of all elements of the decision-making process."

All of which made it easier to understand why Bush had no compunction about answering questions from the reporters who had accompanied him on his tour of Prairie Chapel Ranch, since he wasn't going to pay much attention to the stories they would file.

"Do you want to do it right here?" he said of the impromptu press conference.

"We'll get the camera wherever you want," a journalist replied.

Once the camera was set up, I decided to begin the questioning.

"Another Democrat has thrown his hat into the ring today—John Edwards," I said. "What do you think of the Democratic strategy to essentially say that you're not keeping America safe enough?"

"Oh, you know, I understand politics, and I'm not paying attention to politics," he said. "I'm going to continue doing the job the American people expect, which is to safeguard America and Americans.

"We've got a war on our hands. There is a terrorist network that still is interested in harming Americans and we will hunt them down. There are countries which are developing weapons of mass destruction and we will deal with them appropriately.

"One country is Iraq," he added. "Obviously, we expect them to live up to the U.N. Security resolutions and disarm, and if they won't, we'll lead a coalition to disarm them."

I followed up with questions about North Korea and terrorism. Other journalists jumped in with queries about the economy and tax cuts. At length the president called on the pregnant Bloomberg reporter.

"Yes, Holly," he said.

"Thank you, sir."

"I'm tired of these people calling you Heidi," he deadpanned.

"I appreciate you—"

"And I will correct them," Bush said. "Particularly on camera."

"If we do have to go to war and—"

"With which country?" the president interrupted.

"With Iraq," Holly said. "And with our economy stagnating, what makes you confident that we can afford—"

"First of all, you know, I'm hopeful we won't have to go war, and let's leave it at that," he said.

"But if we do, though, what—"

"Until Saddam Hussein makes up his mind to disarm—see, it's his choice to make," Bush said. "See, you need to ask him that question, not me."

"But the White House is drawing up plans to pay for the war, if we come to that," Holly persisted. "So why—"

"Well, let's leave it at 'if,' for a while then, until it happens."

"So you don't want to talk about whether our economy could sustain it, if that's a possibility?"

Bush pointed out that he had already answered a similar question two days earlier, when a reporter outside a Crawford restaurant said: "Can this economy afford to fight a war?"

"This economy cannot afford to stand an attack," Bush had replied. "An attack from Saddam Hussein or a surrogate of Saddam Hussein would cripple our economy."

Now Bush said to Rosencranz: "Go back to that question, Heidi— I mean, Holly."

Gregory then tried to steer the conversation back to the burgeoning field of Democratic presidential hopefuls, all of whom were taking potshots at the president. But Bush wouldn't bite.

"There's going to be a lot of verbiage and a lot of noise and a lot of posturing and a lot of elbowing," he said dismissively. "To me, that's just going to be background noise. My job is to protect the American people and work to create confidence in our economy so that people can find work."

"On some level, were you getting ready for a rematch and hoping for a rematch with Al Gore?" the reporter ventured.

After much hemming and hawing, Gore had announced in December that he would not mount a second campaign against Bush. Although polls showed the former vice president was the Democratic front-runner with the highest level of name recognition, the party's top strategists and fund-raisers were dubious about his ability to unseat a popular wartime commander in chief. After all, Gore had already lost once to Bush, despite profound advantages like peace, prosperity, the trappings of incumbency, and an opponent widely portrayed as a lightweight. If Gore couldn't push it over the goal line with those sorts of advantages, how could he be expected to win now that Bush was widely admired as the nation's chief prosecutor of the war against terrorism? Bush, who had Gore to thank for the harrowing, thirty-six-day debacle after the 2000 election, was keenly aware of his old foe's decision to sit out the 2004 race. But he wasn't about to come out and admit that to the press pool at the tail end of a hike across Prairie Chapel Ranch.

"Really wasn't paying much attention to it," the president shrugged. "I've got my mind on the peace and security of the American people. And politics will sort itself out."

He added: "One of these days, somebody will emerge and we'll tee it up and see who the American people want to lead. And until that happens, I'm going to be doing my job."

As the press conference wound down, Bush said: "All right, let's go get some coffee."

"One more," a reporter insisted. "Are you satisfied that the inspectors are getting to Saddam's weapon scientists?"

Under intense pressure from Bush, the dictator had ended his four-year ban on weapons inspections in an attempt to avert war. But the president was unimpressed with Saddam's new level of cooperation.

"He is a man who likes to play games and charades," Bush said. "You hear these reports about Iraqi scientists being interviewed, but there's a minder in the room."

Bush was openly skeptical about Saddam getting rid of his chemical, biological, and nuclear weapons programs. Responding to U.S.-led demands that he provide a detailed inventory of these programs, the dictator had released a voluminous report that essentially said he had none.

"The first indication isn't very positive that he will voluntarily disarm," Bush scoffed. "After all, he put out a declaration that the world realized was false."

The president seemed mindful that Saddam had been conditioned by Clinton not to worry too much about American threats.

"Hopefully he realizes we're serious, and hopefully he disarms peacefully," Bush said. "He's a danger to the American people; he's a danger to our friends and allies.

"For eleven long years, the world has dealt with him," the president concluded. "And now he's got to understand: His day of reckoning is coming."

This time the press conference was really over.

"All right," Bush said. "Let's go get a coffee."

As we approached his house, we passed one feature that looked as though it had never been used.

"That's the famous swimming pool, which I dubbed the 'whining pool,'" he said ruefully.

It was a reference to relentless complaints by his twin daughters, Barbara and Jenna, that their new home didn't have an in-ground swimming pool.

"There was a lot of cajoling going on," Bush recalled.

When the teenagers' whining reached critical mass, Bush reluctantly had the pool installed, only to discover that after a few swims the girls grew tired of their expensive new toy. So there it sat, utterly unused, a monument to one man's indulgence of his fickle offspring.

Since Bush had never taken the White House press into his house before, the reporters didn't know quite what to expect as they schlepped up the long driveway. The first impression was underwhelming. Instead of the kind of ostentatious mansion one might expect from a president, the house was a modest affair, almost unnoticeable amid the live oak trees. It was a long and low rancher with a simple tin roof. The walls were made of locally quarried, honey-colored limestone that absorbed the winter sun and transmitted the heat indoors. At the moment, some of that sun was also being absorbed by the jet-black coat of Bush's faithful terrier.

"There's my man, Barney, standing guard," the president said.

Soon the dog was joined by Laura, who came out of the house to greet the approaching press scrum and pose for photos with her husband. When we got to the front door, Bush began knocking his sneakers against the pavement in an attempt to dislodge the mud that was caked to his soles. I bent over and began doing the same to my army boots, only to realize after a few moments that it was hopeless. Our footwear was simply too filthy to be worn indoors. I looked up expectantly at the First Lady, cutting a quick glance at my waffle soles to signal the futility of the effort. She smiled stoically to signify that she was not about to order the national press to remove its footwear. So I suggested it instead, and after a polite protest the First Lady gratefully acquiesced. In the next moment the president and press were unlacing all manner of shoes and boots, tossing them into a filthy heap and parading into the house in stocking feet.

Soon we found ourselves in the dining room, which harbored a table, a buffet, and some upholstered couches and chairs off to one side. A pair of silent stewards handed out bottles of water and cups of coffee, and then the president led reporters into the living room, which boasted expansive views of the lake. A fashionably "fatigued" wooden table stood atop a chestnut floor, which was adorned by a couple of overstuffed couches facing a large coffee table laden with neat stacks of—well, coffee table books. A gas fire burned in an artificial wood fireplace. Above the mantle hung a large, dramatic painting of white ibises with pink beaks. The opposite wall was lined with bookshelves up to the ceiling. Having fulfilled his obligation to talk shop, Bush now took delight in showing off his favorite features of the house, including pocket screen doors that allowed breezes to pass through the 4,000-square-foot structure during the searing heat of Texas summers.

For a president regularly accused of hostility to the environment, Bush lived in a house that would have made a tree-hugger proud. Architect David Heymann, whom Bush had hired after purchasing the property in 1999, had built a large underwater cistern to capture rainwater that cascaded off the galvanized roof. The water was recycled to irrigate the land around the house, which Laura was in the process of restoring to native Texas grasses and wildflowers. Despite his reputation as a macho cowboy, Bush was forever going on about his wife's gardening.

"In the spring, particularly in a year like this year, there will be fantastic wildflowers," he gushed.

After a while, the environmentalist-in-chief spotted a red-tailed hawk in a live oak. Press wrangler Reed Dickens fetched a pair of binoculars so his boss could have a look. The president then passed the binoculars to the journalists, who peered at the bird and murmured their admiration.

At length Bush and his wife led the press outside to a concrete patio, which wrapped all the way around the four-bedroom house. Everyone stood there in stocking feet and gazed at the lake and the grove of trees beyond, where the Bushes said they might build a guest house some day. The president also disclosed that he envisioned making Prairie Chapel Ranch his permanent residence after leaving the White House, although his wife did not necessarily agree.

"That's an interesting conversation Laura and I have had," he allowed. "In my view, this will be the primary residence and we'd have a townhouse somewhere else.

"I think her view might be slightly different," he added. "In which case, her view will prevail."

Although the reservoir of small talk was beginning to run low, most of the reporters stuck close to the president, leaving one or two others to chat up the First Lady, who was accustomed to her husband getting the lion's share of attention anyway. When the collective conversation finally reached a natural pause, it became clear that our audience with the president was over. So we schlepped back outside and pulled on our muddy boots and shoes, thanking the First Couple for their hospitality and bidding them farewell.

We tromped away down the long driveway, congratulating ourselves for having spent an unprecedented amount of time with the president. The get-together had been a rare opportunity to get to know Bush better on a personal level; not every instant with the president, it seemed, had to be an in-your-face display of journalistic hostility—especially when he and his wife were gracious enough to invite us into their personal sanctuary. As I noted in my pool report, though, we had succeeded in getting Bush to discuss all the pressing issues of the day, from Iraq to North Korea, from politics to the economy, from terrorism to illegal immigrants. The president's responses to our questions formed the basis of stories that led the *NBC Nightly News* and other national newscasts that evening, and made the front pages of the *New York Times* and other leading papers the next morning.

Yet later that day I received a call from *Washington Post* media critic Howard Kurtz, one of innumerable beltway types who regularly obtained secondhand copies of White House pool reports. Having perused my lengthy dispatch, Kurtz was preparing a piece for the next day's *Post* on whether the White House press corps, led by one Bill Sammon, was "going soft on the president."

7

"HOSED BY THE STATE OF THE UNION!"

COLIN POWELL WAS IN a panic. Less than three months after his unqualified triumph at the United Nations—where all fifteen members of the Security Council, including Libya, had passed resolution 1441—many of those same countries were now getting cold feet. Although they had threatened "serious consequences" against Saddam if he didn't mend his ways, nations like France and Russia were now increasingly reluctant to pull the trigger. So in late January, Powell found himself under tremendous pressure to shore up international support by making a major presentation to the U.N. General Assembly.

"The president told me that he wanted me to present the case— The Case—because we didn't feel our case was getting out there," Powell explained to me. "And when I looked at the following week and saw the time that I would have to do all this, I went *bleaugh!* And what really scared me is that the material was supposed to have already been done somewhere and all I would have to do is take a look at it and go. Well, the material I was given was not ready for presentation.

"I realized," he concluded, "that the whole thing would have to be done from scratch."

He also realized how difficult it would be to accomplish such a monumental task by Wednesday, February 5, the date Bush had in mind for Powell's U.N. appearance. Yet the president was determined to announce this timetable during his State of the Union Address on January 28, which would be watched by tens of millions.

"And so I said to the White House: 'My God, don't have him say 5 February. Just say next week,'" Powell told me. "And they said, 'Okay, we'll say next week.'"

But Powell's contact at the White House did not realize that fellow administration officials had already begun quietly previewing the president's speech to journalists and others. To suddenly postpone Powell's presentation would be interpreted by the press as weakness.

"Then they called me back twenty minutes later and said: 'Too late, we've already backgrounded the State of the Union and it's 5 February.'

"So I was hosed by the State of the Union!" he said. "It was a bear."

From that point forward, Powell spent every night in Langley, Virginia, huddled with several dozen members of the administration about what to include in his presentation.

"We holed up at the CIA," he told me. "I'd go there every evening and go through all this stuff until late into the night. And it was a very, very dicey, close-run, difficult thing to do."

That's because much of the evidence against Saddam did not meet Powell's standards for an airtight case.

"If it was bad, or screwed up, or didn't sound right, it would be attacked within twenty minutes," he told me. "Everybody would go after it."

Even at this late date, there were some in the administration who did not want Powell to hang his entire U.N. presentation on the issue of weapons of mass destruction. They kept agitating about Saddam's other crimes.

"There was a thought at one time that it would be one day of WMD, one day of terrorism, one day [of human rights abuses]," Rice told me.

Yet this plan was abandoned in favor of a one-day presentation focusing mostly on weapons of mass destruction. Although the presentation retained elements of all three arguments, "the terrorism and human rights got cut back," Rice explained.

Indeed, Powell was determined to excise all but the most unassailable evidence against Saddam. "If there were egregious errors in there that were immediately disprovable, then that would undercut the whole presentation," he told me. "So I had to make sure whatever I put out there was, for the most part, supported by the intelligence evidence."

By now, Powell and everyone else in the administration knew that "making the case" against Iraq was a never-ending endeavor. Although Congress and the United Nations had authorized war more than four months earlier, members of both institutions vacillated as the day of reckoning drew near. For example, Democratic Senator John Kerry of Massachusetts, who was running for president, had voted in October for the aptly named Authorization for Use of Military Force Against Iraq Resolution of 2002. But now, as war seemed imminent, Kerry was disparaging the allies aligned against Saddam—including Great Britain, Australia, and Poland—as "some trumped-up, so-called coalition of the bribed, the coerced, the bought, and the extorted."

The second-guessing was even worse at the U.N., where the Security Council seemed unwilling to hold Saddam accountable to the resolution it had unanimously passed in November.

"We believe that nothing today justifies envisaging war," French Foreign Minister Dominique de Villepin told a news conference at the U.N. on January 20. Accusing Washington of "impatience," he suggested giving inspectors several more months to look for weapons. Countries like Germany and Russia agreed.

"France always liked being the leader of the group, no matter what the cause," Powell told me. "And they were the leader of the group that said: War would be bad. It'll cause turmoil in the region. It'll cause all kinds of problems in Iraq. And we don't want a war."

Ever since the end of the Cold War, Paris had grown increasingly resentful of America's status as the world's sole superpower. While the 1700s had been the French century and the 1800s belonged to the British, the 1900s had been unmistakably dominated by America. And now it looked as though there would be a second American century. Well, not if Paris could help it. French President Chirac seemed bent on turning the European Union into a counterweight against Washington's unchecked power.

"You hear all kinds of rumors as to why the French do what they do," Bush told Brit Hume of Fox News Channel. "And some of it is this notion about having multi-polarity. That means to offset, in Europe, the ambitions of America."

Powell was dismissive of the notion that the United States was a "hyperpower" that must be checked by France.

"There are some thinkers in Europe who like to tout out this theory—and they usually tout it out in French," he told me. "The hyperpower—and it's of course their great fear. And therefore when you have a power that great, it has to be balanced, there has to be other sources of power, there has to be multi-powers, multi-polarity."

"It ain't gonna happen," he told me. "We're too powerful. You can't balance us off.

"And the other reason it won't work is that most of your European friends don't want to be a counter to the United States," he added. "We all have shared values, so we can't be against one another. We all have shared interests. We're all in the same alliances. And you should not be afraid of U.S. power."

Nonetheless, France succeeded in opening a rift between the U.S. and Western Europe. It was exacerbated by German Chancellor Gerhardt Schroeder, who had won a tough reelection in September by taking a hard line against Bush's proposed "adventure" in Iraq. Schroeder's justice minister helped secure her boss's come-from-behind victory by comparing America's president to Germany's ex-fuhrer. "Bush wants to divert attention from his domestic problems," Herta Daeubler-Gmelin told a German newspaper. "It's a classic tactic. It's one that Hitler used." The comment caused such a uproar in Washington that Schroeder fired her after being reelected.

It was no secret that German firms had profited for decades from lucrative contracts to build Iraq's infrastructure and supply Saddam with factories that manufactured nerve agents. Meanwhile, France had a multi-billion-dollar oil contract with Iraq that was in danger of being canceled if the U.S. succeeded in toppling Saddam. So these countries embarked on a sort of "peace for oil" crusade, even as Bush was widely accused of waging "war for oil."

In late January, a Dutch journalist asked Donald Rumsfeld to comment on this growing rift between the U.S. and Western Europe.

"If you look at, for example, France, Germany," the reporter said, "it seems that a lot of Europeans rather give the benefit of the doubt to Saddam Hussein than President George Bush. These are U.S. allies. What do you make of that?"

"You're thinking of Europe as Germany and France. I don't. I think that's old Europe," Rumsfeld shot back. "If you look at the entire NATO Europe today, the center of gravity is shifting to the east."

Indeed, Bush had recently traveled to Eastern Europe to welcome seven former Communist nations into NATO. Addressing 100,000 cheering Romanians in Bucharest's main square, where the body of communist dictator Nicolai Ceauşescu was strung up in 1989 after his execution, Bush asked for help in deposing Saddam.

"The people of Romania understand that aggressive dictators cannot be appeased or ignored—they must always be opposed," he exhorted the rain-soaked crowd. "An aggressive dictator now rules in Iraq. By his search for terrible weapons, by his ties to terror groups, by his development of prohibited ballistic missiles, the dictator of Iraq threatens the security of every free nation, including the free nations of Europe."

While Bush refrained from singling out the complacent nations of Western Europe, Rumsfeld had no such compunction.

"Germany has been a problem and France has been a problem," he told the Dutch reporter bluntly. "But you look at vast numbers of other countries in Europe—they're not with France and Germany on this, they're with the United States."

Still, those smaller Eastern European nations had to live "next door to France and Germany," Powell pointed out. "We can't be insensitive to that," he told me. "What I tell them all is: We don't want you to choose between us and your European friends. But just remember where you'll have to come if you ever really, really get into trouble."

At the same news conference where de Villepin accused Washington of "impatience," German Foreign Minister Joschka Fischer suggested that weapons inspectors be given "all the time which is needed." Incredibly, he asserted that "Iraq has complied fully with all relevant resolutions."

Yet Saddam had been in "material breach" of 1441 from the moment it went into effect, thanks to the numerous "ambushes" Powell built into the document.

"He kept tripping them," Powell told me.

For starters, Iraq did not suddenly "end repression of its civilian population," or stop sheltering terrorists like Abu Abbas, as 1441 required. Nor did Saddam account for weapons like the al-Samoud missiles in a 12,000-page report he submitted to the U.N. Worse yet, Iraqi forces continued to fire on U.S. and British warplanes patrolling the no-fly zones, even though 1441 expressly forbade "hostile acts" against U.N. members enforcing earlier resolutions against Iraq.

Still, the Bush Administration continued to emphasize what it felt was the strongest of all arguments—Saddam's refusal to come clean on weapons of mass destruction. As evidence, they cited a report by Blix to the U.N. on January 27, after inspectors had spent two months getting the runaround from Saddam's regime.

"Iraq appears not to have come to genuine acceptance—not even today—of the disarmament which was demanded of it and which it needs to carry out to win the confidence of the world and live in peace," Blix told the Security Council.

This grim assessment lent new urgency to Powell's diplomatic efforts. "Time is running out," he said after Blix's report. "We've made it very clear from the beginning that we would not allow the process of inspections to string out forever."

Yet the U.N. hesitated. It knew that Saddam's demise would mean an end to the oil-for-food program, a humanitarian effort that had turned into a cash cow for the world body. The U.N. had pocketed more than $1 billion in sales commissions since it began running the program in 1996. This staggering windfall allowed the world body to employ thousands and wield tremendous financial clout by awarding lucrative contracts across the globe.

"The oil-for-food program is no ordinary relief effort. Not only does it involve astronomical amounts of money, it also operates with alarming secrecy," wrote Claudia Rosett, a former foreign correspondent for the *Wall Street Journal*, in an op-ed piece for the *New York Times*. "Putting a veil of secrecy over tens of billions of dollars in contracts is an invitation to kickbacks, political back-scratching and smuggling done under cover of relief operations."

General Tommy Franks derisively referred to the program as "oil-for-palaces." White House Press Secretary Ari Fleischer said instead of providing food for starving Iraqis, the program actually took "resources away from the people" and funneled money to a regime that "builds palaces and builds bombs."

According to Rosett, the U.N.-run program also "facilitated a string of business deals tilted heavily toward Saddam Hussein's preferred trading partners, like Russia, France and, to a lesser extent, Syria."

Ironically, the oil-for-food program was part of an overall sanctions regime against Iraq that began with the best of intentions—to punish Saddam.

"Sanctions are an important tool," Rice told me. "They do have a tendency to grow an underworld, and a corrupt underworld. We need to understand it better."

To that end, she suggested an investigation. "I do think at some point there will have to be a thorough look at how oil-for-food was running and what was happening," she said. "I've heard, we all have, from Iraqi ministers that they're uncovering a lot of contracts that were not fulfilled but the money was paid, a lot of contracts that were where bogus equipment was sent."

Bush himself was deeply skeptical of the oil-for-food program, telling me: "We need to have that investigated until we fully understand the depth of that." Still, he stopped short of linking oil-for-food revenues with international opposition to the war. "It's a hard charge to make," he said. "I'm not going to make a charge against somebody who disagreed with our policy, without knowing all the facts."

Given the president's suspicions about the U.N. and his reputation as a unilateralist, it was not surprising that he chose Powell to make the administration's most comprehensive case to the world body. Powell was the administration's media darling because he was less conservative than Bush, Cheney, Rumsfeld, and Rice. In fact, Powell was almost liberal when compared with his own undersecretary, John Bolton, or Rumsfeld's deputy Douglas Feith. He supported abortion, affirmative action, and even the right of protesters to burn the American flag.

"I'm not as conservative as some of my other colleagues in the administration," Powell told me. "If you looked at all the things I believed in, from the social side of the ledger to the economic and military side of the ledger, and if you put, say, Cheney up around ninety, and Don and Condi and company between eighty and ninety, and you put Bolton and Feith at about ninety-eight, then I'd be somewhere around sixty, sixty-five."

This disparity fueled countless media caricatures portraits of Powell as the lonely voice of reason in an administration teeming with right-wing extremists. He was constantly portrayed as a dove struggling mightily against hawks like Rumsfeld and Cheney.

"The media, from the very first day I took the job, used this difference to create a stereotype," he told me. "It's a stereotype that I fought for two and a half, three years. And now I just say: That's the way it is and here I am. You know, I'm sixty-seven and I can't be sent back to Vietnam for a third tour."

But he could be sent to the U.N., where Bush knew Powell's words would carry greater weight than his own—even though Powell had become every bit as hawkish on Iraq as the rest of the administration. Powell was keenly aware of the historical significance of his presentation, even before he finished the final draft. He recalled the Cuban Missile Crisis of 1962, when Adlai Stevenson, U.S. ambassador to the U.N., asked his Soviet counterpart whether nuclear arms were being stockpiled off the Florida coast. Teetering on the brink of nuclear war, the world was electrified when Stevenson told the Russian at an emergency meeting of the Security Council: "I am prepared to wait for my answer until hell freezes over."

Now it was Powell's turn to electrify the world.

"The greatest challenge was knowing that it was going to be an

Adlai Stevenson moment," he told me. "And every reporter was getting their score sheet out."

The late nights at the CIA finally paid off and Powell finished preparing his case. On February 5, he went before the U.N. and laid out the administration's most comprehensive and damning indictment of Iraq. Using freshly declassified wire intercepts, he played chilling audiotapes of Iraqi officials fretting over the arrival of weapons inspectors.

"We have evacuated everything," said a senior army officer one day before inspectors were scheduled to arrive.

Another official spoke cryptically of "forbidden ammo" before instructing an underling to "destroy this message because I don't want anyone to see this message."

A third official was told by his superior to "remove the expression 'nerve agents' wherever it comes up in the wireless instructions."

Like a prosecutor addressing a jury, Powell used charts, aerial photographs and other visual aids to drive home his points. For an hour and eighteen minutes, he painted a terrifying picture of Saddam's deadly arsenal.

"There can be no doubt that Saddam Hussein has biological weapons and the capability to rapidly produce more, many more," he said. "And he has the ability to dispense these lethal poisons and diseases in ways that can cause massive death and destruction."

He added: "Our conservative estimate is that Iraq today has a stockpile of between one hundred and five hundred tons of chemical weapons agent. That is enough agent to fill sixteen thousand battlefield rockets. Even the low end of one hundred tons of agent would enable Saddam Hussein to cause mass casualties across more than one hundred square miles of territory, an area nearly five times the size of Manhattan."

Powell even tried a tactic Bush had employed during his own speech to the U.N. nearly five months earlier—shame. He pointed out that Saddam spent the previous dozen years flouting no fewer than sixteen resolutions by the world body.

"We have an obligation to this body to see that our resolutions are complied with," Powell said. "We wrote 1441 to give Iraq one last chance.

"Iraq is not, so far, taking that one last chance. We must not shrink from whatever is ahead of us."

8

THE "GET"

DAN RATHER GAZED INTO the mirror and pretended Saddam Hussein was gazing back at him. The seventy-one-year-old anchorman asked aloud the questions he planned to pose to the dictator, who had agreed to give Rather an exclusive interview. Having written out more than thirty queries right there in his Baghdad hotel room, Rather now gave voice to them again and again, sometimes changing their order. It was an invaluable exercise in interview preparation—and not just for Rather. It was also tremendously helpful to Saddam, since—as every Western reporter in Baghdad knew—the rooms in the hotel were thoroughly bugged.

Securing this interview had not been easy. Journalists from all over the world would have given their eye teeth for the chance to chat with one of the bloodiest tyrants of the last half century.

"I'm a reporter who got lucky," Rather explained to the *Washington Post.* Part of Rather's "aw-shucks" persona involved eschewing his highfalutin titles of network anchorman and managing editor of CBS News in favor of the far humble moniker of "reporter." This affected modesty was curious to real reporters, who made a fraction of Rather's multi-million-dollar salary and would have jumped at the chance to upgrade their own lowly titles.

"You work hard, work your sources, make your contacts, not get discouraged, just keep coming," the salt-of-the-earth "reporter" allowed.

One of Rather's key contacts was former U.S. Attorney General Ramsey Clark, a radical leftist who defended Saddam while spearheading a campaign to impeach President Bush. Clark, who had known Rather for many years, vouched for the newsman during his own meeting with Saddam and "was a big help" in landing the CBS interview, Rather acknowledged on CNN.

Also working in Rather's favor was the fact that he had interviewed Saddam in August 1990, just after Iraq's invasion of Kuwait.

"At least I was a known quantity to them," Rather explained to the *Post.* "In 1990 they wanted someone who had a reputation of being independent and had credibility. I came out of the 1990 interview feeling I had done what I said I would do."

Evidently, that entailed asking questions that utterly misjudged the looming U.S.-led attack.

"Mr. President," the newsman had asked the genocidal tyrant. "Do you think this is a Vietnam in the sand for the United States?"

"The harm caused to the invaders who come here will be greater than whatever they suffered in Vietnam," Saddam replied through an interpreter. "Iraq will come out victorious."

More than a dozen years after that prediction was proven ridiculous, Saddam was once again bracing for a U.S.-led attack. Only this time he hadn't invaded any country. This time he hadn't gassed his own people. This time he hadn't even done anything particularly different from what he had been doing all through the Clinton Administration—which is to say, sheltering terrorists, repressing his people, pursuing weapons of mass destruction, and precluding stability from taking root in the Middle East.

Although Saddam was again squaring off against an American president named George Bush, the son seemed more aggressive than the father. As far as Saddam could tell, this brash young president—whom the dictator referred to as "son of the snake"—seemed intent on finishing the job his father had begun. Hoping to avoid that scenario, Saddam arranged to be interviewed by an influential American anchorman. Having failed to get his message across via George Galloway six months earlier, Saddam was now upping the ante by speaking with someone perceived by the West as more objective, or at least more influential—Dan Rather.

Like Galloway, Rather was driven around Baghdad for several hours before finally being taken to Saddam, who was seated at a round white table mounted with microphones and a small Iraqi flag. Although Rather would never dream of allowing the White House to ban a CBS camera crew from one of his interviews with an American president (which had begun with Eisenhower and ended with Clinton), the newsman had agreed to let Saddam's personal camera crew handle all taping of his sit-down with the Iraqi strongman. In an even more unusual concession, Rather agreed that after the interview he would leave Saddam's palace without a copy of the tape, trusting the dictator's camera crew to make a dub (hopefully without any censorship) that would be sent along later to the American anchorman. Rather would have been laughed out of journalism for agreeing to such ground rules in any other country, but swallowed his pride for the sake of the "get"—the TV term for a prized interview. These days, there was no bigger "get" than Saddam Hussein. So Rather acquiesced to the restrictive demands and now was reaping his reward—a private audience with the man responsible for the deaths of more than a million Muslims.

"Mr. President, I do appreciate your agreeing to spend an hour, because I want to ask questions in two categories, please," Rather began. Such deference to one of the most ruthless tyrants on the planet! His politesse was a far cry from the antipathy he showed the elder President Bush during an interview in 1988, when the anchorman berated him over Iran-Contra: "You've made us hypocrites in the face of the world! *How could you do that?!*"

By contrast, Rather was calm, even deferential, as he explained to Saddam the format of the interview.

"Category one would be those questions that I think many, if not most, of Americans would like to have answered about the news of right now," he said. "And in category two, more philosophical questions."

Nothing like a high-minded philosophical discussion with a man whose torture tactics included murdering children in front of their parents.

"Mr. President, do you intend to destroy the al-Samoud missiles that the United Nations prohibits?" Rather said. "Will you destroy those missiles?"

The buzz of the moment was that Saddam had tripped yet another "ambush" in U.N. resolution 1441 by failing to disclose his possession of missiles that could travel more than 150 kilometers. An inventory of these al-Samoud missiles was conspicuously missing from the 12,000-page report Iraq had submitted to the U.N. on December 7. U.N. weapons inspectors went on to find scores of the prohibited weapons, although Saddam was still clinging to the fiction that he was in full accordance with 1441.

"We're implementing that resolution in accordance with what the United Nations wants us to do," Saddam replied. "It is on this basis that we have conducted ourselves, and it is on this basis that we will continue to behave."

"I want to make sure that I understand, Mr. President," Rather said with the utmost respect. "So you do not intend to destroy these missiles?"

"Which missiles are you talking about? We do not have missiles that go beyond the prescribed ranges," Saddam insisted. "The inspection teams have been here. They have inspected every place. And if there is a question to that effect, I think the question should be addressed to them."

He added: "These missiles have been destroyed. There are no missiles that are contrary to the prescription of the United Nations in Iraq."

"What do you consider to be the core issues?" Rather said. "I started with the news of the day. But what do you consider to be the core issue, the basic issue?"

Instead of answering the question by naming his central dispute with the United States and the United Nations, Saddam launched into a rambling theological soliloquy—much to Rather's chagrin.

"In all divine religions, God, the Almighty, has reiterated to man in all his Holy Books and to humanity, in general, that there are two basic, most important things in life, that is, after the issue of the creation and of the issue of faith," Saddam bloviated. "These two important things are food and peace."

Food and peace? This interview was going nowhere fast, and it was only hampered further by the cumbersome and tedious work of the interpreters. Mindful that this dull exchange would soon be airing on national television, Rather was starting to get nervous.

"Boy, I'm in trouble here," he recalled thinking to himself. "This is not going very well."

He later told the *Post:* "It's hard—I'm not complaining about it— to build a rhythm to the interview." So as soon as Saddam finished prattling about food and religion, Rather decided to cut to the chase.

"Mr. President, do you expect to be attacked by an American-led invasion?" he blurted.

"We hope that the attack will not take place, but we are bracing ourselves to meet such an attack, to face it," Saddam replied. "You've been here for a few days, and you've seen how the people live. They live normally. They get married. They establish relationships. They visit each other. They visit their neighbors. They travel around Iraq. They are enjoying life in the manner that life is provided."

He neglected to mention, of course, the countless innocent Iraqis who were arrested, tortured, raped, mutilated, imprisoned, and killed on a routine basis.

"But at the same time, they also hear the news," Saddam continued. "Because the officials in the United States keep talking about attacking Iraq."

Actually, U.S. officials were doing more than talking about attacking Iraq. For months, they had been dispatching large numbers of American forces to the Gulf. Saddam said this mobilization was "done partly to cover the huge lie that was being waged against Iraq about chemical, biological, and nuclear weapons." The dictator also dismissed nations supporting America as "those who would like to ride the bandwagon of evil."

"Are you afraid of being killed or captured?" asked Rather, heartened that Saddam was finally becoming more animated. Perhaps the interview wouldn't be a disaster after all.

"Whatever Allah decides," said Saddam, a committed secularist who cravenly cloaked himself in Islam every time he was about to get walloped. "We are believers. We believe in what he decides."

The dictator rambled on some more before making this inauspicious aside: "Bear with me. My answers are long."

"Mr. President, I have all night," Rather managed, prompting laughter in the room.

"When we were young," Saddam plowed on, "the Iraqi people had suffered a lot of deprivation and backwardness. People did not even find—many people did not even find . . ."

"Are you satisfied with [the] translation?" one of Saddam's handlers murmured to Rather, who had no way of knowing whether the translators were truthfully representing the deluge of unintelligible words pouring from Saddam's mouth.

"Yes, no, the translation is excellent," Rather assured him. "It's superb."

Unfazed by the interruption, Saddam kept talking. He seemed to be reminiscing about his childhood in the tiny village of al-Ouja.

"People generally did not even find shoes to wear, in those days," he said. "And people in the countryside were deprived of most essential things in life. And people even in the city were deprived of the most basic requirements for a decent life, for a simple life.

"We, those days, decided to place ourselves to the service of our people. And I'm not going to indulge in a story about what we did for our people and the sacrifices that we made and the dangers that we went through in order to insure for our people the dignity that our people deserve, because this is a story well known. And I am not going to indulge into that."

Thus did Saddam Hussein, the great defender of Iraqi dignity, spare Dan Rather the story of his bloody rise to power and the unspeakable horrors he inflicted on the Iraqi people for nearly thirty-five years in order to retain that power. Instead, he continued with his tireless account of his heroic sacrifices.

"In those days, we did not ask the question whether we were going to live or die," he mused. "We simply relied on Allah and we moved ahead." In other words, according to Saddam, Allah rewarded selfless devotion with, well, career advancements.

"And now, after having achieved all this march, having reached what we have reached, now we've become leaders of the country. Some of my comrades are ministers and vice presidents and the rest. We're not going to ask ourselves now whether we should change our course or whether we should ask about life and death."

"It's morally unacceptable to ask such a question," one of Saddam's sycophants interjected. Unfortunately for Rather, the interruption did not derail the dictator's self-serving train of thought.

"How could we ask such a question when we, basically, as freedom fighters, did not ask it at the beginning?" he droned. "The people accepted us and accepted the fact of our revolution and the principles of our revolution—and they have committed themselves to them."

The people of Iraq *accepted* Saddam and his henchmen? Maybe back in the balmy days immediately following the 1968 coup, before Iraqis fully realized the depths of Saddam's depravity. But the public's honeymoon with the increasingly cruel dictator had ended decades ago. The only question now was whether Saddam's lieutenants would desert him when the bombs started falling, as Bush was openly inciting them to do. To counter this insidious message from America, Saddam issued a veiled warning to his underlings not to break ranks.

"I do not believe that any officials in this place now should ask a question whether he's going to live or die," Saddam warned. "The question should be how deeply in strength he remains to his commitment to the people, to the basic principles from which we proceeded. And whatever the will of God is, then the will of God will be there. Nothing is going to change the will of God."

When another Saddam toady interjected with an indistinct platitude about "the Iraqi people and humanity in general," Rather saw his chance to retake control of the interview.

"I understand," the anchorman stipulated before segueing abruptly into one of the questions he had practiced in front of the mirror. "Mr. President, Americans are very much concerned about anyone's connections to Osama bin Laden. Do you have, have you had, any connections to al Qaeda and Osama bin Laden?"

"Is this the basis of the anxiety in the minds of U.S. officials?" said Saddam, evidently determined not to directly answer a single question.

"Or is it the basis of anxiety in the minds of the people of the United States?"

"Mr. President, I believe I can report accurately that it's a major concern in the minds of the people in the United States," the humble pollster dutifully reported.

After a disjointed preamble, Saddam finally got down to brass tacks.

"I will answer you now very clearly: We have never had any relationship with Mr. Osama bin Laden, and Iraq has never had any relationship with al Qaeda," he said. "And I think that Mr. bin Laden himself has recently, in one of his speeches, given such an answer—that we have no relation with him."

"Do you or do you not agree, in principle, with the attack of 9/11?" Rather asked.

Again, instead of answering the question, Saddam began another filibuster, this one on his pan-Arab principles. While there might have been a time, many years earlier, when Saddam's dream of being hailed as the leader of the pan-Arab world, a sort of second Nasser, was vaguely plausible, he now seemed unlikely to remain the leader of even Iraq for much longer.

"We believe that the world must seek to find opportunities for peace, not opportunities for war or opportunities for fighting or opportunities for venting or harming others," said the man who had started the Iran-Iraq war, invaded Kuwait, and gassed the Kurds. "There should not be an aggressor while others are silent about the aggression. There should not be a killer while those who watch and applaud the killing [sic]. There should not be an occupier of the land belonging to others while there are those who keep quiet and never move to remove the occupation."

This was evidently directed at fellow Arab nations and Western sympathizers like France, a not-so-subtle plea for them to defend Saddam against the U.S.-led coalition.

"When we are aggressed against, it is our right to face up to the aggression, to confront the aggression," he warned. "And the charter of the United Nations was not actually drafted by Muslims or the Muslim nation. It was drafted by Christian nations, even though we believe in it and we accept it and we go by its articles."

Saddam—who had been stiffing the United Nations for more than three decades—said all this with a straight face. In fact, Rather later told the *Post* that Saddam "was to all outward appearances calm. He was unhurried. He comes across as confident. He has what military people call command presence. Some may argue this was studied; I can only report what I saw, heard, and felt in that room."

Saddam's discussion of Christian and Muslim nations led Rather into another "news of the day" question, based on recent rumblings by the Bush Administration that the dictator might be able to avert war by fleeing Iraq.

"Mr. President, have you been offered asylum anywhere?" the anchorman asked. "And would you, under any circumstances, consider going into exile to save your people death and destruction?"

This must have been unsettling to Saddam, who would have tortured and killed any Iraqi with the temerity to ask such a question. These Americans were an audacious lot. The last one Saddam had met was Bill Richardson, back in 1995, when the U.N. ambassador asked him to release two American prisoners—another brazen request. But now he was being asked by an impertinent American journalist whether he would high-tail it out of his own country. Worse yet was the implication that if he stayed put, he would be responsible for the "death and destruction" of the Iraqi people. And yet somehow Saddam managed to keep his cool. Instead of having Rather dragged off to a dungeon, which would only complicate the dictator's international problems, Saddam adopted the manner of a put-upon parent nobly suffering the travails of a precocious child.

"I can understand the motive behind your question, which is

excitement—this is a very American style," Saddam condescended. "It may not be liked by some, but I can understand. However, I will answer your question.

"After all," added the media-savvy tyrant, "this may be important for television."

Saddam explained that ever since his early days as a "freedom fighter," he had taken a principled stand that Iraq "must maintain the honor of nationalism and pan-Arabism." Having taught his children and grandchildren the same, he said, he was not about to abandon his principles at this late stage of the game.

"I was born here in Iraq," he said. "We will die here. We will die in this country, and we will maintain our honor, the honor that is required, in front of our people.

"You may have asked questions that may be attributed to some excitement to the press," he added. "But let me ask you another exciting question. Let me say something also exciting:

"I believe that whoever asks Saddam to—or offers Saddam asylum in his own country—is, in fact, a person without morals, because he will be directing an insult to the Iraqi people, the Iraqi people who have chosen Saddam Hussein, unanimously, to continue to lead the people of Iraq, and because he will be saying to the people of Iraq: 'Let Saddam leave and leave you without leadership.' "

Rather made no attempt to challenge Saddam's preposterous claim to having been "unanimously" reelected by the Iraqi people. Instead, he let the dictator warm to his theme that Allah, not America, would determine the fate of Iraq.

"However strong a country may be, however powerful, they cannot change the will of other people," he said. "They cannot destroy or direct the will of other people. I live here and we will continue to defend our freedom. We live here in freedom, and our people will continue to defend their freedom, their sanctity, their honor and their country."

"Again, I have plenty of time, Mr. President," said Rather, not wishing to cut short the dictator's filibusters.

Suitably encouraged, Saddam explained his revisionist history of the Gulf War, which he said "might be important to you and the American people. In 1991 Iraq was not defeated. In fact, our Army withdrew from Kuwait according to a decision taken by us. Yes, it withdrew."

When Saddam mentioned the elder "Mr. Bush," he noticed that his translator dropped the courtesy title before relaying the name to Rather. So the dictator corrected his underling.

"I didn't say 'Bush'; I said 'Mr. Bush.' I am being historically accurate in showing him respect," Saddam scolded. "I didn't used to say Mr. Bush when I addressed him when he was in power. But as soon as he left power, whenever I have referred to him, I refer to him as Mr. Bush. And in any case, the law of faith says even your enemy, you have to respect his humanity. For that reason . . . I refer to Mr. Bush."

"I understand now," said Rather, not bothering to point out that Saddam had tried to assassinate "Mr. Bush" after he left office.

"Iraq was not defeated," the dictator repeated. "Iraq was not defeated."

Mindful that it was important for his interview to pass the laugh test, Rather finally felt compelled to express a modicum of skepticism at Saddam's delusional view of the Gulf War. But he did so with maximum deference and journalistic detachment, as if it would be wrong for him, Dan Rather, to personally take a position on the controversial question of whether Iraq had been defeated.

"Mr. President, respectfully, a lot of Americans are going to hear that and say, what is this man talking about, as all of those Iraqi tanks coming out of Kuwait with the turrets knocked out indicated a beaten army on the battlefield," the newsman began apologetically. "There's no joy in my saying that.

"But the point is I'm asking you to explain what you mean that you were not defeated in the war, because I can report to you with accuracy that, overwhelmingly, the American people believe that that was a resounding defeat for you and for Iraq," he said.

Saddam countered that America's periodic, postwar military operations against Iraq—by their very definition—proved he had not been vanquished in the first place.

"Why did Mr. Bush, the father—when he was president of the United States—why did he repeat his attacks on us if we had been defeated? Totally defeated?" Saddam said. "We withdrew our forces inside Iraq in order that we may be able to continue fighting inside our country. And we continued to fight. And the tanks that fought us around Basra, near Basra were defeated. And this is confirmed in writings that have been published by military people.

"And then we had the statement made by Mr. Bush," he added, "that the war had achieved its objective and that he was now stopping it, without preconditions.

"So we have not lost the war and we were not defeated," he insisted. "You know that the fighting between us and Iran continued for eight years. Iran lost battles to us and we lost battles to them. But how do you calculate things? You measure things by the final results."

One of these results, according to Saddam, was that America had stopped short of annihilating Iraq.

"The United States was going to push Iraq back into the pre-industrial age—you remember that, I'm sure," he taunted. "The American onslaught on Iraq continued for more than a month and a half, using warplanes with, of course, the Tomahawks hitting Iraq from everywhere."

He added: "They destroyed bridges, they destroyed churches, mosques, colleges, buildings, plants. They destroyed places, houses, palaces. They killed people, and elderly, but they did not push Iraq back into the pre-industrial age. The Iraqis have subsequently reconstructed everything."

Thus, according to Saddam, did the lesson of the Gulf War become apparent.

"Nobody can sort of take Iraq apart," he said. "We hope that war will not take place. But if war is forced upon us, then Iraq will continue to be here."

Seeking to turn the tables on the current President Bush, Saddam raised the topic of America's own weapons of mass destruction—charging that those weapons were developed to deter aggression from other nations, not to preemptively strike at countries that are minding their own business.

"Did the Americans obtain the weapons in order to control and dominate the world?" Saddam said. "I believe that the scientists of the United States and the people of the United States and the taxpayers of the United States, when they paid that, when they supported that, that was for the basic defense of the United States."

He added: "Is it acceptable that anybody, any official, anyone in power, once he is in possession of a weapon, then he should go and take that weapon to destroy other people?"

Instead of answering Saddam's rhetorical questions, Rather continued to pose his own, some of which were exceedingly solicitous.

"Mr. President, you're being very patient with your time, and I want you to know I consider this a solemn moment in history," the newsman intoned. "If I may take time to have you speak to the American people about questions that I know are on their minds. I just want you to know that I appreciate your patience here.

"Question: You mentioned the Gulf War. You fought the father, George Bush the first. He and the forces he led prevailed on the battlefield. Now you face the son who has an even greater, even more modern, even more lethal military force aimed directly at your throat and heart. Why would you think that you could prevail this time on the battlefield? Or do you?"

"You know that in both situations, then and now, we have not crossed our borders and gone across the Atlantic to commit aggression against the United States, neither by air or by land or by sea," said Saddam, evidently eager to distinguish himself from Osama bin Laden. "And if we were to reverse the question and ask any American, any American citizens, any good, honest American citizen in his own country, including Mr. Rather himself, and we say to him: In any subsequent period or state, if another power, another force were to come across the Atlantic to commit a great aggression against the United States, will you do nothing?"

Before Rather could reply, Saddam filled his own conversational void.

"Let me answer. I say to the honest Americans that if such a thing happens, do not capitulate, do not give in. You have to defend your country, defend your family and your honor."

However, since Iraq had not wronged America, Saddam argued that America should not wage war against Iraq.

"What did Iraq threaten the United States with? Iraq has not committed any aggression against the United States. Nor, nobody in Iraq. Neither an official nor anybody in Iraq says that the United States is our enemy. Or that we must fight the United States."

Saddam suggested the administration "is being pushed or urged by big companies or multinational companies" to attack Iraq in order to engage in war profiteering. It was an argument frequently made by the antiwar movement in the West, which routinely characterized Bush and Cheney of puppets of the military-industrial complex.

"Mr. President," Rather said. "Vice President Richard Cheney of the United States says that if and when an American-led army comes into Iraq, it will be greeted with music. It will be treated as a Army of liberation. If Americans are not to believe that, why should they not believe that?

"There's no Iraqi whatsoever who will welcome any American if that American individual is here in this capacity, as an occupation force," Saddam said. "But all Iraqis will, as they do, welcome all Americans. That is why now you are here, you see that you're being welcomed. Even though you come from a country that is threatening to attack Iraq."

In an effort to demonstrate the support of the Iraqi public, Saddam repeated his boast that he had received 99.96 percent of the vote in his 1996 reelection and a full 100 percent in October 2002. Now presented with a second opportunity to point out the absurdity of such a boast in a totalitarian society, Rather instead murmured "100 percent," as if to say "well I'll be."

"Now, this percentage, I know, may sound very strange to you," Saddam conceded. "May sound strange to you, because you're not used to that. And I can understand that you may find that percentage strange. But even if you take out whatever portion you want to take out of that, then the ratio would remain a high percentage."

He added: "This tells you something about the behavior of the Iraqi people. So, if you want to know how the Iraqi people will behave, or usually behave, you need to look at the elections, and how they behaved during those elections, and how they decided something."

"I understand," Rather assured him. "Mr. President, if it's necessary for you to forgive me, I hope that you'll forgive me. But I have a couple of sort of cleanup questions that I'm not clear about. Number one: Will the new proposed United Nations resolution—the one that's just out this week—will this make any difference at all in your position?"

Although Bush felt that U.N. resolution 1441, passed back in November, cleared the way for him to wage war, he had reluctantly agreed to propose a second resolution for the sole purpose of providing some political cover to allies like Tony Blair of Great Britain.

"The basic position, there is no change," Saddam said. "We will continue committing ourselves to the resolutions. And the inspectors came, and they have seen for themselves that what we've said is true.

We have not pursued any weapons of mass destruction. So, what do they want to issue new resolutions about now?"

"So basically, no change in your position," Rather said.

"We do not compromise our independence or our dignity," Saddam said. "At the same time, we will continue to commit ourselves to what has been decided by the Security Council. If new resolutions that are adopted by the Security Council which may infringe upon our dignity, our freedom, then the position toward such a resolution will be the same—in line with our previous positions."

Abandoning his effort to bring clarity to that issue, Rather returned to an earlier issue that still vexed him.

"And I wanted to ask again, so I'm perfectly clear: You do not intend to destroy your al-Samoud missiles," the newsman said. "The missiles—"

"Al-Samoud," Saddam clarified.

"Yeah, al-Samoud missiles," Rather said. "The missiles that Hans Blix says that he wants a commitment from you that they will be destroyed."

"No violation has been made by Iraq to anything decided by the United Nations," Saddam said. "If what is meant here is to review the resolutions of the Security Council—the resolutions that stipulate that Iraq is allowed to produce missiles with a range of kilometers—if the intention is to rewrite those resolutions, then we will be entering a new framework. A framework in which the United States will be made to forsake its own position."

Saddam's stubborn refusal to acknowledge the existence of the al-Samouds—even though they had already been found by weapons inspectors—cast serious doubt on his other claims to have no weapons of mass destruction. White House Press Secretary Ari Fleischer would later tell CBS that if Saddam "is not facing reality on the issue of the al-Samoud missiles, why would his other statements have credibility?"

But Rather seemed unconcerned with the credibility of Saddam Hussein, whom he continued to treat with maximum deference.

"Mr. President, I know you've been very patient with your time," the newsman said. "Let me go through a short list of additional things. If there is an invasion, will you set fire to the oil fields? Will you blow the dams, or your reservoirs of water, to resist the invasion?"

"Iraq does not burn its wealth," said the man who set fire to Kuwait's oil fields in 1991. "And it does not destroy its dams. We hope, however, that this question is not meant as an insinuation, so that the Iraqi dams and the Iraqi oil wells will be destroyed by those who will invade Iraq."

"Mr. President, I hope you will take this question in the spirit in which it's asked," said Rather, shifting to a more frivolous topic. "First of all, I regret that I do not speak Arabic. Do you speak any English at all?"

"Yes, but I do not speak English fluently," Saddam said. "But I can understand, to a certain degree, the English when spoken."

"Well, would you speak some English for me?" Rather begged. "Anything you choose?"

"My language is Arabic," Saddam demurred.

"I understand," said Rather, abandoning yet another conversational dead end. "Mr. President, again, you've been patient with your time. What is the most important thing you want the American people to understand, at this important juncture of history?"

No longer content to merely serve up softballs to Saddam, Rather was now offering the dictator a no-strings-attached platform for baldfaced propaganda.

"If the American people would like to know the facts," he began, "then I am ready to conduct a direct dialogue with the president of the United States, President Bush, on television. I will say whatever I have to say about American policy. He will have the opportunity to say whatever he has to say about policy of Iraq. And this will be in front of all people, and on television, in a direct, uncensored, honest manner. In front of, as I said, everyone. And then they will see what the facts are, and where falsehoods are."

"Are you speaking about a debate?" Rather said excitedly. "This is new."

Actually, it wasn't new at all. During Rather's 1990 interview, Saddam had proposed a TV debate with the elder President Bush and British Prime Minister Margaret Thatcher. But now that the 2003 interview was breaking so little news, Rather latched onto the debate idea as if it were an earthshaking development. He was so excited he could hardly get the words out.

"You, you are suggesting, you are saying, that you are willing, you are suggesting, you're urging a debate with President Bush?" Rather stammered. "On television?"

"Yes," Saddam said. "That's my proposal."

"Well, that's an interesting. . . ."

"Americans, when they are challenged for a duel, they will not decline the offer," Saddam said. "We are not asking for a duel. We are asking for an opportunity to be seen by the Americans, the Iraqis, and all of the people in the world in a debate that is shown on television, between myself and Mr. Bush, directly.

"This will be an opportunity for him, if he is committed to war," he added, "to convince the world that he is right."

Saddam Hussein had used Stalinesque propaganda techniques to maintain his grip on power for decades. Now he set about to lecture America on free speech.

"Don't you call for the truth to be released in the United States? This is what we read and hear about the American philosophers," he said. "So why should we hide from the people? So why should we discredit ourselves? Why shouldn't we disclose ourselves to the people? We as President of the United States, and President of Iraq, in front of our people."

Saddam explained that the debate might result in war being averted, or at the very least might force Bush "to convince his own people" that war was the answer. Yes, even Saddam Hussein wanted Bush to "make his case."

"This is the gist of my proposal, my idea," he said.

"This is not a joke," said Rather, whose network had described the 1990 debate challenge as "very serious."

"No, this is something proposed in earnest," Saddam said with a straight face. "This is proposed out of my respect for the public opinion of the United States. And it is out of my respect to the people of the United States. And to the people of Iraq. And out of my respect to mankind in general. Humanity at large.

"I call for this because war itself is not a joke. Whoever chooses war as the first choice in his life, then he is not a normal person. I think the debates would be an opportunity for us to ensure peace and safety."

Without a trace of irony, Saddam said that by debating each other, he and Bush "will be respecting our people as the two highest authorities in our countries, the two needed to take the decisions, on the basis of their own, you know, decision-making apparatus. Here in Iraq, we have our own apparatus for reaching those decisions."

Rather didn't even blink at this quaint euphemism for the ruthless implementation of Saddam's every sadistic and paranoid whim.

"And we know that in the United States, you have your own system," the dictator added as if the U.S. Constitution was morally equivalent to Saddam's megalomaniacal tyranny. "But we, as the leaders of the two countries, why don't we use this opportunity in a debate, so that we can show our respect to both our peoples, and to humanity. And then each of us can take the decision that he decides to take, according to what goes on."

"Mr. President, where would this debate take place, that you imagine?" said Rather, pursuing this fantasy as if it were actually feasible. "What would be the venue?"

Saddam explained that he would be in Iraq and Bush would be in the United States. "And then the debate can be conducted through satellite."

"And if Mr. Bush has another proposal—a counterproposal with the same basic idea—then we're prepared to listen to such a proposal," said Saddam, the very picture of reasonableness.

"Would you be prepared to come to the United Nations for this debate?" Rather suggested.

"In the United Nations, voices are not heard—not always," Saddam said. "And I do not mean that I go and I make a speech at the United Nations and then that Bush will make his speech at the United Nations. That is not what I mean. What I mean is that we sit—as we are sitting, you and I, now—I will address questions to him and he will address questions to me. The position of Iraq and the position of the United States. He will explain 'Why I will go to war.' I will explain 'Why we are insistent on peace and we want to maintain peace.' " Lost in the delusion, Saddam began sketching out minor details of the debate, which he said should be held "without makeup, without editing, without prepared speeches, which people do not listen to. The people like listening to live debates."

"How did this—who, who would moderate this debate?" Rather fished.

"You can moderate," the dictator suggested.

"With respect, Mr. President," Rather demurred, "I've got enough problems already."

Indeed, Rather's nightly newscast had been stuck in third place for nearly a decade, badly trailing NBC's Tom Brokaw and ABC's Peter Jennings. Of course, he wasn't about to discuss all that with Saddam, who seemed intent on flattering Rather.

"The responsibility of displaying the truth—as an outstanding man of the media—to carry out this responsibility is something that of course you will do," Saddam gushed.

"Well, first of all, I want to be serious that I—I appreciate your confidence, Mr. President. I'm pausing because I'm tempted to ask a favor of the president," said Rather, now speaking of Saddam in the third person. "He has surprised me. I wonder for my good health if he could denounce me?"

This was Rather's lighthearted way of expressing discomfort at the realization that TV viewers would soon see one of the world's bloodiest tyrants earnestly praising the anchorman of *CBS Evening News.* The nuance, however, was lost on Saddam.

"Denounce you?" he said.

"Yes," Rather replied.

Still not getting the inference, Saddam began spouting disclaimers to assure TV viewers that he and Rather were not somehow in cahoots.

"I met you in 1990 and I'm meeting you now," Saddam stammered. "We have not met—we are not partners in any enterprise or any—not competing with any people for any other—so this is the basics of—"

"I understand," said Rather, backpedaling yet again. "I appreciate your remembering that we met in 1990. And I interviewed you in this great building. Given the sober moment and the danger at hand, what are the chances this is the last time you and I will see each other?"

"You want me to say what I truly believe as it is?" Saddam said.

"Yes," Rather replied.

"I can see that we have other meetings, no matter what happens," Saddam assured the newsman. "And I hope that Iraq and the United States, the people of Iraq and the United States will live in security and in peace."

But Rather pointed out that the United States had formed "a tremendous armada ready to deliver destruction and awe."

"Yes, I understand and I hear and I see," said Saddam, who repeated that God would decide the fate of the Iraqi people.

"I have one last question, Mr. President," Rather said. "Not so long ago, you were clearly hailed by Arabs from Palestinians to Jordanians throughout the Arab world as the, quote, Arab Avenger. Are you still relevant on the Arab street? Or has Osama bin Laden made you, with other Arabs, irrelevant? If you can understand the question. Thank you."

Incredible. Rather was trying to get Saddam's goat by pointing out that bin Laden was a more successful terrorist, having killed 3,000 Americans in a single day.

"This is not our goal," Saddam said. "We want our nation to be happy, not to be spoken of as heroes."

Unfazed by the dictator's reference to bin Laden as a hero, Rather tried to pin down Saddam on whether "Osama bin Laden is now the champion of the Arab street." But the dictator turned the question back on Rather.

"You, how do you see it?" Saddam asked before switching to the third person himself. "Mr. Rather is an intelligent person. I believe that he wants to get to the truth and not merely provoke or to try to get someone to say something that might be held against him."

He added bizarrely: "So if you in America consider Osama bin Laden a hero, we are not jealous of him. And if the Arabs consider him a hero, we are not jealous of him. Jealousy is for women. And men are not supposed to be jealous of one another, especially if this competition is competition in the interests of the nation."

Saddam's chauvinistic asides were surpassed only by his audacious suggestion that bin Laden's handiwork was in the interest of the greater Arab nation. But instead of calling him on either outrage, Rather decided to end the interview.

The event was something of an anticlimax; it had produced little in the way of news. The dictator had spent most of the exchange making absurd, demonstrably untrue claims—that Iraq had not lost the Gulf War, that his government did not possess al-Samouds. A well-documented homicidal maniac, Saddam had portrayed himself as respecting the "humanity" of the elder President Bush, and championing the "dignity" of the Iraqi people. By all objective standards, the interviewee was delusional. Rather would be reduced to peddling the angle about Saddam challenging Bush to a debate, shamelessly hyping it as if the dictator hadn't proposed exactly the same thing more than a decade earlier.

Incredibly, the interview would be portrayed as a journalistic triumph. Rather knew that it wasn't necessary to come away from such an exchange with actual hard news. In the hyper-competitive world of American journalism, sometimes mere bragging rights were enough to carry the day. So Rather contented himself to brag mightily about being the only American journalist to have landed a coveted interview with Saddam Hussein. In the end, it was all about the "get."

"Mr. President, you've been so patient with your time," Rather said. "I appreciate you."

"I'm happy," Saddam said. "And I hope to see you in the future."

"I would like very much," Rather enthused, "to see you in the future—Mr. President."

9
"LET'S GO"

PRESIDENT BUSH'S PATIENCE WITH Saddam Hussein finally ran out at 8 A.M. on Wednesday, March 19. He gathered his war council in the Situation Room of the White House and asked for final thoughts from each adviser—Vice President Dick Cheney, National Security Adviser Condoleezza Rice, Defense Secretary Donald Rumsfeld, Secretary of State Colin Powell, CIA Director George Tenet, and General Richard Meyers, chairman of the Joint Chiefs of Staff. Then he turned to videoconferencing equipment that would allow him to confer with General Tommy Franks at Prince Sultan Air Force Base in Saudi Arabia, along with seven other top commanders in the field. The tension of the moment was broken by Franks, who was supposed to emcee this portion of the proceedings. The general charged with prosecuting the most technologically advanced war in history had trouble figuring out "when to push the button to speak and when not," according to a senior administration official.

"Don't worry, Tommy," Bush deadpanned. "I haven't lost faith in you."

When Franks' underlings stopped laughing, the president turned serious. He wanted to look each commander in the eye—or at least an image of their eye on the teleconferencing screen—and ask two simple questions.

"Do you have everything you need to win?" he said. "Are you comfortable and pleased with the strategy?"

From Qatar to Kuwait, from Tampa to the high seas, the commanders of the army, navy, air force, marines and special forces each answered yes to both questions and assured the president they were ready. When Franks concurred, the commander in chief of the world's sole superpower decided the Iraqi people had suffered long enough.

"For the peace of the world and the benefit and freedom of the Iraqi people, I hereby give the order to execute Operation Iraqi Freedom," Bush announced. "May God bless the troops."

"May God bless America," said Franks as he stood up and snapped a salute.

Bush saluted back and strode from the Situation Room. He walked outside to the South Lawn so that he could be alone to contemplate the magnitude of his decision.

"I knew what I had done and it's not an easy moment," he told me. "I had made up my mind that this was necessary. But to actually give the order, it was a dramatic moment."

The president's fateful decision marked not only the beginning of the military phase of his quest to disarm Saddam, but also the end of the diplomatic phase. In the six weeks since Powell's presentation to the United Nations, France's opposition to war had only hardened.

Although Powell had initially opposed the idea of seeking two Security Council resolutions before attacking Iraq, he now reluctantly reversed course in order to provide some political cover to beleaguered allies like Blair, who were facing intense domestic opposition for their staunch support of Bush. They needed to show their skeptical publics that they were going the extra mile toward seeking a peaceful solution.

"The reason we went for a second resolution is not because the United States needed one. Our friends said they needed one for their political requirements at home and for the domestic public opinion," Powell explained to National Public Radio. "The British and the Australians, the Spanish and the Italians, they all said, 'We really, really could use a second resolution.' The United States could have used one for our own home opinion."

But France, Germany, and Russia were more interested in giving the inspectors additional time to do their jobs. The United States countered that the banned weapons were being concealed by Saddam's regime. In fact, the Bush Administration was so worried that Saddam would use chemical or biological weapons in the coming war that it initiated an effort at NATO to plan for the defense of Turkey, a NATO member on Iraq's northern border. But on February 10 that planning was halted by France and Germany, two NATO members that now seemed determined to thwart America at every turn. The stunning move prompted Turkey to take the rare step of invoking Article IV of the NATO treaty, which called on all members of the alliance to come together whenever one member felt that its security was threatened. Bush was astonished. It was one thing for France to play the role of petulant spoiler at the United Nations, an institution of dubious relevance. But it was quite another to cause a major split in NATO, the mightiest and most effective military alliance in history.

"I am disappointed that France would block NATO from helping a country like Turkey prepare," the president told reporters in the Oval Office. "It affects the alliance in a negative way."

To make matters worse, U.S. efforts to protect Turkey were not reciprocated. On March 1, Turkey's Parliament barred U.S. forces from using Turkish territory as a base from which to launch a northern front against Iraq. The Bush Administration expressed hope that the decision would be reversed in time for war and even left weaponry for the army's 4th Infantry Division on three dozen ships parked off the Turkish coast in the Mediterranean. Most observers speculated that unless Turkey relented, the 4th Infantry would have to sail a circuitous and time-consuming route around the Arabian Peninsula to join other allied forces in attacking Iraq from the south. Assuming the U.S. would never tie up major resources in a holding pattern without a high degree of confidence that Turkey would acquiesce, Saddam positioned significant numbers of his own troops in northern Iraq to brace for an onslaught across the Turkish border.

On March 5, the foreign ministers of France, Germany, and Russia met in Paris and issued a statement that all but doomed U.S. efforts to pass a second resolution. The statement said that France and Russia, both permanent members of the council, would use their veto power to block the U.S.

"We are at a turning point," the statement said. "We will not let a proposed resolution pass that would authorize the use of force."

As far as Bush was concerned, the trio had already passed a resolution authorizing force: 1441. Not that the United States needed the authority of the U.N. to protect its national security.

"We don't need anybody's permission," the president declared the next day in a prime time press conference in the East Room.

Nonetheless, Powell continued to pursue the second resolution. He was hampered by French President Jacques Chirac, a man who had given Saddam a personal tour of France's nuclear research center more than a quarter century earlier. Having sold the dictator $3 billion worth of nuclear reactors in a deal that excluded "all persons of Jewish race," Chirac now attempted to claim the moral high ground on America's push for a second resolution.

"Whatever the circumstances, we will vote no," he announced on March 10.

The next day, the *New York Times* released a poll showing Americans had grown impatient with the U.N. and supported war even without the world body's approval. But Bush was not about to stiff the growing number of allies who did support him, especially those struggling to placate domestic constituencies. These included Blair, Spanish President José María Aznar, and a trio of prime ministers—Australia's John Howard, Italy's Silvio Berlusconi, and Portugal's José Manuel Durao Barroso.

"What it really did was it bound people like Blair and Aznar and myself into tight, close friendships," Bush told me. "John Howard is another one. In other words, these guys—we formed a bond." He went on to group Berlusconi and Barroso with the others as "a series of these people that stood strong."

He added: "I watched these embattled leaders stand their ground. I tried to do the best I could to encourage them. You know, it's an amazing lesson in leadership."

On March 16, Bush flew to the Azores, a string of Portuguese islands halfway between America and Europe, to huddle with Barroso, Blair, and Aznar. The Spaniard confided to Bush that he was under intense pressure to oppose the war.

"I said, stand your ground—I didn't need to tell him that, he was going to do it anyway—but you'll win," Bush told me.

"People are looking for leadership. What they want to know in their leaders is: Is there a sense of backbone and direction and focus?" he said. "And the truth of the matter is, it was an unpopular war in certain aspects. But, nevertheless, it became a test of character for some of these leaders—all of us, as a matter of fact, involved in the process. It was that kind of test of character that brought a lot of us very close."

At the end of the mini-summit in the Azores, Bush announced that the world was approaching "a moment of truth" regarding Iraq.

"On this very day fifteen years ago, Saddam Hussein launched a chemical weapons attack on the Iraqi village of Halabja," he said. "With a single order, the Iraqi regime killed thousands of men and women and children, without mercy or without shame. Saddam Hussein has proven he is capable of any crime. We must not permit his crimes to reach across the world."

As Bush flew back home on Air Force One, he and his aides began drafting a speech that would give Saddam a stark choice—go into exile within forty-eight hours or face attack. He planned on delivering the speech to the American people the next evening, just after the United Nations was scheduled to vote on the second resolution. War was now imminent.

"There were a lot of moments where I was hoping that it wouldn't have to happen," Bush told me. "And of course what happened was 1441; [it] looked like the world was unified, and then we come down to the next resolution. And diplomatic splits started sending wrong messages. And then it became pretty clear to me that the message being received by Saddam Hussein was one that the world isn't unified against him, and, therefore, he thought he could survive."

Halfway through the drafting of the speech, the president and his aides took a break to watch a movie as Air Force One streaked from the Azores toward Washington.

"It was, regrettably, *Conspiracy Theory*," recalled a senior administration official who was with Bush in the plane's conference room. "Not good."

When the film ended, Bush went back to work on the speech, aided by Rice, Card, chief speechwriter Michael Gerson, Communications Director Dan Bartlett, and informal adviser Karen Hughes. Not knowing whether the Security Council would pass the second resolution—or even whether the U.S. would withdraw it to preclude a veto from France—the team built in alternative paragraphs that could be dropped from the speech, depending on how events unfolded.

"I was frustrated, I guess is the best way to put it—extremely frustrated," the president told me. "We lost focus during the second resolution. [It] became almost, 'Who can persuade which country to make this vote?'—as opposed to staying focused on the big picture, which is security and freedom and peace. And so it became a frustrating experience."

Early the next morning, the administration began running its diplomatic traps for the final time at the U.N. When it quickly became apparent that the resolution would be either voted down or vetoed, Bush instructed his diplomatic team to pull the plug. His speechwriters dropped the paragraphs praising the U.N., and replaced them with expressions of disdain.

"Once the second resolution failed and once Saddam had not fulfilled the obligations of 1441, 'serious consequences' kicked in," Bush told me.

"Secondly, we had amassed troops," he added. "There is a point, once you've amassed troops, at which you begin to lose energy and efficiency. You cannot hold troops for long periods of time. My point to you is that I had made up my mind after the failure, after diplomacy wouldn't work."

The president rendered his final verdict from the East Room at 8:01 p.m. on March 17, St. Patrick's Day.

"The United Nations Security Council has not lived up to its responsibilities, so we will rise to ours," he said. "The United States of America has the sovereign authority to use force in assuring its own national security. That duty falls to me, as commander in chief, by the oath I have sworn, by the oath I will keep."

Bush then reminded America of the nightmare scenario that had been vexing him since September 11—the prospect of terrorists gaining weapons of mass destruction from Saddam and unleashing them on the U.S. or her allies. Waiting for Saddam to disarm would be "suicidal," Bush said. He was finally going through with the biggest shift in U.S. foreign policy in half a century—the doctrine of preemption.

"Instead of drifting along toward tragedy, we will set a course toward safety. Before the day of horror can come, before it is too late to act, this danger will be removed," he vowed.

"All the decades of deceit and cruelty have now reached an end," Bush said. "Saddam Hussein and his sons must leave Iraq within forty-eight hours. Their refusal to do so will result in military conflict, commenced at a time of our choosing. For their own safety, all foreign nationals—including journalists and inspectors—should leave Iraq immediately."

Hoping to reassure innocent Iraqis, Bush insisted their future would be bright without Saddam and his regime.

"There will be no more wars of aggression against your neighbors, no more poison factories, no more executions of dissidents, no more torture chambers and rape rooms. The tyrant will soon be gone," the president promised. "The day of your liberation is near."

The next day, Bush received a final, expansive briefing on military intelligence from his war council. He also drafted letters to the House and Senate, notifying them that he was invoking their resolution authorizing war.

Meanwhile, the British House of Commons passed a measure calling for Iraq to be disarmed by "all means necessary." In a major show of support for Blair, Parliament voted down a separate measure opposing military action. It seemed the prime minister was finally being rewarded for standing up to critics like "Gorgeous George" Galloway, who had warned Parliament that "this born again, right-wing, Bible-belting, fundamentalist, Republican administration in the United States wants war."

As far as the White House was concerned, Parliament's rejection of such rhetoric effectively removed the final roadblock to Iraq's liberation. "We were waiting for the British vote in the Parliament," Rice told me. "You couldn't go to war until the British had had their vote in Parliament."

When Bush woke up on March 19, he realized the time for war had finally arrived.

"We ran out of every single option," he told me. "The last hope of hopes was when we were approached by emissaries from a foreign country in that area saying, well, give him a chance to leave."

But it was now clear that Saddam had no intention of voluntarily leaving Iraq. So Bush met with his war council and gave the order to execute Operation Iraqi Freedom. Having unleashed the world's mightiest military force, the president was now walking around the South Lawn running track a couple of times with his dogs, Spot and Barney.

"It was a heavy moment—I prayed, I reflected," he told me. "I got my thoughts and came back in here and started going back to work."

Bush spent the rest of the morning meeting with various officials about how to protect America against possible retaliatory attacks by terrorists. He knew the overt war against Iraq would be preceded by a covert campaign to prepare the battlefield.

"The plan was to start with Special Ops, and hold off on the—as Tommy called it—'shock and awe' until later in the week," the president told me. "The plan was to secure different areas; protect Israel from any potential rocket launches; come up hard from the south to secure the oil fields. But it would be forty-eight hours of clandestine activity."

It was left to Franks to determine how and when to commence open warfare. Although he told the president it would probably begin with air strikes, he reserved the right send in ground forces instead. Such flexibility would allow Franks to study the enemy's behavior until the last possible moment, and then strike with whichever component would be most devastating.

But then something unexpected happened. Late in the afternoon, Bush received an urgent phone call from Rumsfeld, who was with Tenet over at the Pentagon. The two had been putting the finishing touches on a plan for unprecedented battlefield coordination between the CIA and the Defense Department.

"I need to come over," Rumsfeld told the president. "I need to show you something."

Soon both Rumsfeld and Tenet were back in the White House, with a tantalizing piece of information about a farm outside of Baghdad.

"Intelligence came that indicated we had a potential shot at Saddam Hussein, which meant we would have to change the war plan," Bush told me in the Oval Office. "Tenet came in. Rumsfeld came in. We got Colin, Condi—we're all in here. And they're briefing us on eyes-on intelligence about a potential site where Saddam Hussein would be."

The implications were staggering. If the U.S. could launch a surgical strike that killed Saddam and perhaps his sons, Uday and Qusay, Operation Iraqi Freedom might not be necessary after all. By decapitating the regime in one fell swoop, Bush might avert war, or at least shorten it significantly. Much would depend, of course, on how long it took the rest of the Iraqi regime to confirm the dictator's demise. But even if confirmation were delayed, perhaps lives could be spared on both sides of the conflict.

Still, Bush was cautious.

"The risks were that the intelligence wasn't any good—we'd hit a bunker full of children, or we'd disrupt the war plan that Tommy had so meticulously laid out," Bush told me. "In other words, a lot of things that could have gone wrong."

The group gathered in the president's private dining room off the Oval Office and spread out maps of the farm. Those present included Cheney, Richard Myers, and Lewis "Scooter" Libby, Cheney's chief of staff.

"The president was the one who kept saying: 'Well, are you sure that's what that is?' He was really worried about some kind of 'baby milk factory' event," Rice told me. "Or Saddam's grandchildren are going to come out with dead children. So he kept asking question after question."

Having already signed off on a solid war plan, Bush was reluctant to scramble it at the last moment.

"I wrestled with it," the president told me. "I listened and listened and listened and listened and pushed and cajoled. And intelligence kept coming in. General Myers goes out and gets a phone call, more intelligence."

Rice was struck by the freewheeling give-and-take of the afternoon deliberations, which contrasted sharply with the solemn formality of the president's morning decision.

"Imagine the surprise that afternoon when all of a sudden you throw out the playbook and you start again," she said.

After some ninety minutes of deliberations, Bush finally appeared to reach a decision. He approved a launch of Tomahawk missiles by Tommy Franks, who was only a few hours into his forty-eight-hour covert campaign to prepare the Iraqi battlefield with special operations forces.

"He said, okay, all right," Rice recalled of the president. "And they started out of the door. And he said, no, wait a minute. No, wait a minute.

"And they came back," she added. "Then we started again because he just really wasn't comfortable with it."

This time the group moved into the Oval Office proper. With live reports continuing to trickle in from the field, the intelligence was unfolding before their very eyes. It was an extraordinarily fluid situation.

"One of the changes was when they realized that it was actually a bunker, not a surface structure of some kind," Rice said. "So all of a sudden it occurred to people: Well, the ordnance that they planned probably wouldn't destroy it."

So Meyers went down to the office of Deputy National Security Adviser Steve Hadley, where he got on a secure phone line to Franks. He explained that Saddam might be sheltered by steel-reinforced concrete that could be penetrated only by bunker-busting bombs dropped from stealth Nighthawk warplanes.

"This is not looking like it's going to be a good Tomahawk target," Meyers said. "What would you think about weaponeering this thing for bombers?"

"Very, very difficult," Franks replied. "I'll have to get back to you."

The president himself was reluctant to "prepare for bunker-busters to go in via air drop, without any fighter escort," he told me. "We don't know at this point how robust the air suppression assets are of Saddam," he explained.

Nonetheless, when Franks reported back that the bombing mission was feasible after all, Bush ordered the planes sent toward Baghdad. Although the president still hadn't made a final decision, the bombers would have to take off immediately in order to have any chance of hitting their targets with precision-guided, 2,000-pound bombs. They could always be called back if Bush decided not to act on the intelligence.

"Back in the Oval, we're continuing to go through: What if this is wrong?" Condi said. "And the president went around and he said to everybody, should we take a shot?"

All around the Oval Office, the military and intelligence advisers urged Bush to seize the opportunity to kill Saddam. But the president also wanted the advice of Franks, who had successfully prosecuted the Afghanistan war less than eighteen months earlier. Franks was a fellow Texan, a no-nonsense man's man who had attended the same Midland high school as Laura Bush.

"Tommy thought we ought to take the shot," the president told me. "It became very clear to me that the intelligence looked real, felt real. But I would not have done this if Tommy said, This doesn't fit the plan."

Rice was convinced that Franks was the adviser who swayed Bush the most. "One thing about him, he has enormous respect for the commander in the field, the person whose responsibility it is to carry this out," Rice said.

It was nearly 7 P.M. and the deliberations had been under way for more than three hours. Bush was informed he would have to make a decision by 7:15 P.M. in order for the bombers to hit their targets before dawn.

The president went around the room one last time to make sure the decision was unanimous. With three minutes to spare, he gave the order that would set history into motion.

"Let's go," the president said at 7:12 P.M.

Meyers walked out of the Oval Office and relayed the order to Franks. Operation Iraqi Freedom was finally beginning, although in a way the president never could have imagined.

"To complicate matters, once we made the decision to go, I then had to tell the country that the action had begun, thereby disrupting the forty-eight-hour plan that Tommy had put in place," Bush told me.

The president had not planned on addressing the nation until March 21, after Franks would be finished preparing the battlefield and ready to commence the "shock and awe" campaign. That speech, which was not even fully written, now would have to be delivered almost immediately.

"We had to do it that night, because all of a sudden you got Baghdad lit up," Bush told me, referring to the imminent strike by Nighthawk warplanes.

So chief speechwriter Michael Gerson was brought into the Oval Office to help complete the president's address. Rumsfeld even read the text to Franks, to make sure the president's words would be consistent with the revamped military plan.

Bush then went up to the White House residence, where he had dinner with the First Lady. The president had no way of knowing for certain whether Saddam would still be in the structure when it was blown to smithereens. In fact, there was still the remote possibility that Saddam had come to his senses at the last moment and fled Iraq. But then Card telephoned his boss in the living room to say that intelligence officials had no information that Saddam had left Iraq. So the president headed back to the West Wing at 8:45 to tweak the speech one last time with Gerson, Bartlett, and Hughes. He and his aides discussed the imminent attack in his private dining room. They were so determined to prevent the news from leaking that they did not summon outside workers to clear the Oval Office of furniture that would be in the way of TV camera equipment. Instead the couches were hauled out by the president's own senior staff, including White House Chief of Staff Andy Card, his deputy Joe Hagin, and the president's personal assistant, Blake Gottesman.

At 10:05 P.M., just moments before he was to address the nation, Bush received the first reports from Myers and Hadley: the planes had successfully dropped their bombs on the target and were returning to base. The verification was not official—the planes were still in stealth mode—but at least Bush could give his speech with the knowledge that the mission had not been compromised.

"Let's pray for the pilots," Bush told his aides.

Then he sat at his Oval Office desk, carved from the timbers of the HMS *Resolute,* and faced the cameras. Eighteen months and eight days after September 11, when he first publicly uttered the words "war against terrorism" from this very spot, Bush now enacted his foreign policy of preemption. It was a concept unthinkable when he first took office—attacking a sovereign nation that had never attacked America or even harmed one of its own neighbor in years.

"My fellow citizens, at this hour, American and coalition forces are in the early stages of military operations to disarm Iraq, to free its people and to defend the world from grave danger," the president began at

10:16 P.M. "Our nation enters this conflict reluctantly, yet our purpose is sure.

"The people of the United States and our friends and allies will not live at the mercy of an outlaw regime that threatens the peace with weapons of mass murder. We will meet that threat now, with our army, air force, navy, coast guard and marines, so that we do not have to meet it later with armies of fire fighters and police and doctors on the streets of our cities."

The camera slowly panned in on Bush, who wore a crimson tie, bright white shirt—sans French cuffs—and a charcoal gray suit with an American flag lapel pin over his heart. He was flanked by framed photographs perched on tables behind him—one of his twins, Barbara and Jenna, the other of his wife posing with the family dogs, Spot and Barney. The president's demeanor was solemn, his voice calm.

"We have no ambition in Iraq, except to remove a threat and restore control of that country to its own people," he said. "A campaign on the harsh terrain of a nation as large as California could be longer and more difficult than some predict. And helping Iraqis achieve a united, stable, and free country will require our sustained commitment."

Bush felt it was important to emphasize these perils up front, lest his detractors savage him afterward for predicting a cakewalk. Yet he left no doubt about the outcome of Operation Iraqi Freedom.

"Now that conflict has come, the only way to limit its duration is to apply decisive force—and I assure you, this will not be a campaign of half measures," he vowed. "We will accept no outcome but victory.

"My fellow citizens, the dangers to our country and the world will be overcome. We will pass through this time of peril and carry on the work of peace.

"We will defend our freedom. We will bring freedom to others.

"And we will prevail."

After the speech, which lasted just four minutes, Bush went back up to the residence. At 10:40 P.M., he received a call from Rice, who informed him that the U.S. planes had cleared enemy airspace and were headed back to their base. Of course, it was impossible to determine at this early stage whether Saddam had been killed in the attack. So the president resolved to proceed with Operation Iraqi Freedom unless and until he received compelling evidence that Saddam was dead.

"We took the shot," he told me. "We thought we might have gotten him."

10

"MISINFORMING THE WORLD"

"CAN YOU PROMISE IT won't be a quagmire?" a reporter demanded of Defense Secretary Donald Rumsfeld in the press briefing room at the Pentagon.

"I can almost promise you that someone in this room will *say* it's a quagmire," Rumsfeld shot back. "Quite apart from the facts."

This exchange took place not months, weeks, or even days into Operation Iraqi Freedom. Rather, it occurred a full two weeks *before* the first shot was fired. The press set a new land speed record in its desperate race to liken any and all American military operations to the debacle of Vietnam.

The previous record was set less than seventeen months earlier, when the *New York Times* compared the Afghanistan conflict to Vietnam just seven days into the war against the Taliban. The rest of the establishment media quickly followed suit, echoing the *Times*'s assertion that Bush had "underestimated the Taliban's resilience." Soon journalists were deriding the war plan as short on ground troops and oblivious to bad weather. The coverage emphasized military setbacks, civilian casualties, and a potential backlash from the Arab street. But then, a mere month into the war, just as all the gloom-and-doom coverage was reaching a terrific crescendo, the strategic city of Mazar-i-Sharif fell and allied forces swept across Afghanistan. The startled and crestfallen press immediately switched gears and began accusing the Pentagon of being caught off guard by this sudden reversal of fortune. A couple of reporters even tried in vain to lure Rumsfeld and his ground commander, General Tommy Franks, into the gloat trap by asking if they felt vindicated by the quick and decisive victory.

For the most part, though, the press never acknowledged its colossal blunder. That's because American journalists regarded Vietnam, along with Watergate, as their holy grail. Never mind that both stories were thirty years old. The press clung romantically to its tired old 1970s templates, dusting them off religiously and trying to fit them on utterly unrelated stories. Like most Republican presidents, Bush had already been subjected to the Watergate template ("What did he know and when did he know it?") on such news events as the collapse of Enron and even the September 11 terrorist attacks. When neither story line panned out, the press switched to the Vietnam template, frantically trying to apply it to Afghanistan. And even after that comparison proved patently ridiculous, journalists seemed determined to repeat their blunder with Iraq. Having failed to learn its lesson in Afghanistan, now the press was blithely branding Iraq a "quagmire." Never mind that Operation Iraqi Freedom *hadn't actually commenced*. As far as the Vietnam-obsessed press was concerned, *why wait?*

And so, just minutes after one reporter invoked the Q-word in the Pentagon press briefing room, another made it official by uttering the V-word. This time the question was directed at Tommy Franks, who was standing next to Rumsfeld.

"General Franks, let me ask you to reflect on something, if I might," began CNN's Barbara Starr in a pained, earnest tone that signaled the question would be more touchy-feely than nuts-and-bolts. "You're amongst a generation of the last senior military officials in the military today who fought in the heaviest years of combat in Vietnam, who saw a type of combat that many of your troops today have never seen in their lives. And by any measure, certainly Vietnam still hangs as a shadow."

Still hangs as a shadow?! In the minds of media elites, perhaps. Anyone familiar with the U.S. armed forces, which had decisively won plenty of military campaigns over the last three decades, knew otherwise.

"As you begin to think about taking this force into combat, this young force, what's worth remembering about the Vietnam experience for the U.S. military?" Starr emoted. "What comes back to you so many years later that you would like troops to know—good or bad— about the Vietnam experience?"

A triple axel—Starr had managed to mention Vietnam three times in a single question. "Barbara, what pops to my mind is a term called 'decisive engagement,'" said Franks, turning the question around. "And when I think about Vietnam, I think about decisive engagement with enemy forces."

Franks went on to recount several occasions when he, as a young lieutenant in Vietnam, employed decisive force against the enemy. He also reminded Starr of America's use of decisive force in such conflicts as the Gulf War and Operation Enduring Freedom in Afghanistan.

"When one desegregates the theoretical question you ask down to the level where young people are involved decisively with an enemy force, I have no concerns about it," Franks concluded. "I have incredible confidence in weapon systems, the state of training, the state of motivation, the intellectual acuity, and the wisdom of our young people who will do this work, if asked to do so."

Naturally, this upbeat assessment did not satisfy Starr, who wanted Franks to wallow in the horrors and hopelessness of war.

"How, when you have such a young force, do you make them understand how difficult ground combat can be?" she persisted, in the tone of a group therapist.

"Unanswerable sort of question," Franks replied matter-of-factly. "I think we go day by day, in learning from past experience, in thinking about the next experience, in applying our lessons by way of instruction, by way of example to the young people who will be called on to do the work, if necessary. And it's the same as it's always been, Barbara."

"Thank you very much," interjected Rumsfeld, signaling an end to the question-and-answer session.

Rumsfeld fully expected the press to fixate even more obsessively on Vietnam once the fighting actually started. The seventy-year-old warhorse had resigned himself to the reality that he could never stop the East Coast media establishment from portraying war as a quagmire. But this time he had an ace up his sleeve. At the urging of his press secretary, Victoria Clarke, Rumsfeld had agreed to allow some six hundred journalists to accompany troops into battle. Reporters would be "embedded" with various units so they could document the battle's progress from the perspective of ordinary GIs. It was an enormously risky proposition, since the "embeds" might simply reinforce the gloom-and-doom coverage of the East Coast anchors and pundits. But Rumsfeld and Clarke gambled that even if the embeds were predictably liberal cynics, they could not help but be impressed by the courage and dedication of U.S. troops. After all, the reporters would essentially be playing soldiers themselves—dressing up in desert camouflage fatigues, wearing helmets and Kevlar vests, eating military rations, sleeping in tents, and rolling into battle against a dangerous enemy. It would be difficult for the journalists not to bond with the GIs. Perhaps their reports from the front would showcase the bravery and sacrifice of U.S. forces, thereby offsetting some of the negative stateside coverage.

In order for that gamble to have any chance of paying off, of course, U.S. forces would actually have to enter Iraq. But that scenario was scrambled by the last-minute attempt to take out Saddam with a surgical missile strike the evening of March 19. It was difficult to determine whether the dictator managed to escape the daring attack, which left the administration in the awkward position of having begun the war in a manner that was profoundly different than the "shock and awe" campaign that the public had been led to expect. And so, the morning after the surgical strike, Rumsfeld returned to the Pentagon press briefing room—this time with General Richard Myers, Chairman of the Joint Chiefs of Staff—and braced for more maddening questions from the gloom-and-doomers.

"It's apparent that that decision to strike was not in line with what we have been led to believe about the war plan," one reporter said.

"Well, Dick, calibrate me," Rumsfeld asked Myers before turning to the reporter. "But the first thing I'd say is I don't believe you have the war plan—a fact which does not make me unhappy."

Indeed, the reporters had no idea that Special Operations forces had crossed into southern and western Iraq even before the surgical strike. These stealth teams were conducting reconnaissance raids and taking out Iraqi observation towers along the border in order to prepare the battlefield. Although Franks had told Rumsfeld and Bush he would probably begin overt warfare by softening up Iraqi defenses with several days of aerial bombardment, the general now took advantage of his plan's flexibility and decided to switch to a ground game. The change came, in part, because the surgical strike had prompted Saddam's regime to begin sabotaging the oil fields in southern Iraq. Franks figured he could nip this problem in the bud by sending ground troops into the fields before the bulk of Saddam's forces arrived.

As for northern Iraq, Franks had concluded a week earlier that Turkey would never grant basing rights for a second front. But he purposely kept his 4th Infantry ships parked off the Turkish coast as a decoy. In response, Saddam continued to fortify positions in northern Iraq for an invasion that would never materialize. That left him fewer forces in the south, where he believed the allies would not strike until the arrival in Kuwait of the 4th Infantry. But Franks figured the 4th could be deployed later, bringing up the rear in a sort of rolling invasion. Right now he needed the vanguard to secure the oil fields.

There were other deceptions that heightened the element of tactical surprise. Pentagon officials had done nothing to discourage speculation that they would bomb for a full six weeks, even though Franks originally planned no more than a few days of air strikes. Now even that abbreviated bombing campaign was scrapped in favor of a ground invasion—a twist no one had expected.

The invasion began at 10 P.M. Eastern Time on March 20. The speed of the advance was remarkable. By noon on March 21, U.S. troops had pushed nearly one hundred miles deep into Iraq. Then, at 1 P.M., the air war began, finally giving Saddam a taste of the "shock and awe" that had long been promised.

It took just twelve minutes for the press to mischaracterize the bombing of Baghdad, which was shown live on TV. Although the air force scrupulously avoided civilian targets and went to extraordinary lengths to pinpoint only militarily significant installations like Saddam's palaces, MSNBC's Brian Williams immediately likened these precision strikes to the indiscriminate fire-bombing of Dresden, Germany, and the wall-to-wall carpet-bombing of Japanese cities in World War II.

"Looks like Dresden," Williams observed at 1:12 P.M., referring to dramatic video of explosions in Baghdad. "It looks like some of the firebombing of Japanese cities during World War II. There's another one. Still going on. You hear them overhead. Either jet aircraft or cruise missiles, but yet another explosion."

This infuriated Rumsfeld, who happened to be watching MSNBC at the Pentagon as he prepared for his daily press briefing. He decided to chastise the media when he stepped to the lectern at 1:36 P.M.

"Just before coming down, after the air campaign began in earnest at about one, I saw some of the images on television and I heard various commentators expansively comparing what's taking place in Iraq today to some of the more famous bombing campaigns of World War II," Rumsfeld said. "There is no comparison. The weapons that are being used today have a degree of precision that no one ever dreamt of in a prior conflict—they didn't exist. And it's not a handful of weapons; it's the overwhelming majority of the weapons that have that precision. The targeting capabilities and the care that goes into targeting—to see that the precise targets are struck and that other targets are not struck—is as impressive as anything anyone could see. The care that goes into it, the humanity that goes into it, to see that military targets are destroyed, to be sure, but that it's done in a way, and in a manner, and in a direction and with a weapon that is appropriate to that very particularized target. And I think that the comparison is unfortunate and inaccurate. And I think that will be found to be the case when ground truth is achieved."

Warming to his theme, Rumsfeld worried aloud about the media's saturation coverage of the war, which was due in no small part to his own decision to allow hundreds of embedded journalists to roll into Iraq with U.S. forces. In addition to the dramatic footage of bombs exploding in Baghdad, TV screens were also filled with breathless reports from journalists who were racing across the sands of southern Iraq toward Baghdad. One report showed a crowd of jubilant Iraqis cheering a U.S. Marine as he tore down a poster of Saddam. Others showed Saddam's soldiers surrendering by the thousands. While these dispatches were generally positive—sometimes even exuberant—Rumsfeld seemed worried about his gamble to welcome the media with such open arms.

"We're having a conflict at a time in our history when we have twenty-four-hours-a-day television, radio, media, Internet, and more people in the world have access to what is taking place," he cautioned. "You couple that with the hundreds—literally hundreds of people in the free press, the international press, the press of the United States, from every aspect of the media—who have been offered and accepted an opportunity to join and be connected directly with practically every aspect of this campaign. And what we are seeing is not the war in Iraq. What we're seeing are slices of the war in Iraq. We're seeing that particularized perspective that that reporter—or that commentator or that television camera—happens to be able to see at that moment. And it is not what's taking place. What you see is taking place, to be sure, but it is one slice. And it is the totality of that that is what this war is about and being made up of. And I don't—I doubt that in a conflict of this type there's ever been the degree of free press coverage as you are witnessing in this instance."

With that off his chest, Rumsfeld began taking questions. But he soon discovered that his history lesson on World War II was just the pretext the media needed to pivot into a discussion about Vietnam.

"You mentioned earlier the allusions to bombing campaigns in World War II and that they were an inappropriate historical analogy," a reporter began.

"Those were dumb bombs and they were spread across large areas," Rumsfeld interjected.

"Can I finish my point?" the reporter snapped.

"These are very precise weapons," Rumsfeld explained.

"All right, but one thing that characterized those campaigns and the bombing of Hanoi was that the public, their spirit did not diminish; they hunkered down, they pretty much resisted the bombing," the reporter said. "What makes you so certain that in this case, even though it's precise, that 'shock and awe' won't just force the Iraqis to hunker down and wait it out like the Brits, the Germans, the Vietnamese, and the Japanese in World War II—and in Vietnam?"

Rumsfeld couldn't believe it. The air campaign against Iraq had been underway for *less than one hour,* and the press was already comparing it to the bombing of Hanoi! The *New York Times* went a step further by likening the Pentagon's scrupulous targeting of military sites in Baghdad to the Taliban's wanton use of commercial jetliners as unholy weapons of mass destruction against innocent civilians in New York. "Baghdad Bombing Brings Back Memories of 9/11," railed the headline on a story by reporter David Chen, who intoned: "For some, the bombing brought back particularly visceral and chilling memories. They could not help thinking about September 11, and how New York, too, was once under assault from the skies." Over at taxpayer-supported PBS, arch-liberal Bill Moyers added: "Not every patriot thinks we should do to the people of Baghdad what bin Laden did to us."

To many, the profanity of the comparison was staggering. And yet Rumsfeld quickly realized that the gloom-and-doomers were just getting warmed up.

"We keep talking about this overwhelming force," one reporter huffed. "Are you concerned at all that we will be seen as a bully?"

"What we are currently doing could not, by any stretch of the imagination, fit what you just said," Rumsfeld replied with labored restraint. "It would be a—it would be to misunderstand everything that's taking place."

When the briefing finally ended and Rumsfeld stalked from the lectern, the air war was still barely an hour old. And yet a reporter hollered after him: "Could you tell just how long will this war last?"

The questions weren't much better over at the White House press briefing room later that afternoon.

"There was a humanitarian crisis in Iraq even before the bombing began, in terms of food shortages," a reporter told White House Press Secretary Ari Fleischer. "After what we saw today—this massive attack on Baghdad—that situation is clearly going to be much, much worse beginning tomorrow."

"That's not necessarily true," Fleischer said. "You should not necessarily leap to that conclusion based on what you saw on TV today."

The presidential spokesman explained that "the destruction of a palace of Saddam Hussein's, the destruction of a military facility, may not have anything to do with the feeding of the Iraqi people." Besides, he added, "along with the military come massive waves of humanitarian relief in the form of food, in the form of medicine, in the form of everything that may be necessary to help protect and to feed the Iraqi people."

In an apparent quest for self-affirmation, network correspondents wanted to know whether Bush, like Rumsfeld, was watching news coverage of the dramatic bombing on television.

"Ari, has the president watched any of this, the unfolding events in Baghdad?" asked ABC's Terry Moran.

"Obviously, the president, having authorized the mission, was aware of the mission, knew when it would begin, et cetera," Fleischer said. "And I don't think he needs to watch TV to know what was about to unfold."

Indeed, Bush was constantly receiving classified briefings on the latest developments, most of which were not visible on TV newscasts. And yet the correspondents were incredulous that the commander in chief wasn't riveted to their reportage.

"You said the president doesn't need to watch TV to know what's going on in Iraq," scoffed NBC's Campbell Brown. "But you're telling me—these are pretty astounding images—he doesn't have a television on somewhere, he's not watching what's going on?"

"The president, again, understands the implications of the actions that he has launched to secure the disarmament of the Iraqi regime, to liberate the people," Fleischer said.

"Right, right, right," Brown said dismissively. "The question, though: Is he watching TV, or not?"

"The president may occasionally turn on the TV," Fleischer said. "But that's not how he gets his news or his information."

"I'm not suggesting it is," Brown said. "But we just want to try to get an image of—"

"From time to time, he might," the spokesman allowed.

New York Times reporter Elisabeth Bumiller came to the aid of her broadcast colleagues by asking Fleischer what she called "a very direct question."

"Did the president not see the pictures on television?" she said. "The very dramatic pictures of the bombs and the explosions over Baghdad—he did not see those?"

"I was with the president just as the operation was beginning, at about 1 P.M., and he was not watching TV at that time," Fleischer said. "I wasn't with him for the duration of it, so I couldn't answer in all instances about it. I probably shouldn't answer a question like this in this room, but the president does not watch a lot of TV."

"No, but they were very, very dramatic pictures," Bumiller protested. "It's hard to imagine the president of the United States, who had ordered this attack, did not see any evidence of it."

"Elisabeth, I don't know that the president needed to watch TV to understand what it means to authorize military force and to know that the mission has begun and the mission is underway," the spokesman said.

"So the answer is unclear, we don't know if he saw them?"

"I've just described to you where I was with him," Fleischer said. "But I wasn't with him for the entire duration of what you all saw on TV."

Fleischer could scarcely believe his ears. The United States of America had just launched a preemptive war against a sovereign nation, marking the most important shift in American foreign policy in half a century, and yet the most influential media outlets in the world were obsessing over Bush's TV viewing habits.

Even the radio reporters got in on the act. "Isn't it understandable that as the American public is watching the bombardment turning the nighttime sky into light and seeing the gravity of the situation, that he might need to understand what America is seeing and see it with them so he can speak effectively to the American public?" asked April Ryan of American Urban Radio Networks.

"The president of the United States did not need to watch TV to understand what the American people think about the decision to use force to disarm the Iraqi regime," said the exasperated spokesman.

Indeed, TV coverage of Operation Iraqi Freedom was clearly at odds with the 70 percent of Americans who supported the president's handling of the war. On ABC News that evening, former Clinton flak David Gergen fretted that "the war is going so successfully and Iraq is putting up so little resistance. When we win, will it appear that we have been a bully?" The next morning, in a *New York Times* column demanding the resignation of Secretary of State Colin Powell, liberal Bill Keller joined the chorus of media critics accusing the administration of "bullying." In fact, for the first couple days of the war, the press was so "shocked and awed" by the dramatic gains of allied forces that they derided the contest as a colossally unfair mismatch.

But then, over the weekend, at the first sign of resistance to the coalition's march toward Baghdad, the media's mood abruptly shifted. Unable or unwilling to place anecdotal military setbacks into the larger context of a remarkably swift and flexible offensive, reporters seized on each bit of bad news as proof that the entire enterprise was an abject failure. In the blink of an eye, the Pentagon went from "bullying" to "bumbling."

This new story line was fueled by the inevitable tragedies that accompany any war. When dozens of U.S. soldiers in a maintenance convoy took a wrong turn on a desert highway and ended up in a firefight in Nasiriyah on March 23, for example, many of the Americans were killed or injured and half a dozen captured, including a young private named Jessica Lynch. Meanwhile, a U.S. Patriot missile accidentally shot down a British warplane, killing both pilots. Adding to the sense of unease was TV news footage of jubilant Iraqis firing indiscriminately into reeds along the Tigris River in Baghdad, where a coalition pilot was said to have parachuted from his disabled plane. Although the story turned out to be bogus, it reinforced the sense of foreboding being pushed by the media.

Some of the retired generals and other military officers who had been hired by CNN and other news networks as on-air analysts began to second-guess the war plan and accuse the administration of overconfidence, a charge that was parroted by journalists.

"There were some who were supportive of going to war with Iraq who described it as a 'cakewalk,'" Tim Russert admonished Rumsfeld on NBC's *Meet the Press*.

"I never did," Rumsfeld protested.

"You did not?" demanded Russert, a stickler for research who knew perfectly well that Rumsfeld had not. As everyone inside the Washington beltway knew, the word "cakewalk" had famously appeared in a *Washington Post* opinion column the previous month. It was written by Ken Adelman, a former assistant to Rumsfeld during his stint as President Ford's defense secretary from 1975 to 1977. Trying to tie Rumsfeld to a single word written by a man who hadn't worked for him in more than a quarter century was an enormous stretch.

"No one I know in the Pentagon ever did," Rumsfeld said.

"It is far from it?" said Russert, determined to get his guest to repudiate a sentiment he never expressed.

"Oh, my goodness, it's—a war is a war," Rumsfeld said. "It's a brutal thing."

The questions were similarly loaded at the international press center in Doha, Qatar, the forward headquarters of the U.S. military's Central Command (CENTCOM).

"Given the degree of resistance, which I think you concede has been unexpected—the level of casualties, now the prisoners of war—

is it not the case that this is proving to be significantly more difficult than you might have hoped?" asked a BBC reporter.

Lieutenant General John Abizaid's one-word answer drew chuckles from the rest of the reporters: "No."

Although this was the first Doha press conference of the war, journalists wasted no time invoking the V-word.

"We have been seeing reports of U.S. soldiers killed, missing, and captured, and the state of resistance," said a reporter from Abu Dhabi TV. "Are you facing a new Vietnam in Iraq, or are you victims of over–self-confidence?"

"We are not overconfident about this endeavor; we are confident about the ultimate outcome of this endeavor," Abizaid said. "There won't be anything that stops us on the battlefield."

The same reporter asked an even more hostile question the next day: "Are you practicing a strategy of lies and deception, or you just have been trapped by Iraqi army?"

On and on it went. A reporter from *Newsday* wanted to know "if the commanders have somewhat underestimated the tenacity of some of these irregular units—the fedayeen and the Special Republican Guard." A reporter from the Xinhua News Agency of China insisted that "the Iraqi forces are more strong than expected, because the number of casualties of British and American troops is on rise." There was even a reporter from *Popular Mechanics* asking whether Iraq's "regime command-and control network is more resilient and more robust than we had believed when we went in."

The most recognizable face at the Doha press center was George Stephanopoulos of ABC, a self-described liberal Democrat who demanded to know why "there hasn't been more mass surrender." Evidently the capture of 3,000 Iraqi soldiers and dispersal of countless others into the countryside failed to satisfy the ex-Clinton staffer half a week into the war.

Another ABC reporter, Bob Simon, came right out and said the dictator of Iraq was besting the president of the United States. "Saddam has done remarkably well right now," Simon said on *Good Morning America.* "In fact, the most remarkable achievement of the Bush Administration so far has been creating quite a bit of worldwide sympathy for Saddam Hussein."

Over at the White House press briefing room, the gloom-and-doomers were in full battle cry at Fleischer's daily briefings.

"The news gets worse and American casualties mount," wailed one reporter. "Americans are surprised that we haven't seen scenes of widespread jubilation," whined another.

Although Bush had warned all along that the war would not be easy, reporters now tried to blame the White House for their own inflated expectations.

"Is there a concern that the American public might have—at least for the first few days—gotten the sense that this was going to be easier than in fact it is proving to be?" demanded a journalist. Another fretted about "the expectation on the part of some that it would have gone faster." A third actually blamed the White House for responding to the media's own adversarial questions about expectations.

"There's some level of defensiveness," huffed NBC's David Gregory on March 25. "Perhaps the president is worried that the American public may be less patient than he advised them to be."

Still another reporter was openly contemptuous of the White House stance, demanding: "Can you really say that the American people were accurately prepared for the battle that we're now facing?"

Journalists-turned-armchair-generals openly assailed the administration for allowing troops to race toward Baghdad without stopping to secure each and every town along the way. Reporters were positively fixated on militarily insignificant attacks against the coalition's elongated supply lines. Media outlets that had misguidedly called for more ground troops in Afghanistan now renewed that demand in Iraq. And even though Operation Iraqi Freedom was less than a week old, the press kept comparing it to Vietnam, which had dragged on for years.

"You fought in Vietnam," CBS's Leslie Stahl said to one veteran. "Are you getting any feelings of déjà vu?"

Stahl's questions were even more inane when she sat down with Colin Powell on March 25.

"There are now criticisms we're beginning to hear that this force isn't massive enough," she began.

"It's nonsense," Powell scoffed. "It's the usual chatter. I mean, we have commentators everywhere. Every general who ever worked for me is now on some network commenting on the daily battle.

"And frankly, battles come and wars come and they have ups and downs—they have a rhythm to it," he added. "Don't let one day's ups and downs suggest that the battle isn't going well. The United States armed forces with our coalition partners—the British, principally, and the Australians—have gone three hundred miles deep into Iraq in a period of five days. That is a heck of an achievement."

"Yeah, but our—the rear is exposed," Stahl said.

"It's not," Powell said. "Exposed to what? Exposed to small—"

"Exposed to fedayeen, exposed—"

"Fine, so, we'll get them in due course," Powell said. "They are not exposed to a massive Iraqi army that is operating in a coordinated way that could assault our flanks and stop our assault."

"Are you saying you're not worried or concerned about guerilla warfare?" Stahl said.

"Of course we are, and we're trained to handle this," Powell said. "But this chatter for the last twenty-four hours that everything is coming apart because on Sunday we took a few casualties—the casualties for this operation have been low."

Powell went on to explain the simple military logic behind racing past some towns without securing them.

"You don't want to slow your advance to go into a particular city and spend all your time rooting out people that you will get in due course," he explained. "They are not threatening the events."

"But you can't get your supplies," Stahl protested.

"Who said?" Powell demanded.

"Well, you can't get the humanitarian aid in," said Stahl, blatantly switching topics. While the supply lines were stretched across the sands of southern Iraq, the humanitarian aid was coming in on ships through the Persian Gulf.

"Only because the minefields haven't been cleared at the Port of Umm Qasr—but our troops are being supplied," Powell explained. "And as soon as the mines have been cleared, the ships are waiting to deliver the humanitarian supplies to Umm Qasr and the situation will change rapidly."

"How did we get to a place where much of the world thinks that George Bush is more evil than Saddam Hussein?" Stahl blurted inexplicably. "How did this happen?"

"I don't know that that is the case," Powell said. "I think people are unhappy with our policy with respect to Iraq. Now, is there anti-American opinion around the world with respect to this issue? Yes. There's no question about it.

"But when this war is over and we have liberated Iraq and the people of Iraq are facing a better life where their treasure—their oil treasure—is not being used to develop weapons of mass destruction or to threaten their neighbors, I think those opinions and those attitudes will change rapidly."

Stahl persisted. "What I'm looking at is a poll, really not about the war, it's just about the United States and our friends. It makes you feel terrible. India, Mexico—they have negative opinions about the United States."

"You tell me why that I have consular officers all over the world with visa lines going out in all directions—people trying to come to America," Powell countered. "They want to be Americans. They want to go to our hospitals, to our schools and other places."

"But do you admit that we have a problem?" Stahl persisted.

"Yes," Powell said. "We have to go out and take our case to the world. And what we have to do is get this Iraq crisis behind us and show the better life that's waiting for the Iraqi people and then show progress in the Middle East. And this will turn."

That same day, Powell was reminded by Juan Williams of National Public Radio that "Iraqis have mounted fierce armed resistance."

"This war has only been on for six days," Powell marveled. "For the first two days everybody was euphoric: 'Goodness, it's going to be over on day three.' But then on day four, people saw that the Iraqis were going to put up some resistance and they said: 'Oh, [it's] going to go on for much longer.'

"But this war is only in its early stages and I think our troops, the coalition troops, are doing a magnificent job," he added. "Now, there are pockets of resistance. There are some places that have been bypassed that we now have to go clean out. But the remarkable thing is how successful we have been.

"And the other thing I would point out is that Iraqis are not putting up a coherent, coordinated defense. I mean we're not facing trench warfare across the width of Iraq. We're seeing pockets of resistance—sometimes regular army, sometimes Republican Guard, sometimes these fedayeen suicide people. But none of it is going to stop our advance. It may take a little bit longer, don't know how long. The point is we have had a good battle plan, and it's a battle plan that will succeed."

Powell reminded Williams that the press had already been proven wrong about the supposedly Dresdenesque bombing of Baghdad.

"It was fascinating to listen to some of the media commentary in the early days of the war last week when you heard the explosions going off and you could see the bombs dropping and they were saying, 'They are destroying Baghdad.' And the next morning, Baghdad was not destroyed," he said.

"Given your experiences in Vietnam," Williams parried, "when you saw the pictures over the weekend of American soldiers being held as prisoners of war, some of them executed, did you feel as if this effort at liberation had gone astray?"

"No," Powell said. "You never start a war without the knowledge that young men and women will sacrifice their lives. Some young men and women may be captured, others may be missing—hopefully found later, but perhaps never found. That's the cost of war."

"Bill Keller with the *New York Times* wrote over the weekend that you should resign if you really are not in keeping with this administration's way of thinking with regard to this war," Williams said. "How do you feel personally?"

"Personally, I'm very much in sync with the president and he values my services," Powell replied. "And I appreciate Mr. Keller's advice. I also have to take note of the fact, if you would consult any recent Gallup poll, the American people seem to be quite satisfied with the job I'm doing as secretary of state."

"So you're staying?" said Williams, as if surprised that Powell would disobey a *New York Times* columnist.

"Oh, absolutely."

That very day, the *New York Times* trumpeted the word "quagmire" in a front-page, above-the-fold headline. The paper described U.S. forces as "bogged down" by Iraqi sandstorms, spawning another round of press portrayals of the Bush Administration as the gang that couldn't shoot straight.

"Critics are coming out of the walls to criticize this ground campaign," a reporter told Rumsfeld over at the Pentagon. A second journalist chided: "You may have created the impression in the public minds this was going to be over in four days." A third asked:

"Would you say that you have perhaps not adequately managed the expectations?"

"Shhh! Shhh!" Rumsfeld scolded the grown men and women of the Pentagon press corps. "Whoa, whoa, whoa, whoa!"

Taking a deep breath, the grizzled defense secretary reminded the press of its mistakes just seventeen months earlier.

"If you go back to the Afghanistan situation, it was only a few days into it that it was described by one of the newspapers here as a 'quagmire,'" he recalled. "And it was a matter of days later that things looked quite good and, as I recall, Mazar-i-Sharif fell, and then the other cities began to fall."

Rumsfeld didn't bother making the point that Mazar-i-Sharif had fallen more than a month into the war—whereas Operation Iraqi Freedom was just a week old. Yet the perception of time was being distorted by nonstop reportage from the six hundred journalistic embeds, a side effect not foreseen by the Pentagon.

"With as much coverage as we have of the war—primarily because of the decision to embed a lot of reporters with it—we're watching this thing, what happens, pretty much twenty-four hours a day, seven days a week," remarked General Myers, who shared the doublewide lectern with Rumsfeld. "And I think that lends this perception that it's been going on a long time."

Rumsfeld added: "It even seems like weeks to me. But it is really just such a brief period."

Nonetheless, Rumsfeld believed the public was more patient about Iraq than the press or even his own Pentagon. "The American people have a very good sense of what's going on there," he said. "It may be that some analysts might not. But the American people do.

"What do they see? They see young men and women in uniform out there performing incredibly difficult tasks. They're doing it courageously, they're doing it tirelessly, they're doing it with great success. And the fact that a few analysts say, 'well, my goodness, it should have been faster or slower or this or that,' I do not think is affecting the judgment of the American people."

Although the embeds were making the war seem longer, Rumsfeld now felt certain the gamble to deploy them was paying off. Their generally upbeat dispatches from the front lines were indeed mitigating the pessimism of the East Coast media elites. Rumsfeld could not resist tweaking the reporters in the Pentagon press room by telling them the public was seeing the same thing as "your friends and peers, who are out there watching what's happening. And they're seeing that reported every hour of every day."

Alas, the East Coast press was impervious to such rebukes. It was as if the reporters hadn't even been listening to Rumsfeld.

"Is it possible that you did raise expectations beyond reasonable levels by talking about a shock and awe campaign?" persisted one of them. "Do you believe you've shocked this regime?" demanded another. "They continue to broadcast; they continue to issue orders, apparently; they continue to function."

"I guess it depends how you look at it," Rumsfeld mused. "If I were in Baghdad and I was looking south and I saw a U.S. army division that is on the outskirts of Baghdad, I don't know that that would be shock, but I'd certainly be a little concerned. And they'll have a lot more to be concerned about shortly."

Johnny Apple, the *New York Times* reporter who had compared Afghanistan to Vietnam just seven days into that conflict, now reprised his blunder for Operation Iraqi Freedom. Like clockwork, the former Saigon bureau chief compared the "jungles, caves and mountains of Vietnam" to Iraq's desert sandstorms, which he claimed "enable the Iraqis to mount ambushes." He warned that "the North Vietnamese [had] shown how an outmanned, outgunned force can fight back." And, of course, he quoted an anonymous military source grousing that the Pentagon had "underestimated" Iraqi forces.

That evening, at the start of ABC's *World News Tonight,* anchor

Peter Jennings teased, "One marine tells our reporter: Given the landscape and the weather sometimes it is Desert Storm and sometimes it feels like Vietnam."

As Jennings well knew, the United States had been heavily involved in Vietnam for eight long years. The killing of GIs there lasted twice that long, starting in 1959 and ending in 1975. By contrast, Operation Iraqi Freedom was barely eight days old. And yet the press was already pronouncing it a hopelessly protracted debacle.

"War Could Last Months, Officers Say," warned a front-page headline in the *Washington Post* on March 27. Citing unnamed officers, reporter Tom Ricks painted a bleak picture of a "drawn-out fight that sucks in more and more U.S. forces."

That afternoon, reporters renewed their demands for an utterly unknowable piece of information—the war's ending date. The president himself was asked the question during a joint press conference with British Prime Minister Tony Blair at Camp David.

"Given that the resistance has been as strong as it's been in the south, and that we have what you call the most hardened, most desperate forces still around Baghdad, are we to assume that this is going to last—could last—months and not weeks and not days?" asked Ron Fournier of the Associated Press.

"I'll answer that question very quickly," Bush said. "However long it takes to win."

"Months?" Fournier asked.

"However long it takes to achieve our objective," Bush said. "And that's important for you to know, the American people to know, our allies to know, and the Iraqi people to know."

"It could be months?" Fournier persisted.

"However long it takes," Bush said for the third time. "That's the answer to your question and that's what you've got to know. It isn't a matter of timetable; it's a matter of victory. And the Iraqi people have got to know that, see. They've got to know that they will be liberated and Saddam Hussein will be removed, no matter how long it takes."

The hypersensitive press took umbrage at the president's refusal to equivocate.

"Ari, there seems to be some level of frustration on the part of the president with the press coverage and, indeed, our questions," a reporter complained the next day. "One senior official characterized some questions about battle plan and the timing and the press coverage as 'silly.'"

Like Rumsfeld, Fleischer reminded the press of its bogus coverage of Operation Enduring Freedom. "Just several weeks into the Afghanistan theater, people said: 'Why isn't it over?'" the spokesman recalled. "Just like in Afghanistan, one newspaper today on its front page reported that the marines and the army are 'bogged down.' Now, I don't know anybody who would support that notion—from a military point of view—that our troops are 'bogged down.' Yet, that is what one newspaper reported this morning."

"You did very little to lower expectations in the run up to this," a reporter snapped. "Even if you didn't raise them yourself, you did nothing to lower what we were hearing from the Pentagon and from other outside pundits about how well, how quickly, this war would go."

Incredibly, the White House was now being held accountable for what "outside pundits" might have foolishly predicted about the war. Instead of pointing out the folly of the question, however, Fleischer patiently rattled off a long list of public statements in which both he and the president had explicitly warned the nation to expect significant difficulties in any war against Iraq. The first of these warnings came more than six months earlier, during Bush's September 12 address to the United Nations. Another occurred during the president's televised State of the Union Address on January 28, which was watched by 62 million Americans—an enormous audience. As Fleischer pointed out, the warnings of hardship and sacrifice continued right up until the war actually commenced.

Undeterred, a reporter reminded Fleischer that Vice President Dick Cheney told NBC's *Meet the Press* host Tim Russert on March 16 that the war would last "weeks, not months."

"And then what did the Vice President say in the next sentence right after he said that?" Fleischer demanded.

"I don't have that with me," the reporter conceded.

"His next sentence was: 'There is always the possibility of complications that you can't anticipate,'" Fleischer said. "And, obviously, one week into the battle, I don't know that anybody can draw any conclusions."

Indeed, Fleischer pointed out that Cheney's "weeks, not months" line could very well prove true. The spokesman went on the ridicule the press for its impatience.

"On June 13th, 1944, would somebody have said to the Allies: 'You're one week after D-Day, when will it be over?'" he said. "These things are not knowable in the course of war."

This remark seemed to offend *New York Times* reporter David Sanger. "Your use of an analogy to June 1944—I'm just trying to figure that one out—are you saying that this military operation is of the complexity or meeting a resistance similar to what the U.S. forces met after D-Day?" Sanger asked incredulously.

Sensing he had struck a nerve, Fleischer retreated to the safer analogy of Afghanistan.

"After some three weeks into the Afghani theater there were a number of questions: 'How come it's not over yet? Will it be successful? Where's the Northern Alliance? They're incapable of doing anything.' And of course, literally, days after those criticisms were raised people saw Mazar-i-Sharif fall, Kabul fall. So there are plenty of historical analogies people can point to."

"You don't mean to draw an analogy between the complexity of the post-D-Day operations and the complexity of this operation?" Sanger pressed.

"No, not every analogy is a perfect analogy," Fleischer surrendered. "The point I was making is, one week into an operation we are hearing questions about: Why isn't it over yet?"

He added: "When you pick up the front page of one of today's major papers and you see it says that the marines and the army are 'bogged down,' you can only scratch your head."

But it was no use. The reporters remained utterly unmoved by Fleischer's logic.

"The war seems that it may take longer than originally planned," yet another journalist complained.

"Again, you said it may take longer than originally planned," Fleischer said. "How long was the original plan supposed to last?"

"Good question," the reporter shot back. "Would you let us know?"

"See, that's my point," said the exasperated spokesman. "This is the premise of the questions, and it's not something that, as the president said, was knowable. The plan will go on for what the plan's duration will be."

Deaf to Fleischer's explanations, still another reporter gave it a shot.

"This is going to take longer than most people expected a couple of weeks ago," the journalist began.

"There's that magic formulation again: 'Longer than most people expected several weeks ago,'" Fleischer marveled. "I don't know who those people are and what their predictions were a couple weeks ago."

"Vice President Cheney, for starters," a reporter replied. "I mean, the 'weeks, not months' statement."

"And you can say after one week that that's wrong?" the spokesman demanded. "I don't know that you can say that."

Five minutes after Fleischer extracted himself from the clutches of the press, Rumsfeld squared off against their counterparts at the Pentagon. He began by observing that in the "short period of a week, we have seen mood swings in the media from highs to lows to highs and back again, sometimes in a single 24-hour period."

"For some," he added, "the massive volume of television—and it is massive—and the breathless reports can seem to be somewhat disorienting. Fortunately, my sense is that the American people have a very good center of gravity and can absorb and balance what they see and hear."

The press was unembarrassed by this extraordinary, in-your-face rebuke from the defense secretary on national television. Indeed, far from being chastened by accusations of "mood swings" and "breathless reports," the reporters blithely resumed their preposterous insinuations.

"There has been some criticism—some by retired senior officers, some by officers on background in this building—who claim that the war plan in effect is flawed and our number of troops on the ground is too light, supply lines are too long and stretched too thin," a journalist whined.

"Well, we're one week into this, and it seems to me it's a bit early for history to be written," Rumsfeld retorted.

Taking the opposite tack, another reporter expressed dismay at the swift progress of allied forces, which already controlled 95 percent of Iraq's airspace and 40 percent of its land. Soldiers had seized control of oil fields in the south, sailors had demined a crucial Iraqi port, and airmen had blocked all Iraqi planes from leaving the ground. Although Turkey had refused to grant staging rights to U.S. forces who wanted to open a northern front, allied paratroopers had been dropped into position north of the 36th parallel and, along with Special Operations forces, were working with Kurds against Saddam's army. Coalition troops were now within fifty miles of Baghdad.

"Why do you want to be on the outskirts of Baghdad so quickly?" the dismayed reporter said.

General Myers answered bluntly: "Because we could."

Another journalist practically accused the Pentagon of covering up American casualties, which were remarkably low for a war of this magnitude—twenty-eight killed and forty injured. "The proportion of wounded and dead would seem to be historically way out of skew, because the number of wounded is usually far more than the number killed in action," the reporter argued. "Is there any effort to either unreport or underreport casualties from the battlefield?"

"Oh, my goodness!" Rumsfeld exclaimed. "Now, you know that wouldn't be the case. No one in this government—here or on the ground—is going to underreport what's happening. That's just terrible to think that. Even to suggest it is outrageous. Most certainly not!

"The facts are reported," he continued, pounding his fist on the lectern. "When people are killed, they're killed and we face it. When people are wounded, we say so. When people are missing and we know they're missing, we say so. And when we're wrong and they wander back into camp—as several have recently, having been lost or with other units—we say so. Absolutely not!"

Meanwhile, in Britain, George Galloway—whose prewar newspaper column hailing Saddam as a misunderstood scholar had failed to derail the invasion—savaged the U.S.-U.K. coalition in unusually strident terms.

"They attacked Iraq like wolves," he told Abu Dhabi TV. "They attacked civilians. They encountered resistance from Iraqi forces and Iraqi people who are defending their dignity, religion and country."

Incredibly, Galloway even called on other Arab nations to attack U.S. and British troops. "Iraq is fighting for all the Arabs," he complained. "Where are the Arab armies?"

The next day, during an interview with the *New York Times*, Secretary Powell heard the all-too-familiar question: "You did not expect a cakewalk?"

"Well, I saw something in the paper that we were trying to figure out who did say 'cakewalk,' and poor Kenny Adelman took the dive," Powell replied.

"Cakewalk Ken," mused one journalist.

"Yeah," enthused another.

"You can search my speakings and writings for years and you will find I never use expressions or terms or words like that," said Powell, turning serious. "War is not—it is not a game; it is not a slogan. These are young men and women who are being sent to their fate."

But that same day, at CENTCOM forward headquarters in Doha, journalists were complaining about the fate of Iraqi noncombatants, small numbers of whom had been killed by American forces.

"Civilian bloodshed," lectured one reporter, "hands to your adversary the moral high ground which you claim."

Moments later, a reporter asked Major General Victor Renuart whether the conflict would turn "into another Vietnam." Renuart replied: "I really don't think there is any parallel between this operation and Vietnam."

His response was evidently discounted by the *Baltimore Sun,* which published a front-page story the next morning with the headline: "The resemblance to Vietnam War can't be overlooked." From the comfort of the *Sun*'s Washington bureau, reporters Robert Timberg and Tom Bowman began their story as if they were intrepid war correspondents braving Iraqi sandstorms.

"This war in its early stages recalls the pitched battles and bloody skirmishes of the Vietnam War," wrote the journalists, who went on to compare Iraq's fedayeen to the Viet Cong. "Echoes of Vietnam are invariably detected whenever the United States embarks on a course that involves the use of military force."

What they neglected to mention, of course, was that the only people detecting Vietnam echoes were the journalists themselves. However, they did make a passing reference—without a trace of irony—to a fact that managed to utterly obliterate their own thesis.

"Vietnam claimed upward of fifty-eight thousand American lives," the reporters intoned. "At week's end, the death toll in Iraq stood at thirty-six."

Vietnam was also on the mind of *New Yorker* reporter Seymour Hersh, who fretted on NBC's *Today* about the fact that some generals-turned-pundits were disagreeing with the real generals in the Pentagon about the best way to wage war in Iraq. "There's a huge disconnect and so, you know, for us, some of us that went through the Vietnam War, it's sort of terrifying to think it's starting already," he wailed.

Newsweek summed up the media's contempt for the administration with its snide "Conventional Wisdom" feature, which imagined the president saying: "Gee, that little war was easy, just like we told everybody. Now it's on to Iran, North Korea and . . . Wha!! They're fighting back? No fair!" The magazine went on to give "down arrows" to the administration's key players, starting with the commander in chief: "His war cluelessly flings open the gates of hell, making any sort of victory Pyrrhic." Cheney was ridiculed for predicting: " 'We will be greeted as liberators.' An arrogant blunder for the ages." And finally, *Newsweek* mocked Rumsfeld for "taking fire from TV retired generals for flawed war plan. And how did you miss the fedayeen?"

Ex-CNN correspondent Peter Arnett, now working for NBC News, caused a stir on March 30 by appearing on Iraq's state-controlled television network, where he cheerfully provided aid and comfort to the enemy.

"Within the United States, there is growing challenge to President Bush about the conduct of the war and also opposition to the war," Arnett informed an Iraqi "journalist," who was dressed in a green army uniform. "So our reports about civilian casualties here, about the resistance of the Iraqi forces, are going back to the United States. It helps those who oppose the war.

"Clearly, the American war planners misjudged the determination of the Iraqi forces," he added. "And I personally do not understand how that happened, because I've been here many times and in my commentaries on television I would tell the Americans about the determination of the Iraqi forces, the determination of the government, and the willingness to fight for their country. But me, and others who felt the same way, were not listened to by the Bush Administration.

"Now America is reappraising the battlefield, delaying the war, maybe a week, and rewriting the war plan," concluded Arnett, whose remarks were also shown on C-SPAN in the United States. "The first war plan has failed because of Iraqi resistance; now they are trying to write another war plan."

Such treasonous comments were typical of Arnett, whose obsession with Vietnam was so pronounced that he had been fired in 1999 for falsely reporting on CNN, and in *Time,* that U.S. forces had used nerve gas to kill civilians in a Vietnam operation known as Tailwind. That report contrasted sharply with one Arnett broadcast during the Gulf War in 1991, when he parroted Saddam's claim that America had bombed a Baghdad "baby milk factory" that turned out to be a biological weapons plant. The stunt earned him the nickname "Baghdad Pete." After the Gulf War ended, Arnett revealed his true colors on CNN's *Crossfire,* when he was asked the following hypothetical question: If he had discovered information that could save the lives of numerous American soldiers, would he pass it along to U.S. authorities?

"No, I wouldn't have done that," Arnett replied matter-of-factly. "I'm not a spy."

Stunned, host Patrick Buchanan repeated the question: "If there was information that could have saved scores—hundreds—of American lives, you wouldn't have transmitted that information?"

"I wouldn't have transmitted that information," Arnett shrugged. "I was in Baghdad because I was a correspondent for CNN, which has no political affiliations with the U.S. government, thank goodness."

"Your allegiance to CNN comes before your allegiance to the United States?" said Buchanan, incredulous.

"In terms of journalistic matters, yes," came the cavalier answer from this naturalized American citizen.

Despite Arnett's willingness to let U.S. troops die needlessly—and his abysmal journalistic record of covering up Saddam's weapons while falsely accusing his own government of deploying them—the sixty-eight-year-old newsman had no trouble getting hired to cover Operation Iraqi Freedom by NBC News, one of the most influential media organizations in America. Arnett celebrated his journalistic comeback by publicly trashing his former employers at CNN, founder Ted Turner and chairman Tom Johnson.

"I was furious with Ted Turner and Tom Johnson when they threw me to the wolves after I made them billions risking my life to cover the first Gulf War," Arnett seethed to *TV Guide*. "Now they are gone, the Iraqis have thrown the CNN crew out of Baghdad, and I'm still here. Any satisfaction in that? Ha, ha, ha, ha."

Indeed, Arnett seemed to relish reporting for NBC's *Nightly News* and the *Today* show, where anchors Tom Brokaw and Katie Couric reverently lapped up his anti-American rants from Baghdad.

Amazingly, Arnett's Iraqi TV appearance was not the final straw for the media-weary Pentagon. No, the final straw was a pair of page one, above-the-fold articles in the April 1 edition of the *New York Times*. The first quoted anonymous military officers grumbling that Rumsfeld had not deployed sufficient forces. Never mind that there were more than 100,000 coalition troops inside Iraq and twice that many massed on the border.

"Raw nerves were obvious as officers compared Mr. Rumsfeld to Robert S. McNamara, an architect of the Vietnam War who failed to grasp the political and military realities of Vietnam," wrote reporters Bernard Weinraub and Thom Shanker in the story's second sentence.

The piece was paired with a "military analysis" by reporter Michael R. Gordon, who quoted general-turned-pundit Barry McCaffrey as blasting the Pentagon's war plan. "Their assumptions were wrong," railed the NBC talking head. "They went into battle with a plan that put a huge air and sea force into action with an unbalanced ground combat force."

Predictably, the press was clamoring for a piece of Rumsfeld's hide by the time he began his briefing at the Pentagon that afternoon. But it was Myers who stepped in to defend his boss.

"I would love to comment," said the Joint Chiefs chairman before Rumsfeld could speak. "My view of those reports—and since I don't know who you're quoting, who the individuals are—is that they're bogus."

He added: "It is not helpful to have those kind of comments come out when we've got troops in combat, because first of all, they're false. They're absolutely wrong, they bear no resemblance to the truth. And it's just—it's just—harmful to our troops that are out there fighting very bravely, very courageously."

The usually staid general went on to issue a passionate defense of the war plan.

"There may be others that have other ideas of how we should have done it and, you know, God bless them—that's a great sport here inside the beltway," said the agitated air force general. "And I suppose when I retire, I'll probably have my comments, too: 'Gee, they ought to have more air power. I wish the secretary would say we ought to be more air power-centric, perhaps.'"

Turning serious, he added: "I will stick by my statement that this is a great plan and it's one I've signed up to, it's one all the Joint Chiefs signed up to, and it's one we're going to see through to completion."

When Myers finished venting, it was Rumsfeld's turn.

"I don't think there's ever been a war where there haven't been people opining about this or speculating about that or second-guessing on something else," he said. "We're ten or eleven days into this, and these things have kind of a rhythm to them, and right now we're hearing all of the complaints and concerns and questions.

"One of the ways you can get a sense of how knowledgeable people are is if somebody says that they were sent with half of their forces, which I read in one paper. Fact is, that's just not true," he added.

"Before this started, the president sat down in a secure video with General Franks and each of the component commanders before he made a decision to go forward, and he asked them a couple of questions. He said: 'Is this war plan a good one and will it win?' And each single person, every component commander, they said directly to the president of the United States on secure video, 'absolutely.' "

"Well, was—" a reporter interjected.

"Shhh!" Rumsfeld scolded the childish media. "Just listen!"

"Then he said: 'Do you have everything you need?' Simple question. These are adults. They're all four-stars. And they sat there, and they looked at the president in the eye and said: 'Absolutely, we've got everything we need.' "

Rumsfeld explained that this translated into troops on the ground being well armed and well supplied, with minor exceptions.

"They have what they need," he said. "Notwithstanding these little bits and pieces that you keep reading in the paper, most of which are by people who have never seen the war plan—probably never will, until it's all over."

Astonishingly, the press simply refused to believe Rumsfeld's unqualified endorsement of the war plan.

"Mr. Secretary, are you distancing yourself from the plan?" cried one reporter. "Didn't your philosophy have a lot to do with how this came out?" demanded another. "We kept hearing that you kept sending the plan back—wasn't imaginative enough," wailed a third.

"Goodness, gracious!" Rumsfeld exclaimed. "You say 'keep hearing things.' It's the same thing like we 'cut the force in half.' The fact that one person prints it, and then everyone else runs around and copycats it and writes it again, then pretty soon it's been printed sixteen times, and everyone says: 'Well, it must be true.' That's nonsense!"

By now the defense secretary had worked up a good head of righteous indignation. He was openly reproaching the press on live television.

"No one's backing away from anything," he declared. "And the fact that people have been writing this stuff over and over and over again and misinforming the world is really not terribly important. What's important is what we've said and that we're winning this activity, and it is going to end, and it will end with Saddam Hussein gone."

This terrific crescendo of gloom-and-doom coverage crested, appropriately enough, on April Fool's Day.

11
THE RAH-RAHS VS. THE WISEASSES

AT MIDNIGHT ON APRIL 1, U.S. commandos swooped down on Saddam Hospital in Nasiriyah and rescued Jessica Lynch, the Army private who had been captured by Iraqi forces nine days earlier. The Pentagon released almost no details about Lynch's ordeal, but that didn't stop the press from immediately turning her into a poster child for one of the Left's favorite causes—women in combat. Indeed, the dearth of hard facts on the Lynch case only made it easier for the media to indulge in sheer feminist fantasy.

" 'She Was Fighting to the Death,' " blared the front-page headline in the *Washington Post.* Reporters Susan Schmidt and Vernon Loeb conveniently omitted the names of their "sources" for the breathless and utterly fictitious story that followed.

"Pfc. Jessica Lynch, rescued Tuesday from an Iraqi hospital, fought fiercely and shot several enemy soldiers after Iraqi forces ambushed the Army's 507th Ordnance Maintenance Company, firing her weapon until she ran out of ammunition, U.S. officials said yesterday.

"Lynch, a 19-year-old supply clerk, continued firing at the Iraqis even after she sustained multiple gunshot wounds and watched several other soldiers in her unit die around her in fighting March 23, one official said. The ambush took place after a 507th convoy, supporting the advancing 3rd Infantry Division, took a wrong turn near the southern city of Nasiriyah.

" 'She was fighting to the death,' the official said. 'She did not want to be taken alive.'

"Lynch was also stabbed when Iraqi forces closed in on her position, the official said, noting that initial intelligence reports indicated that she had been stabbed to death."

The Pentagon was mortified by this wholesale fabrication. A senior public affairs officer privately reproached one of the *Post* reporters for getting the story so profoundly wrong. Even in public, senior defense officials treated the paper's account as if it were radioactive.

"Can you corroborate the *Post* story pretty much as they described it?" a reporter asked at a Pentagon news briefing.

"No," said Victoria Clarke bluntly. "I can't."

Undeterred, the rest of the press ran with the *Post*'s portrayal of Lynch as Amazon. Almost overnight, the Left transmogrified the five-foot-four, one hundred-pound waif into a plucky female Rambo whose unflinching courage obliterated, once and for all, the quaint conservative argument that women should be kept out of combat. Unsatisfied by Clinton-era half-measures that thrust female support soldiers like Lynch into places fraught with "substantial risk of capture," feminists now demanded full access to the battlefield.

Naturally, this argument was advanced only by elites who had no intention of ever descending from their ivory tower to set foot on a battlefield. It was opposed by the single moms and teenage girls who actually enlisted in the armed forces—"grunts" with a healthy aversion to the idea of being sent to the front.

"Ground combat is the kind of command that enhances career opportunities," enthused liberal *USA Today* columnist Robin Gerber, whose only "combat" experience was on the Democratic National Convention Platform Committee.

"Lynch is a soldier," Gerber intoned. "But she's also a symbol. Her experience shows that the time is right to blast through the armored ceiling that keeps women second-class citizens in the military."

Citing Lynch's "steely heroism," Gerber callously dismissed the usual arguments for protecting women from combat—including "Excuse No. 1: Women lack courage and mental toughness," and "Excuse No. 4: Captured women possibly will be raped."

Actually, both those excuses would have come in handy for Jessica Lynch. Excuse No. 1 might have kept her out of Nasiriyah, where she spent the hourlong firefight closing her eyes, hugging her shoulders, and burying her head in her knees as the men around her fought desperately against the attacking Iraqis. Excuse No. 4 might have spared her the anal sexual assault she suffered after being captured by Saddam's thugs, who no doubt were bewildered and delighted when the world's sole superpower served them up a pretty young blonde in desert fatigues.

Contrary to the heroic yarn in the *Washington Post,* Jessica Lynch was petrified to find herself in combat. Her M-16 rifle jammed before she could chamber even a single round, much less empty it at the enemy, as the *Post* had reported. She spent the entire battle cowering in the back seat of a Humvee, which eventually crashed into a truck. The next thing Lynch remembered was waking up in a hospital three hours later. Her clothes had been removed and she was severely injured, although it was not clear whether her bones had been broken by the crash or her captors. Contrary to the cartoonish *Post* account, Lynch had not been shot or stabbed. Her authorized biographer would later observe that she "seemed ashamed" of her behavior.

"I didn't kill nobody," Lynch told author Rick Bragg in the book *I Am a Soldier, Too: The Jessica Lynch Story.* "We left a lot of men behind."

The *Post* never ran a correction, even after the truth became widely known. In fact, the paper's managing editor, Steve Coll, was "pleased" with the article's "good reporting," according to the *New York Times*. But *Post* ombudsman Michael Getler slammed his paper's reporters for "thin sourcing" and journalistic "propaganda." In a column that *Post* editors buried on page B-6, Getler summed up the episode with a quote from an astute reader: "I smell an agenda." Even liberal *Post* columnist Richard Cohen decided to "take my own paper to task" in an op-ed piece headlined, "On Not Admitting Our Mistakes."

Stung by such criticism, Schmidt wrote a defensive, rambling, front-page article that blamed her initial account not on wishful feminist thinking, but—incredibly—on the Bush Administration. Without a shred of evidence, Schmidt suggested that the White House and Pentagon had cynically exploited the bogus Lynch story to shore up public support for the war. Never mind that public support was already soaring at 70 percent. Never mind that Bush officials had consistently thrown cold water on the *Post*'s ridiculous account. The important thing was to find a scapegoat—preferably a Republican—for the biggest journalistic blunder of the war.

"Neither the Pentagon nor the White House publicly dispelled the more romanticized initial version of her capture, helping to foster the myth surrounding Lynch and fuel accusations that the Bush administration stage-managed parts of Lynch's story," Schmidt harumphed in the follow-up article, which was co-authored by two other reporters.

This was truly a new low, even for the shameless American press. One of the most influential newspapers in the nation was now holding the Bush Administration responsible for correcting the paper's own gross journalistic misdeeds. Instead of just coming clean and admitting its initial story was utterly bogus, the *Post* called it "romanticized," as if someone other than its own reporters had done the romanticizing. Instead of forthrightly acknowledging its story was factually inaccurate, the *Post* tossed around euphemisms like "myth," as if someone other than its own reporters had been the original myth-makers. And instead of taking responsibility for unleashing a wave of misleading copycat stories throughout the rest of the press, the *Post* bizarrely blamed the White House and Pentagon for fueling "accusations that the Bush administration stage-managed parts of Lynch's story." Since the White House and the Pentagon *were* the Bush Administration, the *Post* was accusing the administration of fueling accusations against itself! Even more implausibly, the *Post* was accusing the notoriously disciplined Bushies of willfully peddling a demonstrably false story, the backlash from which would obviously eclipse any short-term public relations gain.

Thanks to this disingenuous piece of "journalism," the rest of the press was soon teeming with conspiracy theories about how the administration had cooked up the Lynch fable for political purposes. The antiwar BBC accused the Pentagon of staging Lynch's rescue mission as a Hollywood-style publicity stunt, complete with Navy SEALS firing blanks for cinematic effect. Liberal *Los Angeles Times* columnist Robert Scheer branded the Lynch story a "fabrication" that was "proving as fictitious as the stated rationales for the invasion itself." Liberal *New York Times* columnist Frank Rich pronounced Lynch "a symbol of Bush administration propaganda."

Naturally, the *Post* reporters never revealed their sources, although Elaine Donnelly of the Center for Military Readiness had her suspicions. The opponent of women in combat figured the story was planted by "Pentagon feminists"—career ideologues willing to cynically manipulate public opinion in order to preempt outrage over Lynch's sexual assault and possible torture, which were not yet disclosed. Others theorized that the *Post* was simply too eager to believe initial intelligence reports from the field, even though those reports were almost always proven wrong. In any event, the bogus reporting had the desired ideological effect. By the time most Americans learned the truth about Jessica Lynch, they were too confused to be outraged about their own government sending a trembling teenage girl into a swarm of marauding Iraqis. So I decided to publicly broach the subject with Bush himself.

"Mr. President, I know you support our women in the military, but sometimes female prisoners of war are treated worse than males," I said during a televised question-and-answer session in the Oval Office. "Is it time to review the Clinton-era rule change that puts women into combat situations?"

"Our commanders will make those decisions," punted the commander in chief. "That's how we run our business here in the White House. We set the strategy and we rely upon our military to make the judgments necessary to achieve the strategy."

Over at the *New York Times,* the Jessica Lynch story was assigned to a reporter named Jayson Blair. Although Blair was only twenty-seven and had racked up what one of his editors called an "extraordinarily high" number of corrections, he kept landing plum assignments because he was black and his boss had an advanced case of liberal white guilt. "As a white man from Alabama," admitted Executive Editor Howell Raines, "I personally favored Jayson." He added that he "gave him one chance too many." That was putting it mildly. Ignoring overwhelming evidence that Blair was simply making up large portions of major news stories—including the Beltway sniper case that paralyzed the nation's capital a mere five months earlier—Raines turned Blair loose on the Lynch story. As a result, the nation's most influential newspaper blithely published falsehoods about an historically significant news event—the first rescue of an American prisoner of war in decades. To make matters worse, Raines and Managing Editor Gerald Boyd assigned Blair to cover lots of other war-related stories, most of which resulted in similarly fanciful dispatches.

When these transgressions were later revealed by the *Washington*

Post, Raines began to panic. He was already under fire for his overt antiwar bias; now the burgeoning Blair scandal was further endangering Raines's career. Instead of renouncing his disastrous pursuit of newsroom diversity—which Raines himself called "more important" than good journalism—he cravenly accused Blair of single-handedly scandalizing the newspaper. "I don't want to demonize Jayson, but this is a tragedy of failure on his part," Raines charged during a defensive interview with National Public Radio. The *Times* also published a lengthy article attempting to shield Raines from blame while hanging Blair out to dry.

"Mr. Blair pulled details out of thin air in his coverage of one of the biggest stories to come from the war, the capture and rescue of Pfc. Jessica D. Lynch," said the story, which called the scandal "a low point in the 152-year history of the newspaper." "In an article on March 27 that carried a dateline from Palestine, W.Va., Mr. Blair wrote that Private Lynch's father, Gregory Lynch Sr., 'choked up as he stood on his porch here overlooking the tobacco fields and cattle pastures.' The porch overlooks no such thing. He also wrote that Private Lynch's family had a long history of military service; it does not, family members said. He wrote that their home was on a hilltop; it is in a valley. And he wrote that Ms. Lynch's brother was in the West Virginia National Guard; he is in the Army.

"The article astonished the Lynch family and friends, said Brandi Lynch, Jessica's sister. 'We were joking about the tobacco fields and the cattle.' Asked why no one in the family called to complain about the many errors, she said, 'We just figured it was going to be a one-time thing.'

"It now appears that Mr. Blair may never have gone to West Virginia, from where he claimed to have filed five articles about the Lynch family. E-mail messages and cellphone records suggest that during much of that time he was in New York. Not a single member of the Lynch family remembers speaking to Mr. Blair."

The *New York Times* and *Washington Post* were not the only major media outlets that behaved reprehensibly when it came to covering Iraq. So did NBC News, which issued a statement defending Peter Arnett's treasonous advice to Iraqi state TV that playing up civilian casualties "helps those who oppose the war."

"Peter Arnett and his crew have risked their lives to bring the American people up-to-date, straightforward information on what is happening in and around Baghdad," said NBC News spokeswoman Allison Gollust. "His impromptu interview with Iraqi TV was done as a professional courtesy and was similar to other interviews he has done with media outlets from around the world. His remarks were analytical in nature and were not intended to be anything more."

But the American public was so outraged by Arnett's shocking remarks that NBC flip-flopped the next morning, unceremoniously firing the thrice-disgraced journalist. "It was wrong for Mr. Arnett to grant an interview to state controlled Iraqi TV—especially at a time of war—and it was wrong for him to discuss his personal observations and opinions in that interview," NBC News President Neal Shapiro conceded. "Therefore, Peter Arnett will no longer be reporting for NBC News and MSNBC."

Even National Geographic was forced to cut Arnett loose, taking pains to emphasize that "the Society did not authorize or have any prior knowledge of Arnett's television interview with Iraqi television." In a hastily issued statement, the magazine added: "Had we been consulted, we would not have allowed it. His decision to grant an interview and express his personal views on state controlled Iraqi television, especially during a time of war, was a serious error in judgment and wrong."

The humiliated journalist made one last appearance on the *Today* show to issue a grudging mea culpa.

"I want to apologize to the American people for clearly making a misjudgment over the weekend by giving an interview to Iraqi television," he began. But in the next breath he cheapened the apology by insisting that his remarks to Iraqi TV merely confirmed "what we all know about the war."

"There have been delays in implementing policy and there's been surprises," he told *Today* co-host Matt Lauer. "But clearly by giving that interview to Iraqi television, I created a firestorm in the United States and for that I am truly sorry, Matt."

"Peter, at the risk of getting myself in trouble, I want to say I respect the work you've done over the last several weeks and I respect the honesty with which you've handled this situation," Lauer fawned. "So good luck to you."

Hours later, Arnett took a job at the *Daily Mirror* of London, a stridently liberal tabloid specializing in virulent anti-Americanism. By the end of the day he had penned his first article, headlined, "THIS WAR IS NOT WORKING." He began by confessing to be "in shock and awe at being fired. There is enormous sensitivity within the U.S. government to reports coming out from Baghdad. They don't want credible news organizations reporting from here because it presents them with enormous problems."

Retreating even further from his "apology," Arnett anguished "that overnight my successful NBC reporting career was turned to ashes. And why? Because I stated the obvious to Iraqi television: that the U.S. war timetable has fallen by the wayside."

Now in full martyr mode, Arnett took a cue from Hillary Clinton. "The right-wing media and politicians are looking for any opportunity to be critical of the reporters who are here," he said. "To be criticized for saying the obvious is unfair. But it has made me a target for my critics in the States who accuse me of giving aid and comfort to the enemy."

Naturally, Arnett—who once won a Pulitzer for his coverage of Vietnam for the Associated Press—couldn't resist comparing that conflict to Operation Iraqi Freedom. He even tossed in a battle story from those golden days, implying it had relevance in Iraq.

"During the Tet Offensive in Vietnam, I entered a U.S.-held town which had been totally destroyed," he recalled. "The Viet Cong had taken over and were threatening the commander's building so he called down an artillery strike which killed many of his own men. The Major with us asked: 'How could this happen?' A soldier replied: 'Sir, we had to destroy the town to save it.' "

Arnett wasn't the only NBC journalist who was forced to backpedal from his own "misjudgment." So was Brian Williams, the MSNBC anchor who had likened the surgical air strikes against Baghdad to the indiscriminate carpetbombing of cities in Germany and Japan during World War II. While it had taken Williams just twelve minutes to make that ludicrous comparison, which was immediately denounced by Rumsfeld, it took him twelve days to correct the record. On April 2, Williams finally reversed course.

"Civilians used to be intentional military targets; the fire bombings of Dresden and Tokyo in World War II were meant to kill civilians and then terrorize survivors," Williams said on NBC's *Nightly News*. "Here we've seen the opposite happen."

Journalists from all the major news outlets were eating similar servings of crow. That same day, the *New York Times* admitted it had falsely accused Vice President Cheney of bragging that Saddam's regime was "a house of cards." Naturally, while the original story had been plastered above the fold of the front page, the grudging correction was buried inside the newspaper.

Ditto for an equally egregious falsehood the *Times* was forced to correct the very next day. It seems the newspaper had conveniently omitted two tiny words from a quote by Lieutenant General William Wallace, who told a reporter: "The enemy we're fighting is a bit different from the one we war-gamed against." In order to sharpen this relatively innocuous utterance, the newspaper dropped the pesky qualifier "a bit." It was just the sort of nuanced "editing" that allowed the *Times* and the rest of the press to falsely portray Wallace as roundly condemning the Pentagon's war plan. Again, the offending story was at the very top of the front page, while the correction was buried inside. Ari Fleischer did his part to raise the correction's profile. "It's worth pointing out there was a rather remarkable correction printed in one of the nation's leading newspapers pertaining to what General Wallace was alleged to have said," Fleischer told reporters from the lectern of the James S. Brady briefing room in the White House. "I can't tell you how many stories are written off of the incorrect quote. I don't yet know how many stories will be written off of the corrected quote."

Virtually none, because the press was too busy mischaracterizing countless other aspects of the war. Despite the fact that allied forces now controlled 50 percent of Iraqi territory and 100 percent of its airspace a mere two weeks into the conflict, reporters simply could not let go of their obsession with Vietnam. On April 2, a journalist at the Pentagon press briefing likened the forthcoming fight over Baghdad with "the battle of Hue in Vietnam." That same day, on the *CBS Evening News,* reporter Jim Axelrod said, "The familiar desert war looked more like the jungles of Vietnam. And this time Iraqi opposition was fierce."

The next evening, NBC News anchor Tom Brokaw managed to sound glum about the allies' remarkable progress.

"After an unexpectedly difficult ground war on the way to Baghdad, American and coalition forces are within nineteen miles of the Iraqi capital," he said. "A lot of progress for the United States and the allies in the last 24 hours, but now the very difficult assignment— taking on Baghdad, with the Saddam Hussein regime showing no signs of folding anytime soon."

Over at CNN, anchor Wolf Blitzer interviewed a rabid Bush hater who voluntarily spent five weeks as a "human shield" at a Baghdad water treatment plant that was never bombed.

"The rage in me has been growing all these years," seethed U.S.

citizen Tom Cahill. "And the anger is another one of the reasons I went to Iraq."

Cahill, who was interviewed in Amman, Jordan, actually considered Bush more of a menace than the mass murderer terrorizing Iraq.

"I didn't see much evidence of a dictatorship there except a lot of soldiers and an awful lot of pictures of Saddam Hussein," he shrugged. "As far as human rights are concerned, President Bush has a problem in the United States."

"Would you agree that the Iraqi people will be better off without Saddam Hussein and his regime in power?" Blitzer asked.

"No, I don't agree!" Cahill snapped.

Meanwhile, many Americans were shocked when Senator John Kerry, a combat veteran, equated the commander in chief with the dictator of Iraq in the middle of a war.

"What we need now is not just a regime change in Saddam Hussein and Iraq, but we need a regime change in the United States," Kerry told an audience in New Hampshire, where he was running for president.

Unfazed by such wartime politicking, allied forces continued to roll across Iraq. When dawn broke on April 4, the coalition was in control of Saddam Airport on the outskirts of Baghdad. At the White House, one reporter began to sense that the press had been overly pessimistic about the war effort.

"Ari, last week, the military plan that has been set in motion for a war in Iraq was very much criticized, including by many ex-generals and colonels and some in active duty in Iraq," the journalist began.

"I noticed," Fleischer deadpanned.

"Does the president feel that the quick taking of the airport and the closing in on the troops in Baghdad vindicates the plan?"

"The president has always felt that what is important, particularly in war, is to be steady at the helm," Fleischer allowed. "He understood that there were going to be some criticisms."

Indeed, most reporters were still reluctant to give the administration credit, even when large numbers of Iraqi civilians began cheering American troops as liberators.

"I am as wary of pro-Saddam sentiment as I am of pro-United States sentiment," sniffed Paul Slavin, executive producer of ABC's *World News Tonight,* to the *New York Times.* "If I had a bunch of fedayeen and Republican Guard around me, I'd say, 'Yeah Saddam!' But if I had a bunch of American soldiers around me, I'd say, 'Yeah America!' We're going to try not to draw any broad conclusions out of any of this."

Incredibly, a major U.S. news executive found moral equivalence between American GIs, who were sacrificing their lives to protect Iraqi civilians, and Saddam Hussein's thugs, who threatened to kill their own countrymen if they refused to take part in staged displays of support for the dictator. Worse yet, Slavin's attitude was rampant throughout the press, as evidenced by questions posed to Brigadier Gen. Vincent Brooks at CENTCOM.

"General, the dancing in the streets that we've seen, is it because they love you or is it because they fear you?" a reporter demanded.

The press seemed more suspicious of American forces than the Iraqi army, which routinely displayed an appalling disregard for international rules of warfare. Some of Saddam's soldiers were dressing up as harmless civilians in order to ambush allied forces. Others stayed in their military uniforms and raised the white flag, only to open fire on approaching Americans. Still others donned British or Australian military uniforms in order to get within deadly proximity of allied forces. They forced terrified Iraqi civilians into service as human shields. They sent suicide bombers to inflict maximum carnage on the allies. All the while, dozens of Iraqi units positioned themselves and their weapons inside schools, hospitals, mosques, and architecturally historic sites to preclude Americans from attacking. Instead of emphasizing these atrocities, though, ABC's *World News Tonight* kept making dubious claims about American GIs killing Iraqi civilians. And no matter how quickly the allies advanced toward Baghdad, the show's journalists seemed determined to characterize Operation Iraqi Freedom as a quagmire.

"This could be, Peter, a long war," Pentagon reporter John McWethy speculated.

"As many people had anticipated," Jennings snipped with an air of I-told-you-so satisfaction.

Over at NBC, Pentagon reporter Jim Miklaszewski brooded, "If the Iraqi regime does not fall quickly, both sides could be in for a lengthy siege of Baghdad."

At CENTCOM headquarters in Doha, CBS radio commentator Dave Ross summed up the media's impatience with a pointed question to General Brooks.

"This is day fifteen," he snapped. "Can you say that Americans at home are safer today than they were fifteen days ago?"

The next day, former NBC correspondent Arthur Kent, whose boyish good looks had earned him the nickname "Scud Stud" during the first Gulf War, was given a platform on CNN to rail against the "shameful situation" in Iraq.

"There is too much civilian death going on here and the U.S. military flunked—flunked!—the test of devising a way to have an inside-out removal of this regime instead of setting up these almost medieval siege situations," railed Kent, who now worked for the History Channel.

Meanwhile, the Department of Defense allowed reporters at the Pentagon to conduct a phone interview with Lieutenant General Michael Moseley, who was running the coalition's air operations from Saudi Arabia. One of the questioners was Tom Bowman of the *Balti-*

more Sun, who earlier in the week had coauthored the article headlined "The resemblance to Vietnam War can't be overlooked."

"You had some critics—retired officers and analysts—say that the initial attack should have been even more violent; you might have been able to end this thing fairly quickly," Bowman chided the Texas-raised general. "Your reaction to the critics?"

"It's a whole lot like listening to a cow pee on a flat rock," Moseley said. "It just doesn't matter."

By this time allied forces had been conducting ground forays into Baghdad for days, a fact that seemed to irritate a *USA Today* reporter at CENTCOM. "Can you tell me what the strategic idea is behind those kind of parades through town?" the journalist agitated at the televised briefing on April 6.

That same day, Tim Russert of NBC dusted off the "cakewalk" canard he had used against Rumsfeld two weeks earlier. "Our soldiers have encountered something much more than a cakewalk," he lectured Deputy Defense Secretary Paul Wolfowitz.

"I have always disliked that term, and no one in the senior leadership in this administration—either civilian or military, and certainly not the president—has ever thought that war is anything other than a very dangerous thing," Wolfowitz said.

Switching to another red herring, Russert cited General William Wallace's quote to the *New York Times* about war-gaming the enemy. Of course, the newsman didn't mention the fact that the *Times* had altered the quote.

"There did seem to be a disconnect for a while from the commanders on the ground saying we didn't game plan for this war," Russert said.

"No, I think the disconnect was [with] how things were being reported," shot back General Peter Pace, Vice Chairman of the Joint Chiefs of Staff. "And in fact I understand that the *New York Times,* for example, has printed a correction of the quote that they had from the very, very capable corps commander who we have out there."

The only bright spot in all this naysaying coverage came from the embeds. By now it was abundantly clear that the Pentagon's decision to send hundreds of journalists into battle with troops was a stroke of genius. The intrepid dispatches from the front lines offset the droning negativity from the East Coast journalists.

On April 7, for example, the networks aired footage of Iraqi Minister of Information Mohammed Saeed al-Sahhaf—better known as "Baghdad Bob"—claiming there were no U.S. troops in Baghdad. But embedded reporter Greg Kelly of Fox News Channel demonstrated the absurdity of this claim.

"The Iraqi Information Minister doesn't seem to think that you guys are winning and that you guys are really here," Kelly said to a soldier with the Third Infantry Division, which had entered Baghdad two days earlier. "What do you have to say about that?"

"Well, he's just across the street from us," the soldier observed. "We'll go over and talk to him."

Americans loved these no-nonsense reports from the embeds, some of whom were clearly moved by the bravery and compassion of U.S. soldiers under fire. For example, CBS correspondent Byron Pitts of CBS gave a stirring testimonial on *The Early Show* that would not have been possible if he had not been embedded.

"For me, one of the great moments was [watching] the captain in charge of Lima company, thirty-one years old from Harrisburg, Pennsylvania, who remained so calm in such a difficult situation," Pitts reported. "Marines were on their stomachs, I was laying on my back, and this guy sat up, ankles crossed, and very calmly made decisions."

With bullets whizzing overhead, the captain refused to lose his cool.

"There was one point when one of his young corporals said: 'Sir, we've spotted where the fire is coming from. There are three people, let me take the shot,'" Pitts recalled. "And he [the captain] said, 'Have you identified their weapons?' He said, 'No, sir.' He said, 'Do not take the shot until you can confirm the weapon.' The corporal pushed. He said, 'No, not until then.'"

At length, the marines "saw three heads bobbing up and down" and assumed they were the shooters, Pitts explained. But "moments later, a man, his wife and daughter stood up. This captain made the right call. Three people are alive today because this marine made the right call."

Such heartfelt dispatches only won the embeds the lasting enmity of non-embedded journalists like Michael Wolff of *New York* magazine, however, who spent the war safely ensconced in CENTCOM's million-dollar, air-conditioned press center in Doha, far removed from the rough and tumble of the Iraqi battlefield. Wolff wrote that he loathed the sanitized press briefings he attended each day, calling them "bullshit" and "obvious disinformation" by lying American generals. But he took comfort in the knowledge that at least he and the other non-embedded reporters were "jaded" enough to "accept that the process of reporting war was a crock."

"We were in on the joke. We were the high-school kids who got it," Wolff explained in his magazine. "The embedded reporters, on the other hand, were the rah-rah jocks."

He added smugly: "The camaraderie of people who understood the joke—who were part of the joke—was very reassuring and comfortable." While mocking "the Tolstoyan reports of the embeds" as "radically dissociated from any larger context," Wolff had to hand it to the "media-savvy" Pentagon planners: "They were smart enough to come up with the embed thing—wherein reporters became soldiers and invaders and liberators."

By contrast, Wolff described non-embedded journalists like himself as "wiseasses," openly wishing that "the wiseasses would triumph and the righteous Bushies would falter." To that end, Wolff mortified millions of TV viewers by posing a breathtakingly inane question to

General Brooks, the brilliant, telegenic African American officer who gave most of the daily press briefings at Doha.

"I'm Michael Wolff from *New York* magazine," he began, mindful that the exchange was being broadcast live on worldwide television. "I mean no disrespect by this question, but I want to ask about the value proposition of these briefings. We're no longer being briefed by senior-most officers. To the extent that we get information, it's largely information already released by the Pentagon. You may know that ABC has sent its senior correspondent home." This was a reference to George Stephanopoulos, at one time the most famous face at the Doha press center.

"So I guess my question is: Why should we stay?" Wolff said contemptuously. "What's the value to us for what we learn at this million-dollar press center?"

The other journalists in the room demonstrated their approval of Wolff's insolence by showering him with what he fondly called "rude applause," although Brooks was witty enough to pretend the clapping was for him.

"I've gotten applause already—that's wonderful, I appreciate that," he said with a good-natured grin. Turning serious, he decided to dignify Wolff's disrespectful question with a respectful answer.

"First, I would say it's your choice," Brooks began. "We want to provide information that's truthful from the operational headquarters that is running this war. There are a number of places where information is available, not the least of which would be the embedded media—and they tell a very important story."

This praise for the embeds only further irritated Wolff, who had nothing but disdain for the brave journalists at the front, some of whom—including NBC News correspondent David Bloom and *Washington Post* columnist Michael Kelly—ended up dying on the job. As if to add insult to injury, Brooks then reminded Wolff that it was not always possible for the military to give the press "very, very precise information about the operations."

"Never forget," he warned, "you're not the only one being informed."

"But is it possible that we can get General Franks on a more consistent basis?" Wolff whined.

"I'm sorry you feel disappointed—I probably need to get a pay raise here," said Brooks, prompting laughter in the room. "General Franks has already shown that he's more than willing to come and talk to you at the right time. But he's fighting a war right now. And he has me to do this for him."

Wolff's bizarre questions touched off a fury back in the States. Rush Limbaugh, the most influential radio talk show host in the nation, was outraged by the journalist's snide effrontery.

"Can you believe the audacity of complaining that Brigadier General Brooks isn't good enough for the press?" Limbaugh marveled. "If this had been a reporter from a conservative news source, the press would point out the fact that Brooks just happens to be the only African American general on the scene. Charges of racism would be made, because this question's underlying meaning is clearly that Brooks can't possibly know anything." Wolff himself seemed acutely aware of the racial undertones, describing his exchange with Brooks as "a white liberal challenging a black general." "Displeased with the service, I was in some sense asking to see the manager," he explained in his magazine. "We were getting briefed by, in effect, middle management." Wolff mocked Brooks as a mere "one-star general" with "hangdog" eyes and an annoying "inexpressiveness." He added: "Brooks was a stiff, rote briefer. Stonewall Brooks."

Snarky insults, of course, were one thing. When Wolff equated Brooks with Baghdad Bob, though, it was another thing entirely. "It seemed to tip back and forth between whose version of the war was wackier," Wolff mused.

Alas, despite Wolff's wish that "the wiseasses would triumph and the righteous Bushies would falter," it was Saddam Hussein's regime that was floundering. By April 9, Iraqi citizens felt sufficiently emboldened by the U.S. presence to begin ripping down portraits of Saddam in Baghdad. They gratefully chanted "Bush! Bush! Bush!" as U.S. troops patrolled the city. Some even took a sledgehammer to the base of a giant statue of the dictator in central Baghdad's Paradise Square, on the eastern bank of the Tigris River. The Iraqis scaled the monolith, erected a year earlier to mark Saddam's sixty-fifth birthday, and threw a noose around its neck. But the statue wouldn't budge, so a column of U.S. Marines advanced into the square to lend a helping hand.

The marines looped a sturdy chain around the statue's neck and attached the other end to a heavy armored vehicle normally used for towing disabled tanks. Jubilant Iraqis crowded into the square, cheering in anticipation of this symbolic toppling of Saddam's hated regime. Sensing the historic importance of the moment, Marine Corporal Edward Chin broke out an American flag that had flown at the Pentagon when the building was struck by terrorists on September 11, 2001. He climbed to the top of the statue and briefly covered Saddam's face with Old Glory. Since brave American troops had given their lives for that moment, it seemed only fitting that the stars and stripes would defiantly obscure the tyrant's terrible visage. Having made his point, Chin removed the American flag after just a few short moments. He then produced a pre-1991 Iraqi flag and draped it around Saddam's neck, prompting raucous cheers from the swelling crowd. At length he removed that flag as well and climbed down.

What happened next electrified the world. The marines pulled down the enormous statue of Saddam Hussein, and the crowd went wild. Jubilant Iraqis leapt upon the fallen tyrant, dancing and crying out in joy. The statue was decapitated and its head was dragged through the streets as Iraqis struck it with their shoes—a sign of maximum disrespect in the Arab world. The extraordinary images were broadcast live to a rapt and relieved world.

"They got it down," marveled Bush as he watched TV in a room just off the Oval Office.

Vice President Cheney was more expansive. "I see the outpouring of joy in the streets of Baghdad today by the Iraqi people at their liberation," he told a gathering of newspaper editors that afternoon. "We were—after great provocation and after twelve years of unsuccessful efforts by the U.N.—acting to eliminate one of the most brutal dictators of our time. A man who probably was responsible for the death of at least a million Muslims, half of them his own people. A man who ran a horrific police state."

Cheney's prediction of "weeks, not months" had come true after all. The gloom-and-doomers of the fourth estate, who had predicted another Vietnam quagmire in Iraq, had been proven wrong again. Baghdad fell a mere three weeks after the first shot was fired. To be sure, there were still pockets of resistance in Tikrit and other parts of the country that would have to be mopped up in the coming weeks. But the vaunted regime of Saddam Hussein, once considered the Arab world's most promising leader, had been thoroughly, unambiguously destroyed. The stubborn determination of George W. Bush to liberate 25 million people and establish a beachhead of democratic reform in the heart of the Middle East had come to pass. It was the first manifestation of Bush's doctrine of preemption—toppling enemies before they had a chance to cause harm to America or her friends.

"Real vindication for the administration," concluded embed Bob Arnot, chief foreign correspondent for MSNBC. "You know what? There were a lot of terrorists here, really bad guys. I saw them. They took women and children hostages, kept them in their own homes."

He added: "This whole idea of Iraqi freedom—the administration may have come up with it at last minute—but I'll tell you, it's like

Paris 1944. Coming into town here, people are yelling and screaming, 'Go, go, USA!' "

Rumsfeld agreed and chided the East Coast press for its misplaced pessimism.

"The scenes we've witnessed in Baghdad and other free Iraqi cities belie the widespread early commentary suggesting that Iraqis were ambivalent or even opposed to the coalition's arrival in their country," he admonished reporters at the Pentagon. "They were not ambivalent or opposed, but they were understandably frightened of the regime of Saddam Hussein and the retaliation or retribution that they could have suffered."

Predictably, the press now tried to lure Rumsfeld and other administration officials into the gloat trap by daring them to crow about the victory.

"Mr. Secretary, in light of the criticisms of the supply line and the pause that was reported a week or two ago, are you feeling vindicated today?" a reporter asked.

"You're right, there have been a lot of people who've suggested that the force was undersized and that they went too fast and they should have had a long air war first," Rumsfeld said. "A lot of experts thought they knew how long it was going to last. But we didn't."

Although Rumsfeld went on to praise everyone from the grunts to the generals, he refused to rise to the reporter's bait. "It's not a matter for me to be vindicated," he said. "The outcome is in the process of speaking for itself and it's not for me to draw conclusions about it."

The same scene was being played out over at the White House.

"There's been a lot of criticism and sniping from this room and elsewhere since the war began of the war plan, of the expectations," a White House reporter reminded Ari Fleischer in the Brady briefing room. "Any feeling of vindication, or 'I told you so'?"

"Well," Fleischer said. "From a personal point of view, all I can say is I'm always glad to be embedded with you."

"Oooohh!" said the wounded reporters.

Bush got the question two days later, while visiting injured soldiers at Walter Reed Army Medical Center in Washington.

"Do you feel any certain sense of vindication after all those people questioned the war plan?" a reporter asked, as if "those people" did not include the press itself.

"I don't take anything personally," Bush replied. "Tommy Franks put together a great strategy. Wonderful thing about free speech and a lot of TV stations is you get a lot of opinions. Some of them were right, and some of them were really wrong. But that's okay. That's what we believe. We believe in free speech, believe people ought to be able to express their opinion."

There was no need for the president to gloat over the media's historic blunder. Why attack the press when it was already self-destructing? That very day, CNN caused a sensation by admitting it had spent years covering up Saddam's atrocities in order to preserve the network's precious Baghdad bureau. The office in question was located, appropriately enough, in Iraq's Ministry of Information—headquarters of Baghdad Bob. But instead of using that unique perch to inform the world of the regime's monstrous reign of terror, CNN had aired reports about Saddam that sometimes bordered on fawning.

"He, too, endures," gushed CNN's Jane Arraf in a 2001 report on the tenth anniversary of the Gulf War. "More than a symbol, a powerful force who has survived three major U.S.-led attacks since the Gulf war, bombing, and plots to depose him. At sixty-three, the president mocks rumors he is ill. Not just standing tall but building up. As soon as the dust settled from the Gulf War, and the bodies were buried, Iraq began rebuilding."

Not to be outdone, CNN correspondent Nic Robertson covered Saddam's sham "reelection" in 2002 as if it were a legitimate news story.

"Iraqi reverence for President Saddam Hussein is rarely more expressive than when their leader calls a referendum," Robertson solemnly intoned on CNN's *American Morning.*

" 'To paint for the president for this special day is important,' explains artist Abdul. 'It shows our love to him,' " the reporter enthused. "Amid even bolder demonstrations of devotion to the Iraqi leader, students at Baghdad's fine arts school, too young to vote in the last referendum in 1995, appear eager now." The network that billed itself as "the most trusted name in news" was dignifying the preposterous charade of a brutal dictator staging a one-candidate election in which he garnered 100 percent of the vote—while failing to remind viewers that any Iraqi who dared to vote against Saddam would be unceremoniously tortured to death.

Later that month, even the liberal *New Republic* noticed the media's shameless kowtowing to Saddam's regime. In a lengthy piece entitled "How Saddam Manipulates the U.S. Media," Franklin Foer singled out CNN for selling its journalistic soul to the Iraqi Information Ministry. "Nobody better exemplifies this go-along-to-get-along reporting strategy than the dean of Western reporters in Baghdad, Arraf," Foer wrote. "And nobody has schmoozed the ministry harder than the head of CNN's News Group, Eason Jordan."

Foer accused Jordan and other network executives of "promising the Iraqi regime that they will cover its propaganda." He even asked Jordan "to explain why his network is so devoted to maintaining a perpetual Baghdad presence."

"Because there's an expectation that if anybody is in Iraq," Jordan replied haughtily, "it will be CNN."

"His answer reveals the fundamental attitude of most Western media," Foer concluded. "Access to Baghdad is an end in itself, regardless of the intellectual or moral caliber of the journalism such access produces."

Jordan was asked about Foer's article a few days later by WNYC radio host Bob Garfield, who wanted to know whether "the Western press is appeasing the Iraqi regime in order to maintain its visas."

"The writer clearly doesn't have a clear understanding of the realities on the ground because CNN has demonstrated again and again that it has a spine," Eason said. "We work very hard to report forthrightly, to report fairly and to report accurately. And if we ever determine we cannot do that, then we would not want to be there."

But as soon as Saddam's statue fell, Eason flip-flopped in a sweeping mea culpa, headlined "The News We Kept to Ourselves," on the op-ed page of the *New York Times*.

"Over the last dozen years, I made thirteen trips to Baghdad to lobby the government to keep CNN's Baghdad bureau open, and to arrange interviews with Iraqi leaders," he began. "Each time I visited, I became more and more distressed by what I saw and heard—awful things that could not be reported."

These things included Saddam's secret police terrorizing innocent Iraqis, some of whom were "hauled off and tortured in unimaginable ways," Jordan revealed. One man's fingernails were ripped off. Another man—who worked as an aide to Uday Hussein—had his front teeth ripped out with pliers. A thirty-one-year-old Kuwaiti woman was beaten for two months for "crimes" such as speaking to CNN on the phone. Her father was forced to watch the torture.

"In January 1991, on the eve of the American-led offensive, they smashed her skull and tore her body apart limb by limb," Jordan wrote. "A plastic bag containing her body was left on the doorstep of her family's home.

"I felt awful having these stories bottled up inside me," he confessed. "At last, these stories can be told freely."

At last, indeed, could the top news executive at CNN—which had been aggressively skeptical of Bush's quest to remove Saddam—admit that several senior Iraqi officials had long ago "confided in me that

Saddam Hussein was a maniac who had to be removed." But the biggest bombshell in Jordan's column was his revelation that CNN had deliberately covered up a plot to kill Iraq's most important and high-profile defectors, Saddam Kamel and Hussein Kamel.

"CNN could not report that Saddam Hussein's eldest son, Uday, told me in 1995 that he intended to assassinate two of his brothers-in-law who had defected and also the man giving them asylum, King Hussein of Jordan," Jordan wrote.

In a move that can only be described as playing God, Jordan chose to warn only one of Uday's three assassination targets.

"I felt I had a moral obligation to warn Jordan's monarch, and I did so the next day," explained the CNN executive, who did not extend the same courtesy to the doomed defectors.

"A few months later Uday lured the brothers-in-law back to Baghdad; they were soon killed," Jordan wrote. The newsman argued that if he had broadcast the story of the plot to kill the defectors, Uday would likely have murdered a translator who was the only other person present when the dictator's son revealed the plot to Jordan. Perhaps. But why hadn't Jordan simply warned the translator and defectors in private, as he had warned King Hussein? Jordan offered no explanation.

Nor did he acknowledge what CNN surely considered the main benefit of deep-sixing the story—that the network avoided permanent expulsion from its coveted perch inside Baghdad Bob's Information Ministry.

After Baghdad fell, it became fashionable for the press to joke about Baghdad Bob's capacity to deny reality, as if he were a harmless clown who had never been taken seriously. But Rumsfeld reminded reporters that they had spent years parroting the lies of this stone evil member of Saddam's inner circle.

"It does look foolish to stand in Baghdad and say that there's no Americans in Baghdad, when everyone is looking at the split screen seeing that there are Americans in Baghdad," he told NBC. "The thing that surprises me is not that. What surprises me is that people are surprised.

"He's been lying like that for years—over and over—and the media carries it as though it's true. It's been happening a month ago, two months ago, three months ago. He's been lying exactly the same way. And yet it's been carried and transmitted across the globe as though it were true. It's only when people had split screens and could see it that they finally said: Oh, my goodness, this fellow lies. Isn't that amazing? There's gambling in the casino!"

Indeed, it was now abundantly clear that Bush's showdown with Saddam had left the American media's reputation in ruins. CNN had admitted covering up Saddam's brutality. NBC had been forced to fall on its sword for airing the blatantly anti-American reports of disgraced journalist Peter Arnett. The *Washington Post* had been caught playing politics with the Jessica Lynch story, publishing a gigantic falsehood that it stubbornly refused to correct. Jayson Blair had resigned from the *New York Times* after fabricating numerous stories about Lynch and other soldiers, while his boss, Howell Raines, had been roundly condemned for his antiwar bias. Even *New York* magazine had openly pined for the failure of Bush and the "rah-rah" embeds.

Yet the media's disastrous coverage of America's conflict with Iraq—itself an enormously compelling story with important societal implications—was virtually ignored by the press. Indeed, the press was the only major institution in America able to dodge such scrutiny. If four or five large corporations had peddled falsehoods and otherwise botched the execution of some high-profile business endeavor, the press would be screaming bloody murder about corporate scandal and corruption. If the White House, Pentagon, State Department and Homeland Security Department had flubbed an important policy initiative, the media would be apoplectic with stories about the sweeping failures and incompetence of the Bush Administration. If any major American institution had mindlessly repeated a colossal blunder in the space of just eighteen months, the press would have gone ballistic. Yet the media—an enormously powerful institution in its own right that largely shaped the American political agenda—decided to give itself a pass.

"Nobody got it quite right," shrugged Johnny Apple in the *New York Times.*

Least of all Apple himself, whose likening of Iraq to Vietnam was merely the first of his journalistic misfires. Three days after publishing his analogy, Apple accused the coalition of "gross military misjudgments" and warned that "the war could last so long that the American public loses patience." He had also predicted a protracted siege of Baghdad, which instead collapsed with only token resistance. But now, as usual, Apple was refusing to acknowledge that he had been wrong about the war. Instead, he tried disingenuously to spread the blame around with vague bromides like "nobody got it quite right." It was precisely the same dodge he had pulled after blowing the Afghanistan coverage.

Apple's behavior was typical of the press. Instead of pausing to engage in some constructive and much-needed soul-searching, reporters raced off to find the Next Big Thing in their tireless quest to disparage the Republican president. Not wishing to dwell on America's historic liberation of 25 million innocents, the press moved on to hyperventilate about something it considered more significant—sporadic episodes of petty looting in Baghdad.

"There's a lot of looting in Baghdad, and it appears that no one is in charge," wailed a reporter at the White House. "You didn't have anything planned for this," cried another. "This crisis of looting and just going—running amuck, the town running amuck—well, the country running amuck," stammered a third.

"This is almost starting to remind me of the stories that said our forces were 'bogged down,' " Fleischer sighed.

Unfazed, the press repeated its ridiculous question directly to Bush.

"Mr. President, some of our colleagues in Iraq are saying while the Iraqis are grateful that the coalition forces freed them from Saddam Hussein, they're frustrated and even scared about the chaos, the looting going on," a reporter on the South Lawn chided.

"You know, it's amazing," Bush marveled. "The statue comes down on Wednesday and the headlines start to read: Oh, there's disorder. Well, no kidding. It is a situation that is chaotic because Saddam Hussein created the conditions for chaos. He created conditions of fear and hatred. And it's going to take a while to stabilize the country.

"But just like the military campaign was second-guessed, I'm sure the plan is being second—but we will be successful. And there will be—"

The reporter tried to interrupt him, but Bush plowed on.

"Let me finish, please," he said. "There will be more stability; there will be more medicine; there will be more food delivered over time. And it's happening as I speak. Have you got a follow-up question?"

"I just want to ask what your message is to the Iraqi people," the reporter said.

"You're free—and freedom is beautiful," Bush replied. "And, you know, it'll take time to restore order out of chaos. But we will."

Unsatisfied, the press went after Rumsfeld at the Pentagon. "Television pictures are showing looting and other signs of lawlessness," Charlie Aldinger of Reuters said. "Are you, sir, concerned that what's being reported from the region as anarchy in Baghdad and other cities might wash away the goodwill the United States has built?"

"Your question," Rumsfeld replied, "suggests that, gee, maybe they were better off repressed."

He added: "The images you are seeing on television, you are seeing over and over and over. And it's the same picture of some person walking out of some building with a vase. And you see it twenty times, and you think: My goodness, were there that many vases? Is it possible that there were that many vases in the whole country?"

"Do you think that the words 'anarchy' and 'lawlessness' are ill-chosen?" a reporter challenged.

"Absolutely. I picked up a newspaper today and I couldn't believe it," Rumsfeld said. "I read eight headlines that talked about 'chaos,' 'violence,' 'unrest.' And it just was Henny Penny—the sky is falling. I've never seen anything like it!"

"Given how predictable the lack of law and order was," a reporter countered, "was there part of General Franks's plan to deal with it?"

"This is fascinating, this is just fascinating," Rumsfeld marveled. "Think what's happened in our cities when we've had riots, and problems, and looting. Stuff happens! But in terms of what's going on in that country, it is a fundamental misunderstanding to see those images—over and over and over again—of some boy walking out with a vase and say, 'Oh, my goodness, you didn't have a plan.' That's nonsense."

So this was Rumsfeld's reward for disproving the media naysayers with a three-week war now he was being blamed for the celebratory looting in Baghdad. It was downright maddening.

"For suddenly the biggest problem in the world to be looting is really notable," he said in exasperation. "And here is a country that's being liberated, here are people who are going from being repressed and held under the thumb of a vicious dictator, and they're free."

"If a foreign military force came into your neighborhood and did away with the police, and left you at the mercy of criminals, how long would you feel liberated?" demanded a reporter.

"But we haven't gone in and done away with any police," Rumsfeld protested. "In fact, we're looking for police in those villages and towns who can, in fact, assist in providing order."

He went on to explain that he and other Pentagon officials were in discussions with various nations about providing international police units for Iraq.

"Is this something that could have been lined up in advance?" a reporter said.

"We have a number of countries lined up already," Rumsfeld explained. "Already a number of countries have things moving into the country."

"You couldn't have done it any faster?" a journalist demanded.

"That's wonderful," Rumsfeld said sardonically. "Are we in a 'quagmire'? Huh? Is that where we are? Come on!"

12
FLY BOY

PRESIDENT BUSH WAS FULLY dressed when he jumped into the swimming pool outside the Oval Office. He landed in the deep end and began treading water as he struggled to remove a harness that had been diabolically fastened around his torso. Beneath the harness was a naval aviator's flight suit, which grew heavy as it soaked up water, although Bush was not allowed to touch the bottom of the eight-foot pool. That would have meant flunking this training session for the president's planned flight to an aircraft carrier at sea.

"You have to have a water rescue exercise, so we go out here in the pool and we put on our flight suits," Bush told me. "Jumped in and practiced chute release."

Also jumping in was White House Chief of Staff Andy Card, clad in an identical get-up. Since he would be accompanying his boss to the aircraft carrier, Card had to go through the same training.

"He did not want to cheat the system at all," he said of Bush. "So what everybody else had to go through, he wanted to have to go through."

Bush and Card soon encountered a few unexpected difficulties that had been cooked up by the naval trainers standing at the edge of the pool.

"They told us how to release the harness, but they always rig it for something to go wrong," Card explained. "So something goes wrong and you have to figure out what to do to get out of the harness."

At length, Bush and Card managed to disentangle themselves without drowning. After practicing the drill a couple of times, the men were cleared for the next phase of training, which would take place in San Diego on May 1. That was the day of their scheduled flight to the USS *Abraham Lincoln*, which was steaming across the Pacific after a nine-month stint in the Persian Gulf—the longest deployment of an aircraft carrier since Vietnam.

Now that Saddam's regime had been toppled, the president wanted to express his gratitude to the troops for a job well done. Although he was painfully aware that difficult and dangerous fighting would continue for the foreseeable future, Bush though it was important to mark the end of major combat operations. Iraq had been liberated, and the commander in chief wanted to personally thank those who had done the liberating.

The *Lincoln* seemed an ideal choice for the presidential visit. The carrier had departed for the Persian Gulf back on July 20, even before Bush began making his case for war. By the end of the year, having completed its scheduled deployment, it departed the Gulf.

"We thought we were headed home," recalled Commander John "Skip" Lussier, one of 8,000 sailors in the *Lincoln* battle group. "But we got turned around on New Year's Day."

With war increasingly likely, the *Lincoln* was ordered back to the Gulf, which left its sailors unsettled.

"At that point we were still unsure whether the president was going to be able, politically, to get the United Nations and coalition and everybody behind him," Lussier told me. "We were wondering if the timeline was just going to continue to get to pushed down the road and we were going to go back and spin our wheels for another three or four months and not make any lasting contribution.

"But as it turned out, as soon as we entered the Persian Gulf on the eleventh of February, we were on a war footing," he added. "We ended up participating heavily in the major combat operations."

Indeed, from the opening salvo of Operation Iraqi Freedom on March 19, warplanes from the *Lincoln* rained destruction all across Iraq. The high performance strike fighter jets—F-14s and F-18s—burned up tremendous amounts of fuel during the nine hundred-mile round trip from the ship to Baghdad, where they dropped a total of six hundred tons of bombs on precise targets. Sometimes the jets lingered over the battlefield to provide support for ground troops, further depleting their fuel tanks. So they had to be refueled in midair by S-3B Viking jets, a squadron of which was headed by Lussier, a navy pilot.

"We would drag a bunch of strike fighters over country—probably a hundred miles into Iraq—and top them off, make sure they'd be as full of gas as possible," Lussier said. "Then they would press on to Baghdad and release their weapons. Meanwhile, we would have gone back to the ship, refueled and launched again. We picked them up on the Kuwaiti border, topped them off one more time and brought them back to the ship."

The day after Baghdad fell, the *Lincoln* set sail for home. On April 25 it made a pit stop at Pearl Harbor, where the commander of the U.S. Pacific Fleet, Admiral Walter Doran, gave a speech thanking the sailors for their long months of service. Remarkably, no one from the *Lincoln* had been killed during the deployment, the longest ever by a nuclear-powered carrier.

"And I've got a special announcement for you," Doran said. "The president is going to come out and give a speech on your ship."

A cheer went up in the hangar bay where the sailors had gathered. "And he's coming out in an S-3," the admiral added.

Lussier was stunned.

"Hey, did you know about that?" he asked his superior officer.

"No, I didn't," replied the boss, who did not fly S-3 Vikings. "I wonder who the pilot is?"

Lussier suddenly realized that as senior pilot of the Viking squadron, he would be the only logical choice to ferry the president onto the *Lincoln*.

"It's going to be me," he said. "Oh crap!" He added sardonically: "No pressure."

Sure enough, Lussier was pulled aside and told he would be piloting the president. Instead of continuing his journey home on the *Lincoln,* Lussier flew directly from Hawaii to San Diego. The navy's risk management people wanted the pilot to be reunited with his wife and daughters, aged ten and six, as soon as possible. They figured it would be better for Lussier to get any emotional reunion behind him so he could concentrate on preparing for the president's arrival.

"My family was in shock," Lussier told me. "But I couldn't tell them why I was coming home."

For the next several days, the pilot was grilled by a variety of White House officials, including Deputy Chief of Staff Joe Hagin, who had cooked up the idea of the presidential landing in the first place. Having witnessed business executives and other powerful people freeze up around Bush, Hagin wanted to size up the man who would have the president's life in his hands. The White House was already being pressured to have Bush flown by various naval officers more senior than Commander Lussier, perhaps someone not even from the *Lincoln*. But that idea was scrapped once Hagin looked Lussier in the eye and concluded he was up to the job.

"The first time I got nervous was when I woke up about four

o'clock in the morning on the day of the flight," Lussier told me. "I turned the television on and the media frenzy's just getting started.

"The commentator that I saw said: 'Well, the president's flying off to the ship today and I don't know who he's flying with, but God, I'd be nervous if I was him. And what if he crashes?'" Lussier recalled. "At that point, I turned the television right off."

Indeed, the press was fascinated by the historic event. No sitting president had ever landed on a moving aircraft carrier. Although Bush had been a pilot in the Texas Air National Guard, he hadn't flown a plane in thirty years. Asked by a reporter whether he would attempt to actually pilot the Viking, Bush remained coy.

"Never can tell what's going to kick in—the urge," he remarked mischievously.

"I make no guarantees about whether he will or will not take the joystick for any portion of the flight," White House Press Secretary Ari Fleischer told reporters on the way to San Diego. "If you see the plane flying on a straight line, you'll know that the Navy pilot is in charge. If it does anything else, it's an open question."

Although landing a plane on a moving aircraft carrier is always dangerous, it is considered even more dangerous to land a helicopter. That's because a heavy wind or heaving flight deck can cause a chopper's wheel or strut to slip off the edge, dooming its occupants, who are unable to eject. By contrast, if a plane's tailhook misses the wires stretched across the flight deck, it can usually fly right off the other end and circle around for a second landing attempt. Even if the plane begins to fall into the sea, its occupants typically have enough time to eject safely. Moreover, when the president's visit was initially planned, the *Lincoln* was expected to be so far out at sea as to be out of range to Marine One, Bush's helicopter.

Still, the White House found itself assuring reporters that Bush was not playing the role of daredevil.

"If it wasn't safe, the president of the United States would not be doing it," Fleischer said. "And I remind you it's done every day, many times a day, by navy pilots whose mission is to fly on an aircraft carrier."

But not all such landings were successful. Just one month earlier, a Viking skidded off the deck of the USS *Constellation*. The two pilots were rescued and the navy was investigating the cause of the mishap.

All these things were on Lussier's mind as he waited for Bush to arrive at Naval Air Station on North Island in the San Diego Bay.

"The other time I got nervous is when Air Force One pulls up, because that's just an amazing sight," he told me. "It pulls up right in front and the door opens and the president gets out."

Lussier's copilot nudged him and said: "Guess there's no backing out now."

"Nope," said Lussier, swallowing hard.

"Where's my pilot?" Bush demanded.

After shaking hands with Lussier and the rest of the crew, the president went into a changing room to put on his flight suit. Then he began the final phase of his training—the ejector seat drill. In the event that anything went wrong during the flight, Bush would have to reach down between his legs and pull an ejector handle from beneath his seat. That would activate a rocket motor that would explode him out of the plane with a force twenty-two times greater than gravity. Since twenty-two Gs can cause severe injuries, the president was told to align his spine with the back of his seat. He was also told to keep his head back, chin up, and feet flat. Both he and his seat would be propelled upward along rails built into the airplane's frame. At the precise moment of ejection, a detonator cord would be activated in the glass canopy above him.

"The explosion shatters the glass and then the seat itself is designed to kind of carve a hole out of the glass as you're going through it," Lussier explained. "There's a metal piece that protrudes over the occupant's head so that as you're going up the rails, it sort of clears out the path of the shattered glass so that you don't get injured from that."

As soon as the president would clear the canopy, another rocket motor—known as an "ear burner" because of its placement behind the occupant's head—would activate, exploding the seat away from Bush. Finally, something called a "ballistic spreader gun" would inflate the president's parachute.

"When it works, which it does ninety-nine percent of the time," Lussier told me, "within four seconds of leaving the airplane, you're swinging in your chute."

The president did not appear fazed by these harrowing possibilities. "How to strap in and eject," he shrugged, recalling the conversation later. "I had had enough flight experience that it wasn't a foreign thought to me."

Nonetheless, Lussier tried to impress on Bush the safety ramifications of what they were about to attempt.

"You know, Mr. President, there's some danger inherent in carrier naval aviation," he intoned. "And 99.9 percent of the time everything goes really smoothly. But there's always that .1 percent chance that something could happen."

"Luce, you don't need to worry about that," Bush replied. "We've got a great vice president."

Lussier appreciated the levity. "You know, the president understood the magnitude of what was going on, but he did absolutely everything he could to make the event as lighthearted as possible," the pilot said. "He's just so down to earth. It came across very quickly that he's just another person who's gonna go flying with us."

When the training session ended, Bush walked out to the Viking, a four-seat airplane that was parked beak-to-beak with Air Force One on the flight line. He noticed a group of sailors and family members gathered behind a fence.

"Hey, who are those people?" the president asked.

Lussier had been warned by the White House advance people not to point out any friends or family on the flight line, because Bush would want to go over and meet them, thereby wreaking havoc with the president's carefully scripted schedule.

"Those are people in our squadron," said Lussier's copilot.

"I want to meet them," Bush said.

Lussier, whose wife was in the crowd, couldn't believe it. "He walks right over and shakes their hands, poses for pictures," he said. "It made their day. It made their lives, actually."

Afterward, Bush walked over to the Viking, climbed up through the crew door and strapped himself into the right front seat. The plane's copilot sat behind Bush.

Meanwhile, on the left side of the plane, Lussier sat in front as a Secret Service agent named Eddie tried to settle in behind him. But the agent was wearing so much gear under his flight suit, including weapons and battery packs, that it was difficult to connect him to the ejection seat fittings.

"I don't think he was very comfortable," Lussier said. "We had to almost stand on him to get him connected."

Since it was important for Bush to always keep an open line of communication with the National Military Command Center in a bunker beneath the Pentagon, Lussier went through the necessary communication protocols.

"Navy One, this is NMCC—radio check," crackled a voice over the radio.

Thus did Skip Lussier's Navy S-3 Viking become the first aircraft in history to be designated "Navy One." For decades, the term "Air Force One" was used whenever a president stepped aboard a plane operated by the Air Force, just as "Marine One" was used whenever a president boarded a helicopter operated by the U.S. Marine Corps. But since no sitting president had ever flown on a navy plane, the term

"Navy One" had never been used. Mindful of the historic significance of the occasion, someone had actually spelled out "NAVY 1" in black characters on the gray fuselage of the Viking that was now taxiing down the runway.

"Navy One for takeoff," said Lussier. For once in his life, he noticed, he didn't have to wait for clearance.

As soon as the plane was airborne, Lussier also noticed that the president's radio was cutting out. So he reached over and pushed in a two-pronged jack that had come loose at the end of Bush's communications wire.

Meanwhile, Eddie piped up from the back seat.

"You're not gonna let the president fly the airplane, right?" he asked Lussier.

"Oh no," Lussier assured him. "No way."

But then, after achieving the desired altitude, Lussier turned to Bush.

"Mr. President," he said. "You want the jet?"

"Yes," the commander in chief grinned. "I do."

With that, George W. Bush become the first sitting president of the United States to pilot an aircraft. He took the stick and assumed control of the jet, which was hurtling over the Pacific at more than four hundred miles per hour. And there was nothing poor Eddie could do about it. The president wasted no time in pressing his advantage over the helpless agent, whose harness was so constructing that he might as well have been wearing a straitjacket.

"All right, Eddie, I've got the controls," Bush taunted. "Don't get nervous."

As Lussier recalled, the president "shakes the airplane around like he doesn't know what he's doing—on purpose."

When Eddie refused to rise to the bait, Bush went a bit further.

"Oh, Eddie, I'm a little off altitude," he said.

The president pushed the stick forward and the plane rapidly dropped three hundred feet.

"We kind of rise up in our seats a little bit," Lussier said. "I mean, he was just yanking the Secret Service agent's chain because I think for the first time he had the upper hand."

Bush was clearly enjoying himself.

"Hey, this flies a lot like an F-102," he said, referring to the jet fighters he had flown in the National Guard.

Lussier's jet was followed by a second Viking containing Card, two pilots and the president's military aide, who carried the nuclear "football"—a briefcase containing codes Bush would need to launch a nuclear attack.

"Hey, Mr. President, you want to fly a little form?" Lussier asked. This was pilot-speak for flying in formation, with one plane very close to another.

"Sure," Bush said. "What do you look at?"

Lussier explained the various visual reference points Bush should watch as they dropped back to let Card's plane take the lead position. Then Bush maneuvered Navy One into the wing position. This meant the tips of the two planes were only five yards apart. One slip of the joystick could have sent them crashing together.

While Bush had enough pilot experience to minimize the chances of such a mistake, Card had now taken the stick of his own plane.

"I have no aviation background—I'm an engineer by training," he told me. "I served in the navy but it was only on college campuses." And yet now Card was flying a highly specialized warplane just fifteen feet from the president, who was also controlling his own plane. The aging flyboys looked through their windows at each other and flashed each other the thumbs-up sign.

"Hey, this is great!" Bush said.

But the president was unable to hold his position that close, and began to drift away.

"It had been awhile," he told me. "I had obviously lost the touch, because we were flying in formation and I was the wing man. And the next thing I know, there's quite a bit of blue sky between the wing man and the lead.

"But it still felt pretty good," he added. "I still had a sense of the stick and the throttle and how to climb in, stay close in. But it was a neat feeling. I enjoyed doing it."

The *Lincoln* had made better time than expected and was now much closer to shore than the White House had originally planned. As a result, the flight only took about thirty minutes, half of which was spent with Bush at the controls. But as Navy One approached the *Lincoln,* Lussier retook the stick and double-checked the president's fittings.

"I wanted to make sure his harness was locked, because if he didn't have it locked his head would have hit the joystick in front of him and he wouldn't have looked too good for the speech that night," Lussier said. "The president with a fat lip would not have looked good on national television."

Card also relinquished control as his own plane neared the ship. His pilot broke into a sharp, 90-degree bank that served to slow the plane down in preparation for landing. The pilot was unusually close to the ship's bow when he executed this maneuver—considered macho in the world of carrier aviation, because it gave a pilot less room to straighten out the plane for the final approach. A cheer went up from the flight deck at this bit of showmanship. The White House aides and journalists on deck were bewildered by the sailors' reaction.

Since Lussier was ferrying the president, he opted not to match the stunt. But he did throttle up to top speed, about 460 miles per hour, and fly low over the 4.5-acre flight deck to give Bush an eyeful of the reception that awaited him. Hundreds of sailors, some dressed in brightly colored jumpsuits to signify their particular jobs on the flight line, had their eyes pinned on Navy One.

"Navy One, Viking ball, 7-point-0," Bush said into the radio. This was his way of telling the ship's control tower that the Viking had made visual contact with the "meatball," a device on the ship with a mirrored lens that projected the plane's glide slope. The term "7-point-0" signified that Navy One had 7,000 pounds of fuel.

Lussier took the plane into a sharp bank, which subjected its occupants to three Gs, and flattened out for the final approach. He lowered the plane's tailhook and aimed for the third of four wires stretched out across the flight deck, each about thirty-five feet apart. A group of F-18 pilots—among the most competitive people in the world—dropped into a collective crouch like baseball umpires to scrutinize the precise point of touchdown. They let out a collective "Ooooooh!" as Navy One came in a little too flat and missed the third wire.

But Lussier snagged the fourth and final wire, and throttled back up to full power as part of his standard safety protocol. That way, if the wire failed to halt the plane, he could simply continue flying off the end of the ship and circle around for another attempt at landing. But the wire held, functioning as a sort of bungee cord that snapped Navy One to a lurching stop as Lussier cut the engine.

"I was very glad we stopped," the pilot told me. "If I hadn't trapped on the first pass, it would have been rather professionally embarrassing. As some of my friends put it, I would have been the Gus Grissom of Naval aviation." Unlike Grissom, the Mercury astronaut who nearly drowned when his space capsule sank upon splashdown, Lussier now sat safely in Navy One and savored the moment.

"Mr. President, thank you for coming out to the ship—this is just a remarkable morale boosting event," he said. "And thank you for bringing grace and dignity back to the White House."

Bush thanked Lussier for landing him safely and then decided to abandon the script that his handlers had prepared.

"The White House did not want to have a Michael Dukakis-in-a-tank-helmet kind of thing, so they wanted him to get out of his flight gear," Lussier said. "But he was so natural in it and he looked so good in it, that he goes: 'You know what? I'm gonna keep this stuff on.'"

Bush climbed out of the plane, pulled off his helmet and grinned from ear to ear. He then plunged into the throng of F-18 pilots, shaking hands and slapping backs for all he was worth. Sailors pressed in from all sides, slinging their arms around the presidential flyboy, who posed for pictures and cracked jokes like just another Top Gun.

"Son, you're on national television," he told Lussier, prompting laughter from the pilot.

Such presidential joshing triggered a spontaneous outpouring of adulation from the weary sailors, who had been away from home so long that they missed the births of 150 of their children. They had steamed 100,000 miles, won a war, and liberated a nation. And now, to cap it all off, they were kidding around with the commander in chief himself.

"It was a joyous moment," Bush told me. "They were just so pleased to see the president. These are sailors who were coming back from a battle. They had been deployed for months. They were anxious to get home, and here comes the commander in chief flying in one of their fighters to greet them, and they were thrilled."

Although Bush was scheduled to spend just five minutes on the flight deck, he ended up lingering for more than half an hour. There were just too many sailors who wanted their pictures taken with the president. The images of Bush strutting around in his flight suit electrified the world. Even the normally jaded media was gushing about the audacious feat of derring-do.

This triggered grumbling among Democrats, who dismissed the landing as an expensive photo opportunity that would show up in TV ads for the president's reelection campaign.

"The president is going to an aircraft carrier far out at sea with military surroundings, while countless numbers of Americans are frightened stiff about the economy here at home," groused John Kerry. He later mocked Bush for "playing dress up."

Still, the day belonged to the president, who went below for a dinner with enlisted sailors and then changed into a suit and tie. He later returned to the flight deck of the *Lincoln*—which had been commissioned in 1989 by Defense Secretary Dick Cheney—to give a major address to the nation.

"My fellow Americans: Major combat operations in Iraq have ended. In the battle of Iraq, the United States and our allies have prevailed," he began under a picture-perfect sky. "The tyrant has fallen, and Iraq is free."

Bush felt strongly that freedom was a gift from God, not governments, and that it was divinely bequeathed to all people, not just those who lived in places like America. To him, the toppling of Saddam Hussein was merely the restoration of the order God always intended.

"Decades of lies and intimidation could not make the Iraqi people love their oppressors or desire their own enslavement. Men and women in every culture need liberty like they need food and water and air. Everywhere that freedom arrives, humanity rejoices. And everywhere that freedom stirs, let tyrants fear."

The president was also careful to place Operation Iraqi Freedom in historical context.

"The battle of Iraq is one victory in a war on terror that began on September the 11th, 2001, and still goes on. That terrible morning, nineteen evil men—the shock troops of a hateful ideology—gave America and the civilized world a glimpse of their ambitions. They imagined, in the words of one terrorist, that September the 11th would be the 'beginning of the end of America.' By seeking to turn our cities into killing fields, terrorists and their allies believed that they could destroy this nation's resolve, and force our retreat from the world. They have failed."

Bush went out of his way to emphasize that U.S. forces were by no means out of the woods. Although the carrier's tower was festooned with a banner proclaiming "Mission Accomplished," the president took pains to point out that "our mission continues."

"We have difficult work to do in Iraq. We're bringing order to parts of that country that remain dangerous. We're pursuing and finding leaders of the old regime, who will be held to account for their crimes. We've begun the search for hidden chemical and biological weapons and already know of hundreds of sites that will be investigated."

Still, Bush maintained a hopeful tone.

"The war on terror is not over; yet it is not endless. We do not know the day of final victory, but we have seen the turning of the tide. No act of the terrorists will change our purpose, or weaken our resolve, or alter their fate. Their cause is lost. Free nations will press on to victory."

The president closed his speech by paying homage to American GIs who had died.

"Their final act on this Earth was to fight a great evil and bring liberty to others. All of you—all in this generation of our military—have taken up the highest calling of history. You're defending your country, and protecting the innocent from harm. And wherever you go, you carry a message of hope—a message that is ancient and ever new."

Bush summed up this message by quoting the prophet Isaiah.

"To the captives: 'Come out.' And to those in darkness: 'Be free.'"

13

"A LONG, HARD SLOG"

LESS THAN SIX MONTHS after journalists hailed the *Lincoln* landing as an unqualified presidential triumph that would undoubtedly show up in Bush's reelection ads, they were deriding it as an embarrassing blunder that would be used against him in Democratic ads. To the administration's horror, the Left transmogrified the event into an act of presidential hubris that symbolized everything that was going wrong in postwar Iraq. And plenty of things were going wrong in postwar Iraq.

"Mr. President, if I may take you back to May 1st when you stood on the USS *Lincoln* under a huge banner that said, 'Mission Accomplished,'" began NBC reporter Norah O'Donnell in a Rose Garden press conference on October 28. "At that time you declared major combat operations were over.

"But since that time there have been over one thousand wounded—many of them amputees who are recovering at Walter Reed," she added. "Two hundred and seventeen killed in action since that date.

Will you acknowledge now that you were premature in making those remarks?"

"Norah, I think you ought to look at my speech," Bush replied. "I said Iraq is a dangerous place and we've still got hard work to do, there's still more to be done. And we had just come off a very successful military operation. I was there to thank the troops.

"The 'Mission Accomplished' sign, of course, was put up by the members of the USS *Abraham Lincoln,* saying that their mission was accomplished," he added. "I know it was attributed somehow to some ingenious advance man from my staff. They weren't that ingenious."

Actually, they were. The banner had indeed been produced by the White House advance team at the request of the sailors. When journalists discovered this fact after the press conference, they turned their wrath on White House Press Secretary Ari Fleischer's successor, Scott McClellan, who backpedaled furiously. It was one of many postwar missteps by an administration that had been so surefooted during the war itself.

"For a while the news was pretty grim," Bush told me.

Indeed, by the summer of 2003 GIs were dying on a daily basis as they struggled to establish order. Remnants of Saddam's regime routinely ambushed U.S. forces with rocket-propelled grenades and small arms fire. Guerillas planted roadside bombs that were detonated as U.S. convoys drove past. Militants from half a dozen Muslim nations streamed into Iraq to kill Westerners in the name of jihad. One American soldier was shot in back of the head at point blank range after buying a soda at Baghdad University. His lifeless body crumpled to the ground as the killer melted into a crowd of stunned students.

"We weren't certain about what kind of resistance there would be," the president told me. "And the truth of the matter is, for awhile the Baathists were intent upon trying to run us out. They transferred their war of direct confrontation to going back to the neighborhoods and coming out and killing when they felt like it. And that was a difficult period, there's no question about it."

Rice was deeply perplexed by the predicament of U.S. forces. "They'd won the war," she said. "Now it was a civil order problem."

That meant replacing tanks, which had worked so well during major combat operations, with lightly armored Humvees that patrolled the streets amid shadowy insurgents. These new patrols became perfect targets for Saddam's "dead-enders."

"It took a little time to restructure our military forces from the forces that had gone in to fight the war, to the kind of forces that you need for law and order," Rice said. "And so you had a period of time which was admittedly very rough."

The administration was also unprepared for one of Saddam's final dastardly acts in office. "He released a hundred thousand criminals," she said. "They went back to doing what criminals do."

The chaos and lawlessness were compounded by the collapse of Iraq's fragile infrastructure, which had deteriorated to a shocking degree during the final years of Saddam's rule.

"No one fully understood how Saddam Hussein, himself, had destroyed the infrastructure of the country," Bush told me. "We had a lot of plans and we had a lot of strategies. But like anything, you really don't know until you're there on the ground."

Adjusting to this unexpected reality proved exasperating.

"We did underestimate the infrastructure deterioration— seriously," Rice said. "In these closed societies, it's hard to tell what's going on.

"Just to give you an example, nobody knew the way that Saddam was keeping Baghdad lit up. If you looked at Baghdad at night, it looked like a brilliant European city. He had a power grid that was only capable of supplying 50 percent of the power to the whole country, but it was all going to Baghdad. The rest of the country had virtually no power supply.

"So when we get in and try to even it out, all of a sudden lights are going off in Baghdad. And you realize the problem is you don't actually have enough power-generating capability. Nobody knew that from inside."

Meanwhile, the man Bush appointed as Iraq's civil administrator—retired Army Lieutenant General Jay Garner—had trouble establishing even rudimentary governmental functions.

"We underestimated the degree to which the institutions and structures would crater," Rice said. "They were really brittle."

Garner devised a plan to remove Baathists from top positions in government ministries and replace them with ordinary civil servants. But "the thing just fell apart instead," Rice said. "They just didn't know what they were doing. Or I think they were just traumatized. A lot of people just didn't show up. Trying to find the Iraqi oil workers was hard. It didn't hold. The structures didn't hold."

Garner was quickly replaced by former State Department official Paul Bremer, who vowed to step up reconstruction efforts. But even when progress was accomplished, it was often undone by insurgents, who bombed oil and water pipelines, causing shortages and riots. The frustration began to show at the White House. At a press briefing on July 1, Fleischer bristled when a reporter asked: "Doesn't it seem that we are ill-prepared to deal with postwar Iraq?"

"You're ignoring the tremendous number of success stories that have taken place inside Iraq," Fleischer shot back. "This is one of these cases where if the glass of milk is nine-tenths full, you'll only see the one-tenth that is empty."

"Success stories?" a reporter said. "You got any?"

"Well, you just haven't aired them, but there are many," the spokesman replied.

He went on to outline the allies' success at setting up a health care system, immunization programs, electrical service and food distribution.

"I see your eyes are glazing over—this is my point," Fleischer chided the press. "When the news is good, it's not something that you pay much attention to."

He added: "Why would anybody think—after all the decades that Saddam Hussein had to build up the hate and the destruction in that country, and how many loyalists he had dedicated to helping him carry out the murders and the torture that he had in that country—that in a mere two months Iraq would look like the United States? It's not the way it works."

Polls showed that while most Americans believed the war had been worthwhile, the size of the majority was beginning to shrink in response to the daily drumbeat of negative news from Iraq.

"The president is not going to make decisions about what to do in Iraq by the polls," Fleischer said. "Polls are volatile; they move. Principles don't, and the president is dedicated to the principle of helping the Iraqi people to have a stable country because that's in America's interest."

He added: "After all, what's the alternative, to let the thugs who ran Iraq before take it over again? No."

Still, the spokesman acknowledged the problems in Iraq were far from over.

"Like the Cold War, it is not something that just goes away quietly overnight," he said. "It is something that will remain a front-and-center issue that will engage the American people and this president—and likely successors to this president."

Rejecting the Cold War analogy, Congressional Democrats clung instead to their old standby. "We can't get bogged down in a quagmire like in Vietnam," warned Representative Eliot Engel of New York, a Democratic member of the House International Relations Committee.

Liberals complained that U.S. forces had failed to uncover weapons of mass destruction, the main reason for invading Iraq in the first place. One of the most outspoken critics was retired diplomat Joseph Wilson, who charged in the *New York Times* on July 6 that "the intelligence related to Iraq's nuclear weapons program was twisted to exaggerate the Iraqi threat."

As evidence, Wilson cited a little-noticed line in the president's State of the Union address back in January. "The British government has learned that Saddam Hussein recently sought significant quantities of uranium from Africa," Bush had said during a lengthy discussion of evidence against Saddam.

Wilson revealed that he had traveled to Niger in February 2002, at the request of the CIA, to look for evidence that Iraq had tried to purchase uranium. "I spent the next eight days drinking sweet mint tea and meeting with dozens of people," he wrote. "Niger formally denied the charges."

The column prompted a rare retraction from the White House. During a presidential tour of Africa in early July, Fleischer told reporters the uranium allegation "was wrong" and "should not have risen to the level of a presidential speech."

But later that day, Bush himself shrugged off the controversy about whether Saddam had tried to buy uranium. "One thing is for certain: He's not trying to buy anything right now," the president said in a news conference in South Africa.

The issue was further confused by Powell and Rice, who were traveling with Bush throughout Africa. Powell told reporters that he had not felt the uranium assertion was strong enough to include it in his own presentation to the U.N. just days after the State of the Union. On the other hand, Rice pointed out that the claim might have been true after all.

"We don't say it's false," she said. "And I heartily object to headlines that say it was false, because nobody has still said that this was false."

Yet Fleischer had said it was "wrong," which merely fueled the impression that the administration's legendary "message discipline" was crumbling. Democrats seized on Wilson's charge because it struck at the very heart of Bush's political strength—his veracity. Presidential hopeful John Kerry challenged Bush to "tell the truth" and admit that the United States was losing control in Iraq.

Until now, Democrats had been reluctant to openly criticize the president's swift and decisive removal of Saddam's regime, which most Americans supported. But the postwar security and infrastructure problems, coupled with new questions about Bush's truthfulness, emboldened Democrats to pillory administration officials.

"It's the first time we've seen them sweat," Jennifer Palmieri, spokeswoman for presidential hopeful Senator John Edwards, marveled to the *New York Times.* "It's the first time anything has ever stuck."

The press gave the story legs by deliberately characterizing Wilson as nonpartisan. Reporters pointed out that he had been the U.S. charge d'affaires in Baghdad under the elder President Bush, and that he was the last U.S. official to meet with Saddam, having sat down with the dictator four days after he invaded Kuwait in 1990.

But Wilson had also worked for President Clinton, and now he was rooting for Kerry to beat Bush. The antiwar Democrat openly railed against Bush's "imperial ambitions" in the stridently liberal magazine *The Nation.*

On July 14, conservative columnist Robert Novak explained how the administration had unwittingly sent a political enemy to investigate the uranium claim. "Wilson never worked for the CIA, but his wife, Valerie Plame, is an Agency operative on weapons of mass destruction," Novak wrote. "Two senior administration officials told me Wilson's wife suggested sending him to Niger to investigate."

Wilson complained that the column blew his wife's CIA cover, and publicly blamed the leak on White House political strategist Karl Rove, although he offered no evidence to support this accusation.

"It's of keen interest to me to see whether or not we can get Karl Rove frog-marched out of the White House in handcuffs," Wilson told an audience in Seattle. "And trust me, when I use that name, I measure my words."

But Wilson later backpedaled from his accusation, explaining that he mentioned Mr. Rove as "kind of a metaphor for the White House." Still, he added: "I have every confidence that Karl Rove condoned it and did nothing to shut this off."

Nor did Wilson do anything to shut off ongoing press speculation that Rove had leaked the name of Wilson's wife. Soon the Justice Department was asked to conduct a full-blown investigation. The FBI subpoenaed White House aides to testify before a grand jury about their conversations with journalists. An administration that had been remarkably free of scandal for nearly three years was suddenly saddled with "Leak-Gate," which Democrats portrayed as yet more evidence of Bush's incompetence.

"This president can't find Saddam Hussein. He can't find Osama bin Laden. He can't even find the leaker in the White House," Kerry thundered.

Bush was not the only world leader to be accused of overstating the case for war. British Prime Minister Tony Blair was savaged by the BBC for publishing a prewar intelligence dossier that claimed Saddam could deploy weapons of mass destruction within 45 minutes.

Quoting an unnamed "British official," radio reporter Andrew Gilligan told anchor John Humphrys that Blair's claim "was transformed in the week before it was published to make it sexier." Later in the broadcast, Humphrys grilled Britain's armed forces minister about whether the claim had indeed been "sexed up."

Blair's spokesman denounced the BBC report as a "lie," and demanded an apology from the publicly financed broadcaster, which refused. Gilligan's source turned out to be Dr. David Kelly of the British Defense Ministry, although the former U.N. weapons inspector made clear that Gilligan did some "sexing up" of his own with their conversation. When the BBC refused to back down from its report, Kelly committed suicide. A senior law lord named Brian Hutton began a wide-ranging investigation into the burgeoning scandal as Blair rejected media suggestions that he resign.

"I predicted before the war that Iraq would be the political death of Tony Blair," Galloway gloated in a column for the *Guardian* on July 14.

Yet Iraq proved to be the political death of Galloway, not Blair. The backbencher from Scotland was expelled by the Labour Party for his wartime interview with Abu Dhabi TV. The party found him guilty of inciting Arabs to fight British troops and inciting British troops to defy orders, among other offenses.

And that was only the beginning of Galloway's troubles. Two newspapers, citing documents found in postwar Iraq, accused him of having profited from the Iraqi regime. When Galloway insisted the documents were forgeries, one of the papers, the *Christian Science Monitor,* agreed that the documents were forgeries and retracted its story. But the other, the London *Telegraph,* stood firm, prompting Galloway to sue for libel. That suit was pending as of this writing.

On July 22, when U.S. forces killed Saddam's only sons, Uday and Qusay, in a hellacious firefight after the men refused to surrender. The dictator's progeny had been personally responsible for many of the hundreds of thousands of murdered Iraqis that coalition forces were now finding in scores of mass graves. Uday and Qusay's bullet-riddled bodies were cleaned up and put on public display to convince ordinary Iraqis they no longer had to fear these sadistic monsters. At long last, there were signs of hope in Iraq.

"A lot of good things happened in that period of time," Rice told me. "The oil infrastructure started to work again. But the biggest thing is that the place didn't break down into sectarian violence. My worst nightmare was that you were going to have huge retribution of Shia against Sunnis and so forth—blood baths. And so it gave you a chance."

Bush had plenty of nightmares of his own that never came true.

"Going in, we had planned for migration movements of people," he told me. "We had planned for sectarian violence; we had planned for the destruction of oil fields; we had planned for food shortages— none of which occurred."

In fact, the biggest challenges in postwar Iraq during May, June, and July entailed salvaging the country's infrastructure, not securing the peace. But as July gave way to August, and the average high temperature in Baghdad rose to 113 degrees, the violence intensified.

"It's ironic because the reconstruction effort gets on its feet," Rice said, "but the security situation then deteriorated."

Insurgents blew up innocent Iraqis at a Najaf mosque, a Baghdad police station, the Jordanian embassy, and even U.N. headquarters. These unpredictable acts of violence alarmed and bewildered U.S. forces. America's resolve was being sorely tested "during the very difficult period of the fall, when troops were dying and attacks were happening," Bush told me.

In September, he asked Congress to allocate $87 billion for reconstruction and security in Iraq and Afghanistan. Although he wanted the Iraqi funds distributed as a grant, some Democrats demanded that it be structured as a loan to be repaid with proceeds from Iraqi oil sales. Bush couldn't believe it. Having been savaged for more than a year by Democrats who accused him of wanting to wage "war for oil," some of those same Democrats were now demanding that he essentially take that oil to pay off the costs of the reconstruction. This towering act of hypocrisy was virtually ignored by the establishment press—in part, perhaps, because reporters were too busy covering another outrageous development: Senator Edward Kennedy was accusing Bush of bribery, a charge first leveled before the war by John Kerry, the other Democratic senator from Massachusetts.

"My belief is this money is being shuffled all around to these political leaders in all parts of the world, bribing them to send in troops," Kennedy told the Associated Press. He added that Bush officials had rationalized the war with "distortion, misrepresentation, a selection of intelligence." Although Bush had never described Iraq as an "imminent threat," Kennedy implied he had done so, and accused the president of willfully misleading the American public.

"There was no imminent threat," Kennedy said. "This was made up in Texas, announced in January to the Republican leadership that war was going to take place and was going to be good politically. This whole thing was a fraud."

Bush later told Brit Hume of Fox News Channel that Kennedy "should not have said we were trying to bribe foreign nations."

"I don't mind people trying to pick apart my policies, and that's fine and that's fair game," he said. "But, you know, I don't think we're serving our nation well by allowing the discourse to become so uncivil that people use words that they shouldn't be using."

Meanwhile, even the irrepressible Rumsfeld began to wonder whether "we are winning or losing the global war on terror," according to a memo he sent to his top advisers in October. While he predicted eventual success in Iraq, he acknowledged: "It it will be a long, hard slog."

The memo was leaked to *USA Today,* resulting in yet another postwar embarrassment for the administration. To complicate matters, Rumsfeld publicly expressed irritation after Bush placed Rice in charge of coordinating the administration's postwar activities.

"It made sense in a complex issue like this—the issue being the rebuilding of Iraq—with a lot of moving parts, even though DOD had the issue," the president told me, referring to the Department of Defense. "We needed a coordinating group to make sure that we're all headed in the same direction.

"And that's how this evolved," he added. "Her job—on my behalf—is to gather the data, coordinate thought."

Working closely with the Pentagon, State Department, CIA, and even the Department of Agriculture, Rice began to make progress.

"Slowly but surely, we kind of got the ministries back up and running," she said. "The problem was that the security situation worsened pretty dramatically in October and November because I think the insurgency got better organized."

Unfortunately for Bush, partisan Democrats back home were also getting better organized, even to the point of playing politics with intelligence that was crucial to national security. In early November, influential radio talk show host Sean Hannity exposed a Democratic plot to embarrass Bush politically with questions about prewar intelligence. The scheme was outlined in a memo by a Democratic staffer for Senator Jay Rockefeller, vice-chairman of the Senate Intelligence Committee, which was conducting an inquiry into prewar intelligence.

"The FBI Niger investigation was done solely at the request of the vice chairman," the memo revealed. "We are having some success."

It was the first public disclosure that Rockefeller, a Democrat, had been the driving force behind the "Leak-gate" probe. But this was only the beginning of the manipulative strategy.

"Our plan is as follows," said the memo, whose author was unnamed. "Pull the majority along as far as we can on issues that may lead to major new disclosures regarding improper or questionable conduct by administration officials."

Bush himself was listed as an official whose conduct was "improper or questionable," because of his State of the Union assertion that Iraq had tried to buy uranium from Niger.

The memo went on to outline an effort to compile "all the public statements on Iraq made by senior administration officials. We will identify the most exaggerated claims. We will contrast them with the intelligence estimates that have since been declassified."

In a particularly chilling passage, the memo writer outlined a scheme to transform the Senate Intelligence Committee into a nakedly political weapon just in time for the reelection campaign.

"Prepare to launch an independent investigation when it becomes clear we have exhausted the opportunity to usefully collaborate with the majority," the memo advised. "We can pull the trigger on an independent investigation of the administration's use of intelligence at any time. But we can only do so once. The best time to do so will probably be next year."

The committee's Republican chairman, Senator Pat Roberts, said he was "stunned" by the memo, which he called a "purely partisan document that appears to be a road map for how the Democrats intend to politicize what should be a bipartisan, objective review of prewar intelligence."

Even Democratic Senator Zell Miller said "heads ought to roll" over the memo. "If this is not treasonous, it's the first cousin of treason," he said. "This is one of those committees that you should never, ever have anything politicized because you're dealing with the lives of our soldiers and our citizens."

The memo was a startling reminder of how prevalent Bush hatred had become since the angry protest in Portland more than a year earlier. And the phenomenon was still growing. One week after Hannity disclosed the bombshell memo, Democratic billionaire George Soros, a Hungarian immigrant, gave $5 million to MoveOn.org, a hard Left activist group with a penchant for Bush-Hitler comparisons.

"When I hear Bush say, 'You're either with us or against us,' it reminds me of the Germans," Soros told the *Washington Post* that same day. "My experiences under Nazi and Soviet rule have sensitized me."

Soros promised to donate significant chunks of his $7 billion fortune to defeating Bush in 2004. "It is the central focus of my life," he said, "a matter of life and death."

The *New Republic* even published a long, serious article celebrating hatred of the president. "I hate President George W. Bush," began senior editor Jonathan Chait. "I hate the way he walks—shoulders flexed, elbows splayed out from his sides like a teenage boy feigning machismo. I hate the way he talks—blustery self-assurance masked by a pseudopopulist twang."

Warming to his theme, Chait added without a trace of irony: "There seem to be quite a few of us Bush haters. I have friends who have a viscerally hostile reaction to the sound of his voice or describe his existence as a constant oppressive force in their daily psyche."

Chait admitted that Bush hatred has "led many liberals not only to believe the costs of the Iraq war outweigh the benefits but to refuse to acknowledge any benefits at all, even freeing the Iraqis from Saddam Hussein's reign of terror."

Finally, Chait could not resist deriding the president as a moron, which was a central tenet of Bush hatred. "The persistence of an absurdly heroic view of Bush is what makes his dullness so maddening," he ranted. "To be a liberal today is to feel as though you've been transported into some alternative universe in which a transparently mediocre man is revered as a moral and strategic giant."

The depth of Chait's antipathy was perplexing to the president's supporters—and particularly jarring to Florida Governor Jeb Bush. "It's painful for me to see it because he's my brother and I love him," Jeb told me. "I mean, this is not an abstract notion for me.

"The absence of new ideas in the Democratic Party has created a void and that void is filled with this vitriolic hate, which is directed principally toward the president. I don't think it helps our democracy much, but I do think it helps the president's chances to be reelected because people don't buy all that stuff.

"The good news is that he takes it all in stride," Jeb added. "I've never seen someone who has [such] a serenity about him when people are screaming and foaming at the mouth all around him."

Card was equally astonished by the ferocity of Bush hatred.

"There is no vision that the Democrats, our opponents, seem to be rallying around," he told me. "There's no, 'we'd like to take America here.' So all they have as a rallying cry is ABB—Anybody But Bush."

I decided to ask the president himself to comment on the phenomenon of Bush hatred, examples of which were everywhere: The Portland protest. Daschle's prewar meltdown on the Senate floor. The Wellstone memorial-turned-rally. Kerry's wartime call for regime change in America. The Bush-Hitler comparisons. Kennedy's accusations of fraud and bribery. The memo on politicizing intelligence. The diatribes by liberals like Chait, who not only hated Bush but also ridiculed him as a dullard.

"That's part of lowering expectations," the president told me with a smile. But he also acknowledged that his quest to elevate the tone of political discourse in Washington had failed. "It is my job to try to unite the country," he acknowledged. "That's hard here in Washington."

Rove described Bush hatred as the "natural evolution of the politics of personal destruction, carried to its ultimate end. And what it becomes, ultimately, is self-destructive."

He suggested that the Hitler references and Kerry's wartime call for regime change in America were rooted in seething Democratic resentment of the president's accomplishments. "They look at him and say: 'He's succeeding and we don't want him to be,'" he explained. "'He won narrowly; we didn't think he had a mandate.'"

Rove added: "He acted as if he did have a mandate. And by God he turned it into something."

Rice speculated that the Democrats were rocked by Bush's self-assuredness after he "didn't win the popular vote" in 2000. "Given the way that he came into the presidency," she said, "they thought he would be kind of afraid of his shadow."

She added: "We have this language in American politics that a certain kind of electoral victory gives you a mandate. And in fact, what this president did was to say, I've got a mandate, seized it, and acted on that mandate. And he created a mandate by doing that. They didn't expect that."

Still, that only partly explains Bush hatred, Rice said. The phenomenon is also rooted in a fundamental misperception of the president.

"I think it is a caricature that says that he doesn't listen, he doesn't care," she said. "I don't understand it because everybody who ever meets the president—even if they don't agree with him—finds him as somebody who wants to listen."

Rice said some people mistake the president's resolute leadership for a dismissive, "my-way-or-the-highway" attitude.

"He's had to do really tough things; I don't think he's felt that he has had the time to do small things," she explained. "Particularly post-9/11, on the security side, sometimes if you have to do very tough things, then people don't like it."

She pointed to the president's trip to London in late November, which prompted a new round of Bush bashing by liberals.

"I actually think that Bush is the greatest threat to life on this planet that we've most probably ever seen," hyperventilated London's mayor, Ken Livingstone. "The policies he is initiating will doom us to extinction."

I accompanied Bush on the trip, and interviewed the handful of protesters who gathered outside Buckingham Palace to protest his arrival. The first person I approached was British artist Raymond Dell, who clutched a full-color placard showing the president with a bloody bullet hole through his forehead. I asked whether he seriously advocated assassination of the president.

"Yes, I do, of course—because he's evil. The American government is evil," the self-described communist replied. "Sorry I have to say that about your country, but you've got to have truth—otherwise you can't fight. I know I'm a bit of an extremist, but that's my view."

The second person I approached was Sergei Jargin, a forty-seven-year-old teacher on holiday from his home in Moscow. He was defiantly waving an American flag just yards from the anti-Bush demonstrators.

"I would like to express my solidarity with President Bush," he said. "Russia is in the same boat with Western countries. We have the same problems, the same political goals. And the more we cooperate, the better."

The juxtaposition of these two men was startling. In the space of ten minutes, I had spoken with a Briton who preferred communism over his native democracy and a Russian who preferred democracy over his native communism.

When I returned to the palace to watch the welcoming ceremony, the place was a ghost town, with even fewer demonstrators than before. But one man with a bullhorn belted out an anti-Bush song just as the president and First Lady Laura Bush were greeted by Queen Elizabeth and the Duke of Edinburgh. The British and American press chortled, but I was secretly pleased when the man's irreverent ditty was drowned out by a stirring rendition of "The Star-Spangled Banner" and the rolling thunder of a forty-one-gun salute. As one hundred black stallions stood by, bearing ceremonial guards in polished brass breastplates, even the jaded White House journalists shook their heads in wonder at Britain's ability to roll out the welcome mat with unparalleled majesty.

By the same token, when Bush arrived in London, even some of his critics were impressed with his presentation. They praised his commitment to pursuing American security through both short-term and long-term strategies in the Middle East. Rice described the dual strategies as transformative.

"In the short term, you hunt down al Qaeda. In the short term, you harden the country. In the short term, you have a coalition of states on intelligence, and law enforcement, and trying to make sure you're dealing with the terrorist threat," she told me.

"But in the long term, you've got to change the nature of the Middle East," she added. "You've got have anchors like Iraq, Afghanistan. We've always thought a democratic Palestine might be one of those anchors. And that's then got to get change in the region. Because if the Middle East remains a place of hopelessness and oppression and frustration, then you're going to have terrorists coming out of there as long as we're all too old to care."

Consequently, after years of reluctance to draw attention to the backward and repressive nature of Middle East regimes like Egypt and Saudi Arabia, the president was undertaking a candid reassessment. It began with admitting a certain degree of Western culpability.

"We must shake off decades of failed policy in the Middle East," Bush told a British think tank devoted to foreign policy. "Your nation and mine, in the past, have been willing to make a bargain to tolerate oppression for the sake of stability. Long-standing ties often led us to overlook the faults of local elites. Yet this bargain did not bring stability or make us safe. It merely bought time, while problems festered and ideologies of violence took hold."

The reference to "elites" such as Saudi's royal family represented an important shift in U.S. foreign policy, which previously had been squeamish about chiding the world's largest oil supplier. But now Bush was putting Riyadh on notice that the threshold for acceptable behavior was being raised.

"As recent history has shown, we cannot turn a blind eye to oppression just because the oppression is not in our own backyard," he warned. "No longer should we think tyranny is benign because it is temporarily convenient. Tyranny is never benign to its victims, and our great democracies should oppose tyranny wherever it is found.

"Now we're pursuing a different course, a forward strategy of freedom in the Middle East," he added. "We will consistently challenge the enemies of reform and confront the allies of terror. We will expect a higher standard from our friends in the region."

As Rice noted, this and another seminal speech the president delivered that month in Washington had an unmistakable effect on Middle East governments.

"People start to respond; people don't want to be on the list of nonreformers," she told me. "I think we've both given a boost to those who were on the way to reform—like Bahrain and Jordan and Oman—and we have gotten others thinking about it, like the Saudis."

She said, in particular, that Crown Prince Abdullah "understands that Saudi can't stay where Saudi is," although she added: "I don't know how far he will go."

In an effort to help Abdullah mollify fundamentalist clerics in the kingdom, Bush began withdrawing virtually all U.S. troops from Saudi soil after the conclusion of major combat operations in Iraq. It was a significant shift for American forces, who had been in Saudi since August 7, 1990, the day they arrived to defend the kingdom against Saddam's expansionism. Their arrival had been a defining moment in the radicalization of Saudi resident Osama bin Laden, whose hatred of the American infidels was so intense that he fled to Afghanistan within a year.

Deputy Defense Secretary Paul Wolfowitz told *Vanity Fair* that the continued presence of U.S. forces in Saudi Arabia "has been a source of enormous difficulty for a friendly government. It's been a huge recruiting device for al Qaeda. In fact if you look at bin Laden, one of his principle grievances was the presence of so-called crusader forces on the holy land, Mecca, and Medina. I think just lifting that burden from the Saudis is itself going to open the door to other positive things."

The move did not affect Bush's commitment to transforming Iraq into a beachhead of democratic reform in the Middle East. But he did acknowledge that the work there was vexing.

"The violence we are seeing in Iraq today is serious," he said in his London speech. "The armed forces of both our countries have taken losses, felt deeply by our citizens."

But the president also highlighted success stories that there downplayed by the media.

"Since the liberation of Iraq, we have seen changes that could hardly have been imagined a year ago," he marveled. "A new Iraqi police force protects the people, instead of bullying them. More than one hundred and fifty Iraqi newspapers are now in circulation, printing what they choose, not what they're ordered.

"Schools are open with textbooks free of propaganda. Hospitals are functioning and are well-supplied. Iraq has a new currency, the first battalion of a new army, representative local governments, and a Governing Council with an aggressive timetable for national sovereignty.

"This is substantial progress," Bush said. "And much of it has proceeded faster than similar efforts in Germany and Japan after World War II."

The president went on to point out that insurgents in Iraq were operating on a decidedly mixed bag of assumptions.

"The terrorists have a purpose, a strategy to their cruelty," he explained. "They view the rise of democracy in Iraq as a powerful threat to their ambitions. In this, they are correct."

But Bush added: "They believe their acts of terror against our coalition, against international aid workers and against innocent Iraqis, will make us recoil and retreat. In this, they are mistaken."

In case anyone doubted America's will, Bush decided to clear the air once and for all.

"We did not charge hundreds of miles into the heart of Iraq and pay a bitter cost of casualties, and liberate 25 million people, only to retreat before a band of thugs and assassins," he vowed. "We will help the Iraqi people establish a peaceful and democratic country in the heart of the Middle East.

"And by doing so, we will defend our people from danger."

14
BONEFISHING IN BELIZE

WHEN JOE HAGIN WAS told to sneak President Bush into Baghdad for Thanksgiving dinner with U.S. troops, he figured the trip would never actually take place. Oh, he went through the theoretical exercise of planning such a journey, and was deadly serious about keeping it secret. But the White House Deputy Chief of Staff doubted the audacious plan could be kept confidential for the full six weeks before Thanksgiving. And he knew that once the story broke, the trip would have to be canceled. Otherwise, every guerilla worth his salt would be camped around Baghdad Airport, just itching for Air Force One to come within range of shoulder-fired, surface-to-air missiles.

Hagin's sense of detachment was reinforced by the president's initial reluctance to sweat the trip's details.

"I don't think about it—I'm a delegator," Bush explained to me. "I trust the people I'm surrounded by."

Although he endorsed the idea when it was first suggested by Chief of Staff Andy Card in mid-October, Bush was preoccupied with problems in postwar Iraq. It wasn't until ten days before the holiday that he began to demonstrate more interest. Instead of making his usual casual inquiry into the status of planning, he pulled Hagin aside and looked him in the eye.

"Are we really going to be able to do this?" the president said.

"Yeah," said Hagin, swallowing hard. "I think we are."

Suddenly Hagin realized the trip was no longer merely a farfetched abstraction. And he had just assured the president that he could pull it off. From that moment forward, the presidential aide started waking up in the middle of the night.

Meanwhile, Bush sought the advice of Colonel Mark Tillman, the pilot of Air Force One. "I don't want you to do this if it's not safe," he said. "Don't push it—for a lot of people's sake."

"Oh, don't worry," Tillman replied. "There's a 99 percent chance we'll get in."

"Why don't you and I spend a little time on the one percent chance?" Bush said. "I need to know: What does it take to get into Baghdad and out? And how risky is it?"

"Sir, I wouldn't take you in there if I wasn't convinced we could do this in a way that would safely bring you to the troops," Tillman said.

The president did not have to wait long to find out what could go wrong at Baghdad Airport. On the Saturday before Thanksgiving, a cargo plane was struck by a surface-to-air missile shortly after takeoff. The left wing of the DHL plane burst into flames, forcing the pilot to make an emergency landing. The Bush Administration promptly suspended all commercial air traffic at the airport.

It was the low point in weeks of furtive planning that had begun with an audacious question aboard Air Force One.

"Are you interested in going to Baghdad over Thanksgiving?" Andy Card had asked Bush.

"Yes, I really am interested," the president replied. "Think about it and get it planned. I'm not going, however, if it puts anybody's life at risk. And I don't want to get there and create an issue. I want to go, thank the troops, and go home."

Just like that, the president of the United States decided to be flown secretly—in his highly recognizable, blue-and-white 747—into Baghdad, a virtual war zone, to have Thanksgiving dinner with U.S. troops. Card delegated the difficult task of making it happen to Hagin. After all, both men had already accompanied a president named George Bush to the Middle East to have Thanksgiving dinner with U.S. troops. In 1991, when Card was White House deputy chief of staff and Hagin the White House appointment scheduler, the elder President Bush had visited troops close to the Kuwaiti border in the wake of the Gulf War. Then again, that trip had not been secret.

"If we go, nobody can know that we're going," Hagin said this time around. "I mean nobody."

Card agreed. In the first instance, he, Hagin, and Tillman, along with Rice, would be the only people besides the president and First Lady to know about the plan. In fact, for the next few weeks, these six were the only people to have any inkling of the president's plan to visit Baghdad. Not even the Secret Service was aware of the secret.

Then, during the first week of November, Hagin called a meeting at the Presidential Emergency Operations Center and sprang the plot on two Secret Service officials and a pair of White House military aides. Although no one blanched, one of the Secret Service officials later feigned umbrage at a separate meeting in Hagin's West Wing office.

"I object," said the official, slamming his hand down on Hagin's desk. "Now that that's out of the way, let's see if we can make this happen."

From the very start, Hagin made clear that if anyone was uncomfortable with the plan it would be summarily scrapped. He wasn't about to put the president in peril for some reckless stunt.

On November 11, Paul Bremer, the top American administrator in Iraq, came to the White House for meetings with Bush and other top administration officials. Hagin pulled him aside and told him about the planned visit. When Bremer responded enthusiastically, his assistant was told he would need to serve as the administration's "eyes and ears in Baghdad."

The planners resolved to discuss the topic only on secure telephones. Even oblique references to the visit were forbidden on regular lines. In an effort to preclude suspicious "spikes" in the number of secure phone calls, the planners in Washington gathered at prearranged times to hold conference calls with their counterparts in Baghdad. Both sides came equipped with lists of questions for maximum efficiency.

Unlike most presidential trips, which were planned months in advance by a small army of White House staffers led by former Fox News producer Greg Jenkins, only a dozen people were even aware of this extraordinarily dangerous trip. Jenkins himself wasn't even told until it was two weeks away. Every time a new person was let in on the secret, a cover story had to be devised to discourage suspicion.

"What are you going to tell people in your office?" Hagin asked Jenkins.

"That I'm going to London with some friends for Thanksgiving?" Jenkins suggested.

"Nope, won't work," Hagin replied. "They can get ahold of you in London. You gotta go where nobody can get ahold of you."

So Jenkins invented something more exotic—bonefishing in Belize. That did the trick.

Soon Jenkins was headed for Iraq with six Secret Service agents and the president's military aide. Packed into a small plane with equipment clogging the aisle, this most miniscule of White House advance teams was told to land in Baghdad—and disappear.

"They slide in as undercover, [like] CIA agents, so nobody will bother them," Bush told me. "And they did the work."

On Monday and Tuesday of Thanksgiving week, the president began to pepper Hagin and others with very specific questions. How grave was the missile threat? How would Air Force One fend off a potential attack? How many people in Baghdad now knew about the visit? What cover story has been devised for the troops coming to dinner?

"I was pushing hard," Bush recalled, "to make sure that my judgment was correct about going, making sure I fully understand the impact of it."

By late Tuesday the president was back at Prairie Chapel Ranch in Crawford, where he was officially scheduled to spend the next five days quietly relaxing with family and friends. On Wednesday morning, Bush reviewed the trip yet again with Cheney and Card, who were in Washington, as well as Rice and Hagin, who were at the ranch.

"I just want to ask one more time: Do you think we ought to go?" the president said.

Rice recalled: "In some ways, he was the most skeptical of all that we could keep it quiet and pull it off. And we went around and we all said, yes, we should go."

Hagin then confided in two more White House staffers—photographer Tina Hager and deputy advance office director Steve Atkiss. Both thought they were being fired as they were summoned into closed-door meetings. But Hagin decided not to inform deputy press secretary Claire Buchan because he didn't want to put her in the position of having to lie to the press corps, which she was scheduled to brief at noon.

"The president will be spending Thanksgiving at his ranch here in Crawford, Texas," Buchan blithely misinformed reporters in the gymnasium of Crawford Middle School, which served as the press filing center. "He'll be joined by family and friends, including his mother and father, former President Bush and Mrs. Bush."

"Menu?" queried an unwitting journalist.

"Menu will be a traditional Thanksgiving dinner, including free range turkey, turkey cornbread dressing, chipotle sweet potatoes, mashed potatoes, asparagus, Texas grapefruit, toasted-walnuts-and-greens salad—that's all one item—pumpkin pie and Prairie Chapel pecan pie, made with pecans from the president's ranch."

"Is the First Lady in the kitchen as we speak?" a reporter asked.

"Are you angling to help cook Thanksgiving dinner?" Buchan parried playfully.

"You bet," the reporter said. "I volunteer."

Laughter filled the gymnasium as the journalists, blissfully unaware of the enormous story taking shape under their noses, prattled on about the presidential menu.

Meanwhile, back at the ranch, the president's biggest worry was the press.

"Have you got the pool put together?" he asked Hagin. "Watch the leak, because if it leaks we're not going."

Normally, whenever the president traveled on Air Force One, he took along the pool of twelve to fourteen journalists who represented the larger White House press corps. Only once during the Bush Administration was the pool reduced in size. That happened on September 11, when the pool was cut to five people as part of an effort to reduce the plane's "footprint" as it hopscotched the nation in the wake of the terrorist attacks. Some Bush aides suggested a similar reduction during the early stages of planning for the Baghdad trip. But the idea was quickly abandoned because the White House knew the press would scream bloody murder.

"We had a discussion about press and I said: Absolutely the press must go. This will be an historic moment," Bush told me. "And therefore, we had to figure out a way to put together a pool—and what looked like a legitimate pool."

The task fell to Hagin, who knew nothing about press pools or how they were formed. He spent ten days studying the maddeningly haphazard way various news organizations rotated in and out of the pool and came to an alarming conclusion. He would be unable to spirit away major components of the pool—the Associated Press,

Reuters, and a TV crew—without raising suspicions among the other reporters in Crawford. Since all the journalists spent their work days together in the press filing center, it would be obvious when some of them turned up missing for an extended period.

So Hagin decided to leave these components of the pool undisturbed in Crawford and instead obtain them from Washington. This entailed contacting news organizations in the nation's capital as early as Tuesday and swearing them to secrecy on a blockbuster story. Card brought in the AP at 8 P.M. Tuesday and Fox News Channel at 11 A.M. Wednesday. These journalists, as well as a Reuters reporter, were told to gather Thursday evening at Andrews Air Force base near Washington, where the president would be changing planes on his way overseas.

That still left the problem of discreetly gathering more than half a dozen other journalists in Crawford without spooking the rest of the press herd. The White House set its sights first on Dick Keil of Bloomberg News, a 6-foot-6 reporter Bush had nicknamed "Stretch." On Wednesday afternoon, Hagin and Atkiss drove to the Crawford Middle School and furtively parked behind the building. Atkiss went inside and retrieved Keil, who climbed into the back seat of Hagin's enormous white pickup truck with the trepidation of a man about to be killed in a mafia hit. Hagin looked in his rearview mirror and almost blew a gasket. Stretch had brought along a dog! Now they would have to find a dogsitter in order to keep the president's secret. The smallest details of this trip were becoming major logistical headaches. Hagin was so exasperated that he refused to corral the newspaper reporter, leaving that task to White House Communications Director Dan Bartlett.

A short time later, *Washington Post* reporter Mike Allen was plucked from the lawn of the school and driven to the parking lot of a nearby church, where Bartlett was waiting with a mischievous smile. He was accompanied by Buchan, who had been let in on the secret now that she had finished briefing the press at Crawford Middle School.

"I have news," Bartlett said. "The president is going to Baghdad."

Allen, like the other members of the pool, was forbidden from telling his editors or family where he was going. He was warned that the president would call off the trip if the story leaked. Although Bush and others in the administration worried that the pool would be the most likely source of a leak, Hagin was relatively confident that would not happen. For starters, the journalists were being given the chance to cover a major story of historic significance. Secondly, they risked becoming part of the story if they got too cute and somehow nixed the president's Thanksgiving visit to the troops. Finally, the reporters were just as wary as White House officials about doing anything that might get them shot in Baghdad.

The only remaining members of the pool were the photographers, who always traveled in a pack. They were cryptically instructed to wait in an alley behind a Waco hotel. Since one of the photographers, Larry Downing of Reuters, was a practical joker, the others figured Downing and Atkiss were trying to pull one over on them. Hagin had always worried that the entire trip could be blown by the very real possibility that someone would simply refuse to believe his farfetched story. But when he and Bartlett showed up behind the alley, serious as a heart attack, the photographers believed. After waking up a fifth and final photographer with just five minutes to spare, the group was taken to Air Force One, where Hagin instructed them to remove the batteries from their cell phones so that their movements could not be tracked. He also warned them not to turn the phones on in Washington.

"Do you believe it now?" one photographer said to a skeptical colleague.

Bush waited until an hour before he was scheduled to depart the ranch to break the news to his twin daughters, Barbara and Jenna.

"Their first reaction was, 'that's fine, Dad.' And all of a sudden, as it came closer to the departure time, they became a little more—more solemn," Bush told me. "They began to wonder whether this was the last time they'd see me. That sounds a little overdramatic, but nevertheless, I'll just say their hugs—and the hug of Laura—were intense."

Normally, when Bush traveled from his ranch to the airport in nearby Waco, he flew on Marine One, the presidential helicopter. During weather inclement enough to preclude chopper travel, he rode in a specially armored limousine, accompanied by an identical decoy and more than a dozen other vehicles packed with Secret Service agents, staff, and press. But both methods of transportation were impossible now, since they would blow the president's cover. So Bush got dressed in jeans, boots, and a work coat and climbed into the back seat of an unmarked red van with tinted windows.

"I slipped on a baseball cap, pulled 'er down—as did Condi. We looked like a normal couple," the president joked. "We were a casual yuppie couple."

Although there were two Secret Service agents in the front seat, they did not tell their fellow agents guarding the ranch that George W. Bush, for the first time in his presidency, was about to sneak off his own property.

"Nobody else knew who was in the car," he explained to me. "One-car motorcade. Out we go. And I hadn't been outside my gate in one car in—I can't remember when. Never."

Bush passed right under the noses of the guards at the gate. "The guys guarding the house did not know I had gone," he told me. "This was done in incredible secrecy."

Rice added: "None of the agents on the ranch knew, which is really pretty extraordinary if you think about it."

The president, who was accustomed to riding in an imposing motorcade that barreled along highways cleared of ordinary motorists, was now an ordinary motorist himself, cruising with Condi in the back seat of a solitary van. The one-vehicle motorcade drove unmolested into Waco, turning north on Interstate 95. It was evening now, and the highway was so crowded with vehicles headed toward Dallas that Bush's van soon slowed to a crawl.

"What's this?" Bush asked.

"It's traffic, Mr. President," Rice replied.

"Is this what a traffic jam looks like?" he deadpanned.

Rice later recalled: "We looked at each other and we thought, the night before Thanksgiving, 6:30 P.M. rush hour—why didn't someone think of this?"

The president was remarkably exposed to the random collection of holiday drivers who happened to be stuck in traffic alongside him. But since would-be terrorists had no way of knowing his whereabouts, the Secret Service figured the risk was manageable. Besides, Bush knew his red van was the most closely watched vehicle on the road. He noticed the shadowy, unmarked security vehicles that kept appearing and then melting into traffic.

"Occasionally you'd see these cars on the side of the road, drop in behind—this thing was incredibly well organized," the president told me. "There [were] relays and hand-offs, and guys going by. You kind of look over and all of a sudden guys in black uniforms who I'd seen before, kind of speeding ahead."

The traffic caused the usually punctual president to arrive ten minutes late at Texas State Technical College Airport in Waco. Then, according to Rice, "All of a sudden there was another glitch because somebody realized there was a guard at the gate."

Eddie, the same Secret Service agent whom Bush had tormented during the flight to the *Lincoln,* now craned around to give the president some last-minute instructions on their latest adventure.

"There's going to be a guy at the gate," Eddie said. "We don't want him to know who you are."

Bush said he and Rice pulled "the hats down over our head, kind of feigned sleeping." The guard fell for it and waved through the van, which made a beeline for Air Force One.

"It's okay, Mr. President, you're fine—wake up," Eddie announced. "Get out of the car and go straight up the stairs."

But Bush was not dropped off at the front stairs that he normally used, for obvious reasons. Instead he was unceremoniously deposited at the rear stairs like any other member of the crew, which routinely flew Air Force One back to Washington without the president for maintenance.

"Footman's entrance," Bush later joked. "Glad to know how the people live."

The president was now actively deceiving large numbers of people to preserve the integrity of his stealth mission. The White House even filed a false flight plan so that air traffic controllers would think the massive 747 was a much smaller Gulfstream 5.

"It's exciting," he told me. "I mean, this is dramatic. This is dramatic. And we were doing it for the good of the troops."

Shortly after takeoff, the president sat down in the plane's conference room to compose the speech he would deliver to the troops in Baghdad. Since he hadn't brought along any speechwriters, Bush wrote the address out longhand on a white legal pad. He was joined by Hagin, Rice, and Bartlett, who threw out ideas as the president scribbled. Bush went through several drafts, each time handing the pad to his personal assistant, Blake Gottesman, who typed up drafts until the president was satisfied.

There was an electric air of excitement on Air Force One as it streaked toward Washington. Even back in the press cabin, where the usually jaded journalists were watching the film *Terminator 3: Rise of the Machines,* the sense of adventure was almost palpable.

"The president of the United States is AWOL, and we're with him," marveled Keil with a grin. "The ultimate road trip."

Upon landing at Andrews, Air Force One taxied inside its super-secret hangar and parked alongside an identical blue-and-white 747 that would actually fly the group into Baghdad. At 10:45 P.M., Bush emerged from the first plane and began climbing up a staircase that descended from the belly of the second plane. At the top of the stairs, he noticed the journalists getting ready to make the switch.

"A crucial moment in this trip, frankly, was in between changing planes," Bush explained later. "I wasn't sure people would be able to tell their loved ones: 'I can't see you on Thanksgiving, I can't tell you why.' I was worried about that. But I was fully prepared to turn this baby around and come home."

Since the hangar was too noisy for the president's voice to be heard, he raised his hand to his ear in the motion of someone talking on a cell phone. He mouthed the words, "No calls, got it?" In case any-one missed the point, he crossed his arms in front of him, made a slashing motion to his throat and again mouthed "no calls." He had the demeanor of a stern but good-humored father admonishing his untrustworthy teenagers.

It was after 11 P.M. by the time Air Force One took off, so Bush sacked out in his bed in the nose of the plane, sleeping for two-thirds of the 10.5-hour flight. In fact, he was still asleep when the 747 crossed over England and Tillman heard an interesting exchange on the radio.

"Did I just see Air Force One?" asked a pilot with a British accent.

After a pregnant pause, a British-sounding air traffic controller replied, "Gulfstream 5."

After an even longer pause, the hawk-eyed pilot said, "Oh," as if he had just been let in on a secret. Tillman figured the pilot was radio-ing from a British Airways jet nearby, which had been cruising behind and slightly above Air Force One for fifteen or twenty minutes. He mentioned the conversation to Hagin, who passed it along to Bartlett.

As Air Force One continued eastward, Bush woke up and inquired whether he needed to abort the mission.

"Three hours out, I checked with our Secret Service and checked with the people on the ground," Bush said. "They assured me that we still had a tight hold on the information."

Indeed, even when Air Force One was less than an hour away from Baghdad, the information continued to hold. At 8:35 A.M. Eastern Time, CNN White House correspondent Dana Bash stood outside Crawford Middle School and authoritatively assured the world that the president "will be having a quiet day on his ranch." Bash had no way of knowing that instead of relaxing seven miles down the road at his ranch, Bush was traveling 7,000 miles away in the Middle East.

"For dessert," she said by way of update, "we are told that the president will be having some Prairie Chapel pecan pie— and that will be made from some pecans grown right there on his 1,600 acre-ranch."

"Wish I was going to be there," enthused CNN anchor Heidi Collins. "Sounds pretty good."

"Me too," said Bash, unaware that her arch-rival, Jim Angle of Fox News, was accompanying the president on a story of historical significance halfway around the world.

Twenty-two minutes before the scheduled landing, all unnecessary lights—both interior and exterior—on Air Force One were extinguished. The window shades were pulled down tight to prevent the escape of any light that might provide a target to insurgents. No one on board could see outside except the pilots and the president, who had walked upstairs to the cockpit as the sun was setting over Iraq.

"I want to watch us fly into Baghdad," Bush told me. "Tillman is up there. And there's an air of excitement in there. These guys are doing something historic. They're driving the president of the United States into a war zone."

At length, Air Force One made contact with a surprised air controller in the Baghdad tower.

"He's a little confused about what's going on at this point in time, and then it dawns on him what's happened—he'd been given some code," Bush told me. "Tillman says: 'He got the code. Don't worry, Mr. President.'"

Although it was getting dark, which minimized the risk of a surface-to-air missile strike, Bush was acutely aware that the next few minutes would be fraught with peril.

"Had the security been broken, that would have been the moment when we would have been most vulnerable," he said. "This plane is well equipped for air defenses. And I'm watching the red light.

"If the red light comes on," Bush told me, "it's an indication of a launch. And I kind of had my eye out there, watching the Baghdad sky kind of darken."

As a former pilot, Bush could not resist peppering Tillman and the rest of the flight crew with innumerable questions. "Can you see the runway? Can you see? No, where is it? Where is it?" he remembered saying. "Everybody is craning their neck, looking around. Oh, there it is, a guy says. And there it sure enough was."

Bush could see Apache helicopters fanning out across the airport. They were pushing back the security perimeter so that Tillman would have plenty of room to bring the big 747 down in a wide, looping corkscrew. As Tillman made his descent, Bush headed back downstairs.

"The plane is totally blacked out now," the president told me. "It was like you had no idea that you were kind of orbiting down in— couldn't feel it."

At 9:31 A.M. Eastern Time, Air Force One landed safely at the most dangerous airport in the world. It was 5:31 P.M. local time and a sliver of moon hung over Baghdad.

"It's dark by the time we get down and we pull into a remote part of the airport," Bush told me. "I wear a flak jacket."

A Secret Service agent instructed the president to exit via the retractable stairs from the plane's belly. In the next moment Bush was standing on the wet, dark tarmac, where a dozen SUVs and an ambulance had formed a convoy. The shock was evident on the faces of the drivers, who were accustomed to picking up VIPs but had no idea this job would involve the commander in chief.

Bush jumped into a white vehicle with Army Lieutenant General Ricardo Sanchez, commander of U.S. forces in Iraq and one of a handful of people in Baghdad who had known about the visit. The convoy began to bump along rutted, muddy roads through a blacked-out section of the airport.

Hagin was riding on the open tailgate of one of the vehicles, facing backward toward Air Force One. He was worried about the plane's tremendous recognizability. A terrorist with a shoulder-mounted missile launcher, even a poor shot, might be able to hit the massive aircraft, which measured over two hundred feet in both length and wingspan. The behemoth's tail towered sixty-three feet above the tarmac, practically inviting the bad guys to engage in target practice.

But as the convoy pulled about two hundred yards away, something amazing happened. Air Force One suddenly vanished into a strange mix of dust and fog and mist that clung to the rain-drenched tarmac. By some miracle of meteorology, the world's most recognizable airplane simply disappeared into the night. For the first time in weeks, Hagin got the feeling that the trip might go smoothly after all.

After driving past an assortment of Humvees and dog teams, the president arrived at an enormous, soft-sided, white building known as the Bob Hope Dining Facility. He entered through the rear door and stood behind a screen of camouflage that separated him from six hundred unsuspecting soldiers who had gathered for Thanksgiving dinner. Before the president could gather his wits, Sanchez was out at the lectern introducing Bremer, whom the troops assumed was their VIP guest.

"Thank you, general—and happy Thanksgiving to all of you," Bremer began. "I can't tell you how much those of us on the civilian side appreciate the sacrifices all of you are making to make this place safer for us. Now General Sanchez, it says here I'm supposed to read the president's Thanksgiving proclamation. But I thought the deal was it was the most senior person who reads it. Is that you?"

"I don't know," Sanchez shrugged.

"Let's see if we have anybody more senior here to read the president's Thanksgiving speech," said Bremer, craning around toward the camouflage screen.

"They just announced you," Andy Card prompted his boss, who still didn't budge.

"Is there anybody back there who is more senior than us?" said Bremer, repeating the president's cue. He was hamming it up for all he was worth.

"I really haven't had time to collect my thoughts that much," Bush explained to me later. "It's a whirlwind at this point."

When he finally stepped from behind the screen, the room exploded in thunderous cheers and applause. The soldiers leapt to their feet at the site of the commander in chief, punching their fists in the air and clambering atop chairs and tables for a better view of this incongruous image—the president of the United States joining them in war-torn Baghdad.

"It was an emotional moment to walk into that room," Bush said later. "The energy level was beyond belief. I mean, I've been in some excited crowds before, but this place truly erupted. And I could see the first look of amazement and then look of appreciation on the kids' faces."

He added: "There's this sense of wonderment and then the place just goes very emotional."

Indeed, while the lone TV camera at the rear of the room captured the jubilation of the GIs from behind, Bush was astonished to seen another emotion from his own vantage point.

"There were people weeping—it was a very, very dramatic moment," he recalled. "It was a new experience for me to see tears streaming down soldiers' faces—not everybody, of course—or to see this kind of: 'My God, the commander in chief has bothered to come.' "

Bush, himself an emotional man, was so taken aback that he wondered whether he could deliver the speech. As the soldiers watched, a tear appeared on the president's cheek.

"I did become emotional," he told me, "because I felt the emotion of the crowd."

He added: "I had to take a step back, collect my thoughts. This was one of those moments where it's very important for the president to stay focused on the message."

The president seemed to gather strength by momentarily turning toward Secret Service agent Nick Trotta, to whom Bush had grown close during the campaign of 2000. Fortunately, the president could not see Hagin and Card and Rice and the rest of his aides, who were just as overcome with emotion as they peeked through the camouflage screen behind him. Even one of the younger Secret Service agents choked up.

Bush figured the best way to get himself and everyone else in a better frame of mind was with a joke.

"I was just looking for a warm meal somewhere," he deadpanned, sparking a round of raucous laughter and applause—along with some whooping and even barking—that bought him some time to compose himself.

When the noise died down, the president turned serious. He knew he could not come all this way without paying homage to the U.S. soldiers who had been killed in Iraq over the previous eight months.

"On this Thanksgiving, our nation remembers the men and women of our military, your friends and comrades who paid the ultimate price for our security and freedom," he said.

But Bush also made clear that the deaths of those soldiers would be meaningless if the U.S. abandoned its mission now.

"We will prevail," he said. "We will win because our cause is just. We will win because we will stay on the offensive. And we will win because you're part of the finest military ever assembled."

Defiant shouts of *"Hoo-ah!"* the military's all-purpose expression of approval, filled the air. One of the soldiers was struck by the difference between Bush and former President Clinton, who had visited U.S. troops near the border of Kosovo in 1999. The soldier later wrote an e-mail, which ended up at the White House, remarking that while he had been visited by a president in the Balkans, he had been visited by the commander in chief in Baghdad.

Seeking to maximize the impact of his visit, the president devoted a portion of his remarks to an audience much larger than the six hundred soldiers in the room.

"I have a message for the Iraqi people," he said. "You have an opportunity to seize the moment and rebuild your great country, based on human dignity and freedom. The regime of Saddam Hussein is gone forever."

The place went nuts again as Bush plunged into the crowd, shaking hands and slapping backs like a man possessed. It quickly became apparent that the president had no intention of following the itinerary that his aides had carefully scripted.

"The drill was for me to go through, and then sit down with kind of the select group of soldiers—I'm sure they went to great pains to eventually kind of figure out the right mix," Bush told me with a roll of the eyes. "But no, I wasn't about to do that."

Instead, he decided to work the room. "It was the ultimate presidential event," he explained. "Wading in crowds and shaking hands and pictures and hugs."

He added: "They wanted me to sit down. I wasn't about to sit down. As a matter of fact, my instincts were to go serve food."

The president made a beeline for the cafeteria counter at the other end of the room. Along the way he noticed a picture-perfect turkey on a platter, and picked it up for the benefit of the photographers. Bush was so accustomed to having his every move recorded on film that he often tried to accommodate photographers by giving them shots he knew they could use, preferably images that went beyond him standing behind yet another lectern. So he posed with the turkey for a fleeting moment.

"I knew it would be a funny picture," he told me.

Then he handed the platter off and hustled behind the cafeteria counter to start serving dinner to the soldiers. "How many do you want, one or two?" he asked a soldier while doling out sliced turkey with all the trimmings. "What do you want?" he asked another. All the while, he joshed with his fellow servers, ordering them to give more food to the hungry soldiers.

"I've never been so surprised—I had no idea, not a clue," marveled Private Stephen Henderson, who had been in Iraq just ten days. "I feel uplifted. I almost forgot I was even here."

Private Mark Hansen added: "I never thought he would be here. I'm proud to have him as the commander in chief. You can't beat it."

Staff Sergeant Gerrie Stokes Holloman said the president's visit "shows that he cares about us and is thinking about us. It's not easy being here. Every day you're over here, you feel depressed anyway. But it's especially hard on a holiday."

Bush spent more than an hour waiting on the soldiers. Although he didn't eat anything himself, he chatted up the group that had been selected to have dinner with him. Then he worked his way back across the room, posing for more pictures and shaking hands. He stepped up on the stage for a final wave, which prompted a deafening roar.

The president was then taken to another building to meet with members of the Iraqi Governing Council. He also met with a group of Baghdad officials, including the city's mayor, before giving a pep talk to two dozen members of the U.S. command staff. While these meetings were taking place, Hagin stepped outside to confer with other Bush aides.

"Do we know if the story's broken?" he asked.

"There's a CNN feed in this room downstairs," replied one of the aides, who promptly disappeared inside the building.

A few minutes later, the aide radioed Hagin with an update. "CNN is reporting," the aide began, which caused Hagin's heart to sink. "CNN is reporting that the president is having pecan pie at the ranch."

The Bush aides erupted in euphoric laughter—and no doubt a little relief. Even if the story broke now, there would be almost no time for insurgents to attack. A few minutes later, Bush emerged from the building and headed for Air Force One.

"It was just dark and I'm kind of looking around—where in the heck is the airplane?" he told me. "This plane was, like, shrouded in this mist."

He added: "And all of a sudden, the big Air Force One just emerges—big 747. Nobody could have seen it. It was really mysterious."

A guard with an enormous gun scrutinized the credentials of the journalists before letting them back on board. The plane was heavy with fuel for the long ride home, so Tillman had to use a lot of runway to get it airborne. But once in the sky, he throttled up to peak power and climbed at the steepest angle since September 11. It was another moment of vulnerability for the plane, which was well within missile range.

"Well?" Bartlett said to Hagin, who was staring at the digital clock in the senior staff compartment with Rice and Card.

"Too soon," said Hagin, noting that the plane had been in the sky for only four minutes.

After letting another two minutes pass in uncomfortable silence, Hagin said: "All right, we're okay." The group emitted a collective sigh of relief.

Everyone on board had been told the plane would remain blacked out until it ascended above 10,000 feet. "It seemed like it took an eternity to get to ten thousand," Bush told me. "Everyone was exhilarated."

When the lights finally came on, journalists were given access to telephones so they could break the news—which was greeted with skepticism by some editors back in Washington.

"No, I'm telling you, we just left Baghdad!" one reporter could be heard exclaiming to an incredulous boss.

By now the president's top aides had moved to the plane's conference room to monitor media coverage. Although they had no television images, they gathered around an audio speaker to listen to CNN. It was 12:27 P.M. Eastern Time; the president had been airborne for twenty-four minutes.

"The White House has now confirmed that President Bush did, indeed, secretly fly to Iraq this Thanksgiving Day," announced Senior International Correspondent Walt Rodgers in Baghdad. "We're not even clear whether he is still in-country—that is, whether he's still in Iraq—or whether perhaps he's left the country, or whether, indeed, he may be visiting U.S. troops around the country.

"Regardless of the circumstances of the visit, it was still an extraordinarily intrepid thing for the president to do, because this remains a very, very dangerous place—and it took some rather clever execution to get the president in here so quietly," Rodgers continued. "No one here knew it was happening, Miles."

"Walt, it comes less than a week after a cargo plane was struck by—apparently—a shoulder-launched, heat-seeking missile at that airport," said anchor Miles O'Brien. "Do you know much about the security precautions they took when bringing Air Force One in there?"

"Well, we don't even know that he came in on—that the president came in on Air Force One," Rodgers said. "There are more than a few choppers going over here. And you have to wonder if, indeed, one of those may not have the president on it. That's unusual helicopter activity at this moment."

Moments later, he added: "As the president moves about, he's moving about on a helicopter. Helicopters get shot down here with a fair amount of frequency."

"I can only imagine what the meeting was like with the Secret Service when this idea was broached," O'Brien said.

Although most Bush aides were howling with laughter at this report, Bartlett was peeved. Rodgers was making it sound like the president might be in trouble—perhaps even lost in a war zone. Not wishing to cause a national panic, he snatched up the phone in the conference room and called Claire Buchan, Scott McClellan's deputy, in Crawford.

"Tell them the president is fine, he's on Air Force One, he's out of Baghdad," Bartlett instructed.

But when Buchan called CNN to explain the president's whereabouts, the frantic journalist on the other end of the line misunderstood the purpose of the call. It seemed the entire network was in an uproar over Bush having spirited a crew from Fox News Channel to Baghdad.

"We don't know where he is!" the journalist exclaimed. "We have no idea where he is! We're just f---ed!"

At the Crawford Middle School gymnasium, reporters at first didn't believe the booming baritone of CBS radio correspondent Mark Knoller as he read aloud the AP bulletin that Bush was in Baghdad. But in the next moment, pandemonium broke out. Journalists scurried in and out of the gym, hollering, screaming, cursing the realization that they had been hopelessly hoodwinked by the Bush White House.

Knoller later said he realized he had been "filing radio reports that amounted to fiction." "Even as President Bush was addressing U.S. personnel in Baghdad," he added, "I was on the air saying he was at his ranch making holiday phone calls to American troops overseas."

Such reports perplexed Laura Bush, who forgot that there would be a delay of nearly two hours between her husband's visit to the troops and the media's coverage of that visit. All morning in Crawford, she kept checking the TV news stations and wondering what happened to her husband. Finally, she picked up the phone and called the Secret Service command center at Prairie Chapel Ranch.

"Where's the president?" she asked.

"Oh ma'am, he's forty-five minutes away," the Secret Service agent informed her.

Laura realized he was referring to the elder President Bush, who was scheduled to come over for Thanksgiving lunch with his wife Barbara. Laura's in-laws, who did not know about the visit to Baghdad, were driving in from College Station, Texas, site of the elder George Bush's presidential library.

"No, no, I meant *my* George," Laura said to the agent.

"Oh, we've got him in the house, ma'am," replied the agent, unaware that the president had slipped out of the ranch nearly eighteen hours earlier.

Not wishing to blow the secret, Laura feigned forgetfulness. "Oh, yes, that's right," she said. "What am I doing? Thanks."

A short time later, as journalists were frantically calling their Washington editors from aboard Air Force One, the president was calling his wife in Crawford to "let her know I was okay," he told me.

Then Bush walked through the plane, thanking the aides who had pulled it off. After posing for pictures, the group headed into the conference room for a big Thanksgiving dinner of turkey, stuffing, mashed potatoes, and all the trimmings.

Afterward Bartlett went back to the press cabin, where reporters pressed him for some colorful details about the flight. So he told them about the sighting of Air Force One by the pilot with the British accent. Later, the reporters were invited up to front of the plane to talk with the president himself in his office.

"I thank you for honoring the confidentiality necessary to pull this off," he told them. "Thanksgiving has got to be hard for young troops that know that their families are gathered and having dinner and the turkey feast and everything. It's got to be a lonely moment for them.

"I felt like at this point, that it would be hopeful for them to see their president. And I recognize I can't see every troop in harm's way, scattered throughout the region. But the word will get out that I came, thanks to you all."

He added: "I understood the consequences and risks. And over time, I was assured by our planners and, as importantly, our military people and the pilot here, of this airplane, that the risk could be minimized if we kept the trip quiet."

"Was there any point along in your planning for this trip when you said, you know, this might be too risky?" a reporter asked.

"Yeah, all along," Bush said. "I mean, I was the biggest skeptic of all."

"Yes!" grinned Card, who was standing in the doorway.

"We can attest to that," added Rice, who was sitting on a sofa across from the president's desk.

At 4:30 A.M. Eastern Time on Friday, thirty-two hours after it had departed Waco, Air Force One returned to Texas State Technical College Airport. Bush headed back to Prairie Chapel Ranch, fully prepared to regale his father—"41," as he called him—with the story of the Baghdad adventure.

"And sure enough, the guest lights come on, and there's old forty-one wanting to relive every moment of the trip," Bush told me. "So it was a great end."

So great, in fact, that the president's approval ratings spiked by five points. After months of negative news from Iraq, where the insurgents seemed to have the upper hand, Bush had staged an audacious, in-your-face visit that proved Baghdad wasn't completely out of control after all.

"It was a fantastic experience—I'm really glad I did it," the president told me. "I was speaking to troops, not only in the room, but everywhere around the world, it turns out. And it was a good thing to do."

Even the Democratic presidential hopefuls, who had assailed Bush for his dramatic landing on the USS *Lincoln* seven months earlier, generally gave him a pass on the Baghdad visit. Experts at finding something negative in almost everything the president said or did, they instead tipped their hats in grudging admiration of the daring visit.

National media coverage of the visit bordered on adulatory, which gradually began to annoy the smaller universe of reporters who covered the president on a full-time basis. These White House correspondents were irked that Bush had pulled off the stunt in absolute secrecy. It was bad enough that the administration was practically leak-proof on everyday stories about policy and politics. But to deceive the press on an event of this magnitude was adding insult to injury. And so, with the passage of time, reporters found a few nits to pick.

For starters, it turned out the turkey Bush had picked up on a platter had been placed in the chow hall for decorative purposes, which prompted a 900-word expose by Mike Allen, the *Washington Post* reporter who had been part of the pool.

"Bush picked up a decoration, not a serving plate," Allen wrote a full week after the trip. "A contractor had roasted and primped the turkey to adorn the buffet line, while the 600 soldiers were served from cafeteria-style steam trays."

Allen called it a "sign of the many ways the White House maximized the impact" of the visit.

"White House officials do not deny that they craft elaborate events to showcase Bush," Allen intoned. "The foray has opened new credibility questions for a White House that has dealt with issues as small as who placed the 'Mission Accomplished' banner aboard the aircraft carrier."

On the day the story was published, the rest of the press corps assailed White House Press Secretary Scott McClellan over another tempest in a teapot. It turned out that the pilot with the British accent who'd spotted Air Force One over England had actually been flying a German plane in front of the president's plane, not the British Airways jet flying just behind. The press seized on this innocuous mixup as if it were Watergate.

"How could the White House be so wrong?" hyperventilated Norah O'Donnell of NBC. She demanded to know whether the mixup "takes some of the shine off the president's surprise visit to the troops."

A senior White House official who had worked for Bush since the beginning of his presidency happened to be watching this exchange on a TV monitor in the West Wing. He shook his head and muttered to the president: "That is the stupidest thing that I've heard since I've been here."

15
"WE GOT HIM"

"CONGRATULATIONS," THE ELDER PRESIDENT Bush told the younger President Bush. "It's a great day for the country."

"It's a greater day for the Iraqi people," George W. replied.

It was also a great day for this unlikely father-and-son presidential team, whose combined efforts to bring Saddam Hussein to justice had spanned more than a dozen years. After the eight-year interruption of the Clinton Administration, their efforts finally came to fruition at 12:36 P.M. ET on Saturday, December 13, 2003, when U.S. forces pulled the once-mighty dictator of Iraq from a squalid "spider hole" on a farm outside Tikrit.

"I got the call from Donald Rumsfeld Saturday afternoon and made the decision then—until I was more certain about the facts— that I would talk to very few people," Bush said. "Because what I didn't want to have happen is that there would be this rush of enthusiasm and hope, and then all of a sudden it turned out not to be the person that we would hope it would be."

Indeed, there had been plenty of false reports about Saddam's fate since Bush ordered the daring but unsuccessful surgical strike nearly nine months earlier. The dictator went on to elude a second strike, and kept showing up in taped messages designed to incite remnants of his regime. So Bush was not about to share the unconfirmed news of his capture with anyone except Vice President Cheney and Condoleezza Rice, although he did ask Rice to alert Andy Card.

"I didn't talk to my family—I told Laura, of course—and pretty much went to bed early Saturday night," he said. "And Condi woke me at 5:15 in the morning, which was okay this time."

Rice explained that she had just received a call from Paul Bremer. "They were prepared to say this was Saddam Hussein," Bush said, adding that he "got dressed and hustled over to the Oval Office to start making calls. One of the calls I did receive was from my dad. And it was a very brief conversation."

After everything that had transpired, what could the two men say that hadn't been said before? The elder Bush had never second-guessed his decision to leave Saddam in power after the Gulf War, although he was proven wrong about Iraqis being able to overthrow the dictator afterwards. The younger Bush, mindful of his father's unfulfilled wish, had spoken of Saddam in unusually personal terms during the run-up to Operation Iraqi Freedom.

"After all," he said, "this is the guy who tried to kill my dad."

But the president later insisted he took no familial satisfaction in the capture of his father's would-be assassin.

"None," he told me in the Oval Office. "Because I still lived with the death of American soldiers. And I mourn for those deaths. The decision I made is much greater than petty revenge. It's a decision based upon doing my most solemn duty, which is to protect the security of the country."

Shortly after talking with his father, the president watched live TV coverage of a press conference in Baghdad. The first speaker was Bremer, who hadn't lost his dramatic flair in the seventeen days since announcing Bush's Thanksgiving surprise.

"Ladies and gentleman, we got him," he said, prompting jubilant cheers and applause from U.S. officials and Iraqi journalists in the room. "The tyrant is a prisoner."

Bremer then directly addressed the people of Iraq.

"This is a great day in Iraq's history," he said. "For decades, hundreds of thousands of you suffered at the hands of this cruel man. For decades, Saddam Hussein divided you citizens against each other. For decades, he threatened and attacked your neighbors. Those days are over forever."

Moments later, Lieutenant General Ricardo Sanchez took the lectern to explain how the vanquished dictator had made no attempt to use the pistol he was packing when he was apprehended.

"In fact, not a single shot was fired," the general marveled. "Saddam Hussein, the captive, has been talkative and is being cooperative."

Sanchez then narrated a short videotape showing the crude "spider hole" where the ex-palace dweller had been living. The briefing room was silent until the tape showed an image of Saddam himself. Suddenly the Iraqi journalists leapt to their feet and cried out in anguished joy.

"Death to Saddam! Death to Saddam!" several of them screamed in Arabic, punching their fists in the air. Others shouted their thanks to U.S. forces.

But one Iraqi journalist, Fatah al-Sheikh, didn't say a word. Having been tortured for two years by Saddam's henchmen, Sheikh now sobbed uncontrollably as he watched the video of his tormentor being subjected to a medical examination. A U.S. Army medic matter-of-factly stuck a tongue depressor into the gaping mouth of the compliant dictator. Wearing rubber gloves, the American searched for lice in Saddam's unkempt hair and beard, which had grown bushy during his nine months on the lam.

"When I saw Saddam's long beard, how he looked like a defeated man, it reminded me of the two years I spent in jail, how his agents tortured me in every way you could imagine," Sheikh told a Reuters reporter.

Like most Iraqis, Sheikh had been heartened when American forces ousted Saddam's regime in April—but he was unable to feel completely safe without proof of Saddam's death or capture. When proof finally arrived in the form of this video, it was incredibly cathartic. As Sheikh sobbed in the press room, Iraqis across the country poured into the streets to dance with joy and fill the air with celebratory gunfire.

"The capture of Saddam Hussein is a defining moment in the new Iraq," said Sanchez, now showing before-and-after photos to illustrate how the dictator had been ignobly shaven and shorn.

"I expect that the detention of Saddam Hussein will be regarded as the beginning of reconciliation for the people of Iraq—and as a sign of Iraq's rebirth," the general added. "More importantly, this success brings closure to the Iraqi people. We now have final resolution. Saddam Hussein will never return to a position of power, from which he can punish, terrorize, intimidate, and exploit the Iraqi people—as he did for more than thirty-five years."

Sanchez and Bremer had taken four Iraqi officials to see Saddam shortly after his capture. One of them was Adnan Pachachi, acting president of the Iraqi Governing Council, who now approached the lectern to tell reporters about his extraordinary encounter with the fallen tyrant.

"He tried to justify his crimes by saying that he was a just but firm ruler," Pachachi said. "Of course our answer was he was an unjust ruler, responsible for the deaths of thousands of people."

Pachachi also spoke confidently about Iraq's future as a free and democratic state.

"Before the end of June, there will be an Iraqi government with comprehensive sovereignty to rule Iraq with total independence," he said. "I will call upon the Governing Council to declare today as a national day, as a holiday for all Iraqis, to be announced as the official Independence Day of Iraq."

The next day, Bush treated himself to a press conference. He returned to the room where he had faced reporters more than a year earlier, flush with midterm victory and a crucial U.N. resolution. But this time the president allowed himself to express a measure of satisfaction about the day's headlines. In fact, he pretty much called the fallen dictator a coward.

"What is your greeting to him?" a reporter asked.

"Good riddance," Bush shot back. "The world is better off without you, Mr. Saddam Hussein. I find it very interesting that when the heat got on, you dug yourself a hole and you crawled in it. And our brave troops, combined with good intelligence, found you."

He added righteously: "You'll be brought to justice—something you did not afford the people you brutalized in your own country."

Less than a week after Saddam's capture, Libyan leader Moammar Gadhafi abruptly announced he would relinquish his own weapons of mass destruction programs, the existence of which had not been known to the rest of the world. He even gave international weapons inspectors something they had never received from Saddam—unfettered access. The Left tried to portray Libya's dramatic move as the natural culmination of a decade of diplomacy initiated by the Clinton Administration. But Gadhafi had approached U.S. and British intelligence agencies just nine months earlier—at the opening salvo of Operation Iraqi Freedom.

"I will do whatever the Americans want because I saw what happened in Iraq, and I was afraid," Gadhafi told Italian Prime Minister Silvio Berlusconi, according to a Berlusconi spokesman who was quoted in the London *Telegraph*.

This account was not disputed by Vice President Cheney.

"It's no accident that they we were contacted by Colonel Gadhafi to begin those negotiations for him to give up his weapons of mass destruction about the time that we began military operations in Iraq, and that he announced his willingness to follow through and implement such an agreement a few days after we dug out Saddam Hussein out of his spider hole," Cheney said. "It's a direct result of strong U.S. leadership, backed up by U.S. military force."

The exposure of Gadhafi's weapons programs helped uncover a global proliferation network masterminded by a Pakistani scientist named A. Q. Khan, who had been brazenly peddling nuclear technology to Libya, Iran, and North Korea. This led to a major U.S. crackdown on Khan's customers.

"It's a very different profile on counterproliferation than the world has had, which was sort of going with the Nonproliferation Treaty, pretending that the Nonproliferation Treaty was actually working—when, of course, it was working for countries like Japan, but it wasn't doing anything for countries like Iran or Libya," Rice told me. "It's all about credibility, resoluteness, and the willingness to take up action." Indeed, after Saddam's capture, Iran—which had previously refused to cooperate with the International Atomic Energy Agency (IAEA)—suddenly allowed inspections of its own nuclear facilities.

"We're watching history be made," Bush told me. "This is a transforming event. I believe a free Iraq will have an effect on the freedom lovers inside of Iran."

Rice said Iran was equally affected by fears of an attack by the U.S. military.

"When you establish that you're serious about a problem and you're prepared to take tough action, people start to reassess their options," she said.

"That's true for the Iranians, who suddenly thought: Well, maybe the IAEA should come in," she added. "But especially for the Libyans, who I think decided to take advantage at this moment to get out of this business."

Rice insisted that none of these developments would have been possible without the president's stubborn determination to oust Saddam. But she acknowledged that Bush's blunt rhetoric was not always appreciated by the international community. She cited "the 'Axis of Evil' speech, which everybody hated." And yet within two years of coining that phrase to describe Iraq, Iran, and North Korea, Bush had made progress with all three.

"Just look at where we are," Rice enthused. "Massive progress in Iraq. Progress in Iran. Progress in getting the Chinese to take the North Korean threat seriously."

And yet, despite such progress, Bush continued to irritate a number of nations.

"In international politics, he will stake out ground, and then bring others to it—I think that's sometimes hard," Rice explained. "It's dissonant for a world that's accustomed to extremely slow movement. Diplomacy tends to be glacial, and the president is not satisfied with glacial."

While Saddam's capture reverberated around the world, it also had profound ramifications inside Iraq's own borders. Ordinary citizens were no longer terrified that the dictator would somehow regain power. Tipsters flooded coalition forces with intelligence about guerilla activities.

"After Saddam is captured, the insurgency kind of loses heart," Rice said.

One of its main organizers, al Qaeda leader Abu Musab Zarqawi, admitted as much in a letter he wrote to a top lieutenant of bin Laden. The letter was intercepted by U.S. forces just weeks after Saddam's capture.

"Our enemy is growing stronger day after day, and its intelligence information increases," Zarqawi complained. "By god, this is suffocation!"

The Jordanian-born terrorist was particularly peeved that the United States was training and fielding Iraqi security forces. "With the spread of the army and police, our future is becoming frightening," he wrote. He cautioned that if it continued, "we will have to pack our bags and break camp for another land."

In a particularly telling passage, Zarqawi said the gradual American withdrawal would mean that foreign terrorists would be reduced to inciting a sectarian war between Iraq's Sunnis and Shiite Muslims. But the two groups were loath to fight each other, especially after U.S. forces widely distributed the Zarqawi letter.

"That was a very illustrative letter," Bush said, "basically saying, 'this is tough sledding.'"

The document renewed the president's hope that freedom was beginning to take hold in Iraq.

"I truly believe that the Almighty God's gift to every person is freedom," he told me. "And if you believe that, then you must act on that belief, and you must have confidence in that belief.

"And the rebuilding of Iraq is a difficult period because that is being challenged at times. It's being challenged by killers on the ground. It's being challenged by the new politics of Iraq, where people are beginning to show some interest in the process because they think they may be able to win over the other person.

"In other words, it's what happens when you've been suppressed—a bubbling of democracy shows up," he said. "What I'm telling you is I think freedom will prevail, so long as the United States and allies don't give the people of Iraq mixed signals, so long as we don't cower in the face of suiciders, or do what many Iraqis still suspect might happen, and that is cut and run early, like what happened in '91."

It was a reference to his father, who in 1991 stopped short of ousting Saddam and then urged the Kurds and Shiites to "take matters into their own hands and force Saddam Hussein, the dictator, to step aside." When Saddam crushed the uprisings, the elder Bush stayed on the sidelines, fearful that further meddling might lead to a takeover by Islamic fundamentalists.

Now, a dozen years later, the younger Bush was vowing not to "cut and run early." The remark crystallized the difference between him and his father.

"I happen to think they were the right presidents for their times," observed Andy Card, who worked for both men. "They came to office with the same moral character, but with different perspectives of America's problems."

"Forty-one was an extremely important president for the time, managing without bravado or braggadocio—even though there was great temptation," he said. "I remember being in the White House, in the Roosevelt Room, when word came that the wall had been breached in Berlin. I was one of those who got to go into the Oval Office and tell the president the wall came down.

"And his first reaction was: This is not a time for us to be standing on the wall dancing. We have to be very measured in our response to make sure that the world reacts to this change the right way.

"And I was struck by that," Card marveled. "He was trained as a diplomat. He was there to help manage the extremely challenging change in the world when the wall came down and diplomacy had to be practiced in a different way than it has to be practiced today. He was the right president for the right time.

"But this president came from west Texas," Card said of the younger Bush. "And west Texas was his home for a lot longer than it was for the former president.

"He was the governor of Texas; he wasn't the first envoy to China or the U.N. ambassador or the CIA director. His training was dealing with problems on the streets of Laredo or Dallas or Houston or Midland or Austin. This president came with kind of street smarts and recognition of the importance of the resolve of America."

Those traits came in handy after terrorists savaged America on September 11.

"He had to act," Card said. "He preferred to act with allies around the world, but if there were no allies, he still had to act. Because the oath that he took didn't say protect and defend the Constitution of the United States if the U.N. says it's okay or the French say it's okay. It just said protect and defend the Constitution of the United States. So that became the paramount responsibility," Card concluded. "He could not shirk that responsibility that he accepted on behalf of all of us."

16

VIETNAM ELECTION

HAVING SPENT MONTHS BEING savaged by Democrats like John Kerry for failing to find Saddam, Bush now found himself accused of timing the capture to score political points. This bizarre charge was leveled by Representative Jim McDermott of Washington, the Democratic congressman who had gone to Baghdad before the war to say that Bush would lie to the American people in order to justify military action. Now McDermott insisted that U.S. forces could have captured Saddam "a long time ago if they wanted."

Asked by interviewer Dave Ross on KIRO-FM in Seattle whether the capture was timed to help the president, the congressman replied: "Yeah. Oh, yeah. There's too much by happenstance for it to be just a coincidental thing."

Pressed on the point by Ross, McDermott said: "I don't know that it was definitely planned on this weekend, but I know they've been in contact with people all along who knew basically where he was. It was just a matter of time till they'd find him. It's funny, when they're having all this trouble, suddenly they have to roll out something."

The comments earned McDermott the scorn of even some in his own party.

"With all due respect to my colleague, that is a fantasy," Representative Norm Dicks, Washington Democrat, told the Associated Press. "That just is not right. It's one thing to criticize this administration for having done this war. I mean, that's a fair question. But to criticize them on the capture of Saddam, when it's such a big thing to our troops, is just ridiculous."

The next day, former Secretary of State Madeleine Albright floated a new conspiracy theory by suggesting Bush would spring an "October surprise" before the 2004 election.

"Do you suppose that the Bush Administration has Osama bin Laden hidden away somewhere and will bring him out before the election?" the former Clinton cabinet member asked journalist Mort Kondracke while waiting to appear on Fox News Channel.

Kondracke recounted Albright's remark on the air, which prompted a public outcry. Albright then claimed she had been joking, although Kondracke insisted "she was not smiling" at the time. Several witnesses supported Kondracke's version of events.

Not to be outdone, Senator John Kerry came up with his own conspiracy theory. He accused Bush of delaying his announcement of the Libya deal until it could help his reelection bid. "Gadhafi's been trying to get back into the mainstream for several years now. There's evidence that we could've had that deal some time ago," Kerry pooh-poohed. Colin Powell called Kerry's charge "absurd," "offensive" and "political" during an interview with Fox News.

Clearly, leading Democrats viewed Saddam's capture (and attendant national security dividends) not as an historic triumph for America, Iraq, and human liberty, but as an unfortunate political development that redounded to the benefit of the Republican president.

Polls showed Americans believed 2-to-1 that going to war had been the right decision, despite continuing casualties. The frustration was beginning to show on Democratic front-runner Howard Dean, who built his entire candidacy on an uncompromising opposition to the war.

"The capture of Saddam has not made America safer," Dean harumphed.

That improbable claim came shortly after Dean mused aloud whether Bush had advance knowledge of the September 11 attacks. When I asked for the president's reaction at a press conference, he replied: "It's an absurd insinuation."

It was the first time that Bush had directly responded to an attack by a Democratic challenger in the presidential campaign. By contrast, Dean's own Democratic rivals had long ridiculed the front-runner's mounting gaffes. They were given fresh ammunition the following week, when Dean was asked by the *Concord Monitor* in New Hampshire whether Osama bin Laden deserved the death penalty.

"I've resisted pronouncing a sentence before guilt is found," Dean allowed. "I still have this old-fashioned notion that even with people like Osama, who is very likely to be found guilty, we should do our best not to, in positions of executive power, not to prejudge jury trials."

The remark raised grave doubts about Dean's grasp of national security. After all, Osama bin Laden had boasted on videotape about masterminding the September 11 terrorist attacks, saying he was pleasantly surprised at how the World Trade Center towers collapsed for maximum carnage. Bush treated such atrocities as acts of war, not infractions of the criminal code, as Clinton had done. Dean was talking about going back to the old way of fighting terrorists—with subpoenas and indictments instead of missiles and tanks.

Yet the Dean juggernaut rolled on, aided by the coveted endorsement of former Vice President Al Gore, who had opted out of the race a year earlier. By the time caucusgoers gathered in Iowa on January 19,

Dean was enjoying a five-month run as the undisputed front-runner of a crowded and fractured Democratic field.

But then he shocked the political establishment by finishing in third place. Dean compounded his defeat by delivering a disturbing, highly emotional rant that laid bare, once and for all, the frightening face of Bush hatred. Dean's strange, guttural growl grew otherwordly as he angrily spat out the names of states where he would continue to campaign defiantly. He concluded with a bloodcurdling, primal scream that instantly became fodder for late-night comics. Matt Drudge, the most influential journalist in America, summed up the spectacle on his "Drudge Report" website with the headline: "DEAN GOES NUTS!"

Even Bush weighed in on the meltdown.

"Boy, that speech in Iowa was something else," he said during a stand-up routine at the Alfalfa Club dinner in Washington. "Talk about shock and awe. Saddam Hussein felt so bad for Governor Dean that he offered him his hole."

One month later, after losing all seventeen states in which he competed, the humiliated candidate withdrew from the race. Drudge's prophetic headline was then confirmed by one of Dean's most influential supporters, union boss Gerald McEntee.

"I think he's nuts," the president of the American Federation of State, County and Municipal Employees (AFSCME) told the *New York Times*.

Karl Rove, the president's top political strategist, said he was not surprised by Dean's outburst, which pundits dubbed the "I Have a Scream" speech. "That was not the first night he had a screed," Rove told me.

He cited Dean's speech to the California Democratic Convention in Sacramento on March 15, 2003. "We want our country back!" Dean had thundered, drawing cheers from the party faithful. "I'm tired of being divided! I don't want to listen to the fundamentalist preachers anymore! I want America to look like America, where we are all included, hand in hand, walking down! We have a dream! We can only reach the dream if we are all together—black and white, gay and straight, man and woman! America! The Democratic Party! We are going to win in 2004!"

I asked Rove if he considered the California speech as bad as the Iowa meltdown ten months later.

"Worse, worse, absolutely worse," he told me. "In fact, we tested the dang thing. The peroration at the end is, like, twenty-seven seconds long, so you can use it for television spots. And you just show it to people without any commentary," he added. "We showed it to people and Democrats would say: 'Why does he hate gay people?' And it was because he was just so angry.

"And yet read how the press wrote it up: 'Dean energized them; took the campaign to a new level,'" Rove concluded. "What it tells us is, the press misses it."

Dean's demise, widely considered the most spectacular political flameout in American politics in at least half a century, paved the way for the emergence of John Kerry, who just weeks earlier had been trailing even the unelectable Reverend Al Sharpton in a poll by the *New York Times*. Kerry's sudden surge into front-runner status stirred hope among Democrats that the party would finally be able to counter Bush's formidable credentials on defense and national security. After all, Kerry had earned Silver and Bronze stars and three Purple Hearts in Vietnam.

The press, fresh from erroneously equating both Afghanistan and Iraq to Vietnam, rejoiced in the selection of a bona fide Vietnam war hero as the presumptive Democratic nominee. Kerry's ascension allowed journalists not only to resume their fixation with Vietnam, but to attempt something much more ambitious—the morphing of the 2004 presidential election into some tortured referendum on a thirty-year-old conflict. Left-wing filmmaker Michael Moore got the ball rolling by denouncing the president as a "deserter." This was a reference to unconfirmed reports that Bush had failed to report for some of his duties after transferring from the Texas Air National Guard to its Alabama counterpart in the early 1970s. On February 1, Democratic National Committee Chairman Terry McAuliffe upped the rhetorical ante by accusing Bush of having been "AWOL," or absent without official leave, a felony.

"George Bush never served in our military in our country," McAuliffe told ABC News. "I look forward to that debate with John Kerry, a war hero with a chest full of medals, standing next to George Bush, a man who was AWOL."

When Republicans countered that Bush had received an honorable discharge, Kerry was not impressed.

"Was he present and active on duty in Alabama at the times he was supposed to be?" he demanded. "Just because you get an honorable discharge does not, in fact, answer that question."

Kerry's eagerness to play up his Vietnam record while challenging Bush's military service was a dramatic departure from his rhetoric of a dozen years earlier. In 1992 he had taken the opposite argument in order to defend Bill Clinton, whose evasion of the draft was being criticized by Democratic presidential rival Senator Bob Kerrey of Nebraska, himself a Vietnam veteran.

"I am saddened by the fact that Vietnam has yet again been inserted into the campaign," Kerry said on the Senate floor. "Leadership requires that one help heal the wounds of Vietnam, not reopen them."

He added: "We do not need to divide America over who served and how."

So when Kerry reversed course in 2004 by demanding to know exactly how Bush had served, conservatives started looking more closely at the Democrat's post-Vietnam record. As a result, Americans soon learned that Kerry had made some controversial remarks just after returning from Vietnam, during his first run for Congress.

"I'm an internationalist," Kerry told the *Harvard Crimson* in February 1970. "I'd like to see our troops dispersed through the world only at the directive of the United Nations." He added that he wanted "to almost eliminate CIA activity."

After losing his congressional bid, Kerry became a spokesman for the radical leftist group Vietnam Veterans Against the War (VVAW). The organization was bankrolled in part by actress Jane Fonda, later nicknamed "Hanoi Jane" for her infamous visit to North Vietnam. In early 1971, Fonda sponsored the "Winter Soldier Investigation" at a Howard Johnsons in Detroit, where VVAW members heard "testimony" about "war crimes" by disaffected veterans.

"They relived the absolute horror of what this country, in a sense, made them do," Kerry told the Senate Foreign Relations Committee in April of that year. "They told stories that at times they had personally raped, cut off ears, cut off heads, taped wires from portable telephones to human genitals and turned up the power, cut off limbs, blown up bodies, randomly shot at civilians, razed villages in fashion reminiscent of Ghengis Khan, shot cattle and dogs for fun, poisoned food stocks, and generally ravaged the countryside of South Vietnam."

Although Kerry would later admit that he never actually witnessed atrocities, the ex-lieutenant told the Senate committee: "These were not isolated incidents but crimes committed on a day-to-day basis with the full awareness of officers at all levels of command."

That same day, at an antiwar rally, Kerry made a show of throwing what journalists assumed were his medals over a barricade in front of the U.S. Capitol. It later was revealed that he had actually thrown the medals of a fellow veteran while retaining his own, which were still displayed in his Senate office a third of a century later.

In 1972, Kerry wrote an antiwar book entitled *The New Soldier*. Its cover photo showed a scrum of long-haired men irreverently manhandling the American flag, which was flying upside down. The idea was to mock the legendary photo of U.S. Marines raising Old Glory at Iwo Jima.

When these and other unflattering stories began to surface in February 2004, Kerry claimed he was being personally maligned by the president. On February 21, the man who had once railed against dragging Vietnam into politics actually challenged Bush to a debate on Vietnam.

"Over the last week, you and your campaign have initiated a widespread attack on my service in Vietnam, my decision to speak out to end that war, and my commitment to the defense of this nation," Kerry wrote in a letter to the president that he shared with the press.

"As you well know, Vietnam was a very difficult and painful period in our nation's history, and the struggle for our veterans continues. So it has been hard to believe that you would choose to reopen these wounds for your personal political gain. But, that is what you have chosen to do.

"I will not sit back and allow my patriotism to be challenged," he wrote. "America deserves a better debate. If you want to debate the Vietnam era, and the impact of our experiences on our approaches to presidential leadership, I am prepared to do so."

Bush ignored the challenge, instead highlighting Kerry's long record of voting to cut defense and intelligence funding. Republicans also noted that when it came to prosecuting the war against terrorism, Kerry sounded a lot like Dean. In early 2004, the Massachusetts Democrat said the titanic struggle should be "primarily a law-enforcement and intelligence operation" and only "occasionally military."

Such comments astonished and delighted Rove, who insisted that Kerry brought such scrutiny upon himself by assailing the president's national security credentials in the first place. "He backpedaled from the AWOL thing," Rove said of Kerry. "He began to distance himself from that because at some level he realized, or the people around him realized: Hey, this is backfiring."

However, Kerry refused to back away from his effort to make the election about Vietnam.

"He's blatant about it," Rove told me. "He says: Our Democratic

Party has appeared weak on defense and I can deal with that by demonstrating that I was a war hero in Vietnam—which he was. I mean, the guy served with honor."

But Rove added: "This is a guy who opposed every major weapons system we used to win the war on terror. This is a guy who after we were struck in '93 at the World Trade Center bombing said: Let's cut the intel budget. This is a guy who says the war on terror is primarily a law enforcement and intelligence matter. It ain't. It's a war."

Rice explained that the barbarity of the September 11 attacks fundamentally altered America's response to terrorism.

"You can do one of two things," she told me. "You can go back to treating it like it's just your basic law enforcement problem. And maybe you can go bomb Afghanistan a little bit.

"Or you can decide: Okay, this is the true battle. We have to mobilize this country for a struggle against an extremist jihadist that wants to bring down civilization.

"Now, when you decide that it's that, then you can't worry about the headline that says: Did you underestimate electrical supply in Baghdad?" she added with a shrug. "Maybe you did."

Kerry's greatest vulnerability, according to Republicans, was his inconsistency on major policy issues. They pointed out that he voted against the 1990 Gulf War resolution, even though Saddam had invaded Kuwait. A dozen years later, however, when Saddam wasn't even contemplating such an invasion, Kerry voted in favor of war. He then proceeded to rail against that war and even voted against Bush's request for $87 billion to pay for reconstruction and security in Iraq and Afghanistan. Much of that money was earmarked for desperately needed armor to protect American troops in Iraq.

"I actually did vote for the $87 billion before I voted against it," Kerry explained, which merely gave the president further occasion to ridicule him as a flip-flopper.

There were other inconsistencies in Kerry's record, which the president began to highlight in a February 23 speech to the Republican Governors Association.

"For tax cuts, and against them. For NAFTA, and against NAFTA. For the Patriot Act, and against the Patriot Act. In favor of liberating Iraq, and opposed to it," Bush said. "And that's just one senator from Massachusetts."

The governors roared with laughter, which helped convince Bush that his attacks on Kerry should be leavened with humor whenever possible. The president was betting that optimism and humor would prevail over the seething resentments of the Bush haters.

"Our opponents have not offered much in the way of strategies to win the war, or policies to expand our economy," he told the Republicans. "So far, all we hear is a lot of old bitterness and partisan anger. Anger is not an agenda for the future of America."

Republicans relished pointing out that Kerry was a strident Massachusetts liberal who once served as lieutenant governor to Michael Dukakis. On February 28, the *National Journal* ranked Kerry as "the most liberal senator in 2003, with a composite liberal score of 96.5." Remarkably, the Democratic Party had selected someone to the left of both Ted Kennedy and Hillary Rodham Clinton.

Still, some Democrats never forgave Kerry for authorizing Operation Iraqi Freedom. While defending the vote to *Rolling Stone,* he exclaimed: "Did I expect George Bush to f—— it up as badly as he did? I don't think anybody did."

I asked Bush to respond to Kerry's description of the anti-Saddam coalition—which included Great Britain, Australia, and Poland—as "some trumped-up, so-called coalition of the bribed, the coerced, the bought, and the extorted."

"Yes, well sometimes people say some things they regret," the president told me. "In the course of a campaign, there will be great scrutiny of people's words. I'm sure that is the kind of quote that will eventually be in the public arena. We'll let the American people decide whether or not it has any merit."

As for the media's willingness to turn the election into a referendum on Vietnam, Bush merely shrugged. Having waged two successful wars that were prematurely and erroneously equated with Vietnam, the president was accustomed to this peculiar press obsession.

"That's an inevitable part of this culture we're in, which is there's a lot of writers that remembered Vietnam and were legitimately concerned that the nation would get bogged down in another Vietnam," he said. "On the other hand, I've got a different perspective."

The president vowed never to repeat the central blunder of Vietnam-era politicians—trying to micromanage military operations.

"I'm talking to our commanders, who bring great expertise, and unlike Vietnam, I'm not going to be making military decisions unless asked," he explained. "I made a military decision on the first shot of the war, but I was asked to make that. In the meantime, I'm checking whether or not the plans are going well."

Indeed, Bush had been so hands-off when it came to the military tactics of Operation Iraqi Freedom that he deferred to Tommy Franks about whether to begin with air strikes or a land assault. Although Bush wanted civilian casualties kept to a minimum, he refused to curb the Pentagon's quest for decisive force.

"I want 'decisive,'" Colin Powell told me. "Why wouldn't you want 'decisive'? You want to go in with indecisive force? If you can gang up on somebody, don't you gang up on somebody? Why do we buy all this stuff?"

Himself a Vietnam veteran, Powell was dismissive of the media's preoccupation with the conflict.

"The press is fixated on Vietnam," he said. "Everybody says Powell and all those generals still suffer from Vietnam Syndrome. No, I don't."

He called the media's use of the Vietnam template "an incorrect characterization of the thinking within the U.S. military. I think the press is more sycophantic with respect to Vietnam than any general I've ever served with."

Card, another veteran, agreed.

"I don't think the press learned as much by what happened in Vietnam as the government did," he told me. "There were tremendous mistakes made in governance around Vietnam, and those mistakes have not been repeated. They were not repeated in Grenada; they were not repeated in Panama; they were not repeated in the first Gulf War; they were not repeated in Afghanistan; and they're not repeated in Iraq.

"And that's because the people who are governing learned from what wasn't done well in Vietnam—starting with political leadership making tactical decisions of war. You let the military take charge. You respect the chain of command. And this president understands that."

He added: "The media, in my opinion, kind of wants to relive the Vietnam experience, where it was less about what worked and what didn't work, [and more about] what was fun to cover. So it's more about the story and less about the actions."

No one in the White House understood this better than Rice, the former provost of Stanford University. Rice was convinced most Americans did not share the media's view of Vietnam as some mystical "open wound."

"I don't think there's an open wound for the country," she told me. "I think the country has moved on." The Left, on the other hand, seemed stuck in place. "I come out of the university," she said, "and look, for the intelligentsia, there's still an open wound about Vietnam. It's a huge deal, and it's like it's unresolved still. I see it in my colleagues at Stanford. I see it in the press. It's just unreconciled."

To liberals, she explained, Vietnam came to symbolize more than just an unsuccessful military venture.

"For people of that generation," she said, "it became the lodestar for the questioning of authority. And authority was never to be trusted again. And so whenever people say 'Vietnam,' what they mean is 'authority is not to be trusted.' " Because the government had "lied about the Gulf of Tonkin, they must be lying about weapons of mass destruction in Iraq. Despite the fact that every reasonable person who knew anything about Iraq said there were weapons of mass destruction there," Rice added.

So as winter 2004 gave way to spring, the Left kept harping on missing weapons, lingering violence, and Kerry's Vietnam bona fides—all of which served to keep national security at the forefront of the campaign. And yet poll after poll showed most voters trusted Republicans over Democrats on national security. Liberals seemed to be repeating the mistake they had made during the midterm elections. Even when they managed to wrest the conversation over to the economy, it was no longer such an easy issue to demagogue. In the seventeen months since Daschle had accused Bush of botching the economy in 2002, the Dow Jones Industrial Average rose a staggering 45 percent. In fact, the entire economy was booming in the wake of the president's aggressive tax cuts, which he enacted with nearly annual regularity. Having inherited a recession from Clinton, Bush was now boasting more than two years of economic growth, including the largest quarterly GDP jump in nearly two decades.

Meanwhile, the president turned to second-tier issues to cement his reputation as a "compassionate conservative." To satisfy the "compassionate" portion of his constituency, he pushed through a prescription drug entitlement for senior citizens as part of a major overhaul of Medicare. He also relaxed U.S. prosecution of illegal immigrants from Mexico, which infuriated many law-and-order conservatives.

"He is a compassionate conservative, and sometimes his compassion runs up against the old biases of some of the conservatives," Card told me. "So I think the conflict between a compassionate Republican and a conservative Republican invited a little bit of clash."

To pacify the right wing, Bush waded into the culture wars. He signed a ban on partial-birth abortion and called for a constitutional amendment banning homosexual marriages. The political dividends were substantial.

"Our party is more united in this cycle than most times," Card said.

He spoke from experience, having witnessed firsthand the elder President Bush's failed reelection campaign a dozen years earlier.

"In '92, Pat Buchanan was out there, stirring the pot," Card recalled. "He got 37, 38 percent of the vote in New Hampshire, and created a climate that attracted Ross Perot. We do not have that."

Indeed, the lack of a primary challenger allowed the younger President Bush to concentrate on the Democratic opposition. He resolved to cast the election as a stark choice between two profoundly different sets of priorities.

"You make it about big issues," Rove said when I asked him how Bush planned to beat Kerry. "The president is right on the war on terror; Kerry is fundamentally wrong. The president is right on what's necessary to keep the economy gaining strength and creating jobs; Kerry's wrong. The president's right on where the country is with regard to values; Kerry's fundamentally wrong."

Rove said he planned to portray the candidates as "two men who have a fundamentally different attitude." This entailed framing Bush as a rugged individualist and Kerry as a condescending elitist.

"One guy who comes from Midland, Texas. You know: The sky's the limit. I trust you, not the government. I respect the individual," Rove said. "And another guy who says: Hey, I'm better than you. I know better than you. The government knows better than you."

Perhaps no one in the Bush White House knew Kerry better than Card, a native of Massachusetts who once served in the state's legislature.

"Senator Kerry is someone who has aspired to be in politics and to run for president, I believe, ever since he was at St. Paul's in Concord, New Hampshire," said Card, referring to the elite prep school. According to Card, the word among Kerry's contemporaries even in those days was that "he wants to be JFK. So I guess I'm not surprised that he is kind of in the wannabe mode."

Nor was Card impressed by Kerry's political accomplishments.

"He's not as successful as some of the other politicians that I know from Massachusetts. He didn't always have as much stick-to-it-iveness in some of his missions as others did.

"He took advantage of political opportunities—I don't fault anyone for doing that. He was lieutenant governor and abandoned that to be able to run for the Senate.

"He's got a record that reflects very liberal-leaning Massachusetts tendencies," Card concluded. "And I don't think that is what most people across the country want as the direction the country should be headed in."

Furthermore, Kerry was beginning to exhibit a penchant for gaffes that recalled the failed candidacy of Howard Dean. Not realizing his microphone was on while working a rope line in Chicago, he derided the Bush team in unusually strident terms. "These guys are the most crooked, you know, lying group I've ever seen. It's scary," he said in March.

That same month, while snowboarding in Idaho, Kerry tumbled into the powder after colliding with his Secret Service agent. When a reporter asked him about falling down, Kerry lost his cool. "I don't fall down," he snapped. "The son of a bitch knocked me over." Having cursed out the man sworn to take a bullet for him, Kerry proceeded to fall down six more times all by himself.

But perhaps the worst gaffe of all came when Kerry told a group of donors in Florida: "I've met more leaders who can't go out and say this publicly, but boy, they look at you and say, 'You've got to win this, you've got to beat this guy, we need a new policy.'" When Bush called on him to identify these leaders, Kerry refused, prompting Republicans to lampoon him as an "international man of mystery." The controversy raged for weeks, but Kerry still refused to name the foreign leaders. His position deteriorated even further when he began to receive unsolicited endorsements from foreign leaders like the communist dictator of North Korea, the socialist prime minister-elect of Spain, and the anti-semitic ex-dictator of Malaysia. Vice President Cheney railed: "American voters are the ones charged with determining the outcome of this election, not unnamed foreign leaders." The next day, Kerry did an about-face and issued the following statement through his foreign policy adviser, Rand Beers: "This election will be decided by the American people, and the American people alone. It is simply not appropriate for any foreign leader to endorse a candidate in America's presidential election. John Kerry does not seek, and will not accept, any such endorsements."

Kerry's larger problem stemmed from his seeming inability to inspire passionate support among Democrats, many of whom had lost their inspiration when Dean flamed out. While most Republicans were genuinely enthusiastic about Bush, many Democrats seemed to view Kerry as simply their best hope of ousting the president. Blinded by Bush hatred, the Democrats chose a generic nominee who utterly failed to excite their imaginations with a positive vision for America.

During my final interview with Bush in the Oval Office for this book, I asked him directly: "Why do you deserve a second term?"

"I deserve a second term because, first, I've showed the American people I'm capable of handling tough times," he said. "The thing about the presidency is you never know what's going to be around the corner, and you'd better have a president who is capable of making decisions when times do get tough.

"And secondly, we're changing the world. Let me rephrase that: The world is changing, and we're helping to change it. And there's still a lot of unresolved issues regarding the security of the United States and peace of the world: North Korea. Iran. We've got to make sure that the Libyan initiative is fulfilled. It's essential that the Iraqi people hear a message that 'America will stay with you as you develop a free country.' Same in Afghanistan."

The president also seemed determined not to repeat his father's mistake of seeming to focus too much on foreign affairs.

"At home, this economy must continue to grow in order to achieve a lot of national objectives," he said. "And there is a big difference of opinion on this issue.

"Some will raise taxes in order to feed the appetite of the federal government," he added. "I think we need to make the tax cuts I passed permanent."

Bush was mindful of his father's disastrous decision to break his "no new taxes" pledge.

"This president learned from the 1992 campaign," Card said. "He learned a lot while feeling great pain, because he did not like what was happening to his dad.

"I know his dad observes very closely what is happening today, just as the son observed very closely what was happening to his dad in 1992," he added. "So I think there is a high degree of empathy—not just sympathy—but a high degree of empathy from both of them."

Indeed, the lessons from the 1992 campaign were seared into the younger Bush.

"He learned not to allow himself to be so far removed from the campaign that he isn't able to allow his instincts to have an impact on how the campaign is run," Card said. "So I think he's more closely engaged as the strategy is discussed and considered.

"He is not bound by the beltway mentality," he added. "It's pretty remarkable that you can have an incumbent president running for re-election who is not an insider. In fact, the Democratic challenger is likely to be the insider."

Finally, the younger president was determined not to fall prey to complacency. "Nothing will be taken for granted," Card vowed. "This president learned by what happened in 1992 and we are better positioned and we are cognizant of the challenge."

Having also learned from his success in the 2002 midterms, Bush decided to ignore those who advised him once again to adopt a Rose Garden strategy, keeping himself above the fray as long as possible. Instead, he began attacking Kerry by name a full eight months before the election, racing to define him as a tax-raising, flip-flopping, liberal opportunist who was soft on terrorism and on the wrong side of the culture wars. By mid-March, Republicans had launched an extraordinarily aggressive series of coordinated attacks by the Bush campaign, Republican National Committee, and White House, unleashing an army of high-profile surrogates and an avalanche of well-finance TV advertising.

On March 20, Bush headlined his first official campaign rally in Orlando, where he reminded voters of the enormous ramifications of his looming showdown with Kerry.

"Great events will turn on this election. The man who sits in the Oval Office will set the course of the war on terror and the direction of our economy. The security and prosperity of America are at stake," he said.

"For all Americans, these years in our history will always stand apart. There are quiet times in the life of a nation and when little is expected of the leaders. This is not one of those times."

Bush knew that not even Kerry could deny the transformative effect of September 11 on the presidency and the nation.

"None of us will ever forget that week when one era ended and another began," Bush said. "On September the 14th, 2001, I stood in the ruins at the Twin Towers. I'll never forget that day. One guy pointed at me and said, 'Don't let me down.' Workers in hard hats were shouting, 'Whatever it takes.' And as we all did that day, these men and women searching through the rubble took it personally.

"I took it personally," he concluded. "I have a responsibility that goes on. I will never relent in bringing justice to our enemies. I will defend the security of America, whatever it takes."

While the president pressed forward with his campaign, he hoped Kerry would make the same mistake that Gore and his Democratic supporters had made four years earlier.

"They misunderestimated me," Bush had said on November 6, 2000, the day before the election that would make him the 43rd president of the United States.

The president and his top advisers would laugh about this quintessential malapropism for years. The word neatly summed up the success of George W. Bush, who was simultaneously misunderstood and underestimated by terrorists, Democrats, and the press. In fact, by early 2004, the geopolitical landscape was littered with vanquished figures who had made the mistake of misunderestimating George W. Bush. The body count was considerable.

In the Middle East, Saddam Hussein, who had once derided Bush as "the son of the snake," was rotting in jail. His only sons, Uday and Qusay, once widely expected to be Iraq's future rulers, were dead. Of the U.S. military's fifty-five most-wanted Iraqis, forty-four had been killed or apprehended. So were two-thirds of al Qaeda's top operatives around the globe. Abu Abbas, the Palestinian terrorist who had been sheltered by Saddam, was captured five days after the fall of Baghdad and later died in U.S. custody. Libyan leader Moammar Gadhafi, frightened by the opening salvo in Operation Iraqi Freedom, had relinquished his own weapons of mass destruction. Iran had agreed to allow nuclear inspections. Pakistan's unauthorized export of nuclear secrets had been scuttled. Saudi Arabia was planning free elections.

In Europe, "Gorgeous George" Galloway had been kicked out of the Labour Party. German Justice Minister Herta Daeubler-Gmelin, who had compared Bush to Hitler, was fired. Germany, France, and Russia were excluded by Bush from lucrative reconstruction contracts in postwar Iraq, even as they acquiesced to American pressure to forgive Iraq's debts.

The United Nations, after being shamed into passing resolution 1441, ended up proving itself the feckless "debating society" that Bush had warned against at the outset. Its corrupt oil-for-food program was now a burgeoning international scandal. Even Secretary-General Kofi Annan was forced to admit the need for a massive, high-level investigation.

In the United States, the Democratic Party was in disarray. Representative Richard Gephardt, who ran for president by denouncing Bush as a "miserable failure," finished a miserable fourth in Iowa, a state he had won sixteen years earlier. Since Bush's midterm triumph had already blocked Gephardt's ascension to speaker of the House, the Missouri Democrat quit politics altogether. Howard Dean, once considered all but certain to win the Democratic presidential nomination, had become a political punch line, mired in debt after squandering a $40 million war chest. Al Gore, whose endorsement of Dean had sparked talk of a secretary of state appointment, now lost all political relevance. To make matters worse, by endorsing Dean, Gore had forsaken his own former running mate, Connecticut Senator Joe Lieberman, who also failed to wrest the presidency from the man he claimed had stolen it. Meanwhile, Bill Clinton's support for Democrats had proven disastrous in both the midterms and the subsequent recall drive in California—which resulted in the ouster of Democratic Governor Gray Davis and election of Republican Arnold Schwarzenegger. Clinton's handpicked chairman of the Democratic National Committee, Terry McAuliffe, had overseen far more defeats than victories since taking office, and was likely to lose his own job if he failed to finally deliver in November 2004. Day after day, McAuliffe and the rest of the Democratic Party had to live with the depressing reality that Republicans, led by George W. Bush, controlled American government at every level—the White House, the Senate, the House of Representatives, the governorships and state legislatures. Even when Senate Democrats managed to block a handful of the president's nominees to federal courts, Bush installed them through recess appointments. As for the Supreme Court—where several elderly justices were expected to retire—the president was poised to make appointments that would shape landmark court decisions for a generation of Americans.

The president was also besting the media. Liberal editor Howell Raines, who had used the ostensibly objective news pages of the *New York Times* to crusade against the war, was unceremoniously fired in the wake of the humiliating Jayson Blair plagiarism scandal. Peter Arnett, the NBC correspondent who gave aid and comfort to the enemy, was also dismissed in disgrace. CNN, the liberal network whose top news executive, Eason Jordan, covered up Saddam's crimes, continued to lose market share to Fox News Channel, which had risen to dominance during the Bush era. The BBC, which had accused Tony Blair of having "sexed up" prewar intelligence on Iraq, was forced to apologize after Lord Hutton concluded the only thing sexed up was the network's own reporting. The castigated reporter, Andrew Gilligan, was forced to resign, along with the BBC's editor-in-chief, Greg Dyke, and chairman of the board of governors, Gavyn Davies. It was the most humiliating journalistic debacle in the seventy-eight-year history of the vaunted network. Even Helen Thomas, the liberal doyenne of the White House press corps, lost her coveted front row seat and chance to grill the president at press conferences.

"I think that anybody who misunderestimates this president is going to have egg on their face in a few years," Rice told me. "People ought to go back and look at Harry Truman, because that's another president who was misunderestimated."

Democratic Yale historian John Lewis Gaddis agreed.

"There certainly has been a tendency to underestimate Bush himself and to view him in the way that Reagan was viewed when he first came in—as being a cypher, manipulated by his own advisers," Gaddis told me. "That turned out not to be true of Reagan and it's turning out not to be true of Bush as well."

In March 2004, Gaddis published *Surprise, Security, and the American Experience,* a book that credited Bush with instituting one of only three "grand strategies" in U.S. history by trading in the doctrine of containment for preemption.

"The Bush team really did, in a moment of crisis, come up with a very important statement on grand strategy, which has not been taken as seriously as it should have been taken, particularly within the academic community," the eminent historian told me. "The academic world is of course predominately liberal, predominately Democratic, so there is a predisposition to be less critical of a Democratic administration than there is a Republican administration."

Gaddis explained that America's three grand strategies were instituted by Bush, John Quincy Adams, and Franklin Delano Roosevelt. All three strategies were prompted by rare, catastophic attacks on American soil by foreign enemies.

In 1814, after the British burned the White House, Secretary of State Adams resolved to secure America through expansionism, a grand strategy that endured for a century.

In 1941, after the Japanese attacked Pearl Harbor and the United States responded by winning World War II, Roosevelt and his successors went about securing America through a grand strategy that came to be known as containment. But that strategy became obsolete when the Cold War ended shortly before Clinton took office.

"The Clinton administration was somewhat like the Harding and Coolidge administrations after World War I," Gaddis said. "There was the sense that the war had been won, the fundamental processes in world politics were favorable to us, and therefore you could just kind of sit back and let them run."

But the processes of globalization and self-determination during the Clinton era did nothing to stop terrorists from using minimal resources to inflict massive death and destruction against the U.S. and her interests. The former president did not act decisively to head off this gathering threat, Gaddis said. "It just seems to me that any good strategist would be unwise to sit back and assume that things are going our way," he said. "You ought to be thinking through how what appear to be favorable trends can produce backlashes."

Such a backlash occurred on September 11, necessitating a new grand strategy that was implemented by Bush. The strategy entailed preemption, an aggressive push to democratize the Middle East, and an unwillingness to be constrained by international organizations like the United Nations. While Gaddis faulted the president for not gathering sufficient international support before the invasion of Iraq and underestimating the challenges of postwar Iraq, he concluded that Operation Iraqi Freedom was both necessary and just.

But it might not have occurred if someone other than George W. Bush had been president, according to Rice.

"Go back and you ask yourself: What could have been the responses to 9-11?" Rice said. "They could have been a lot less surefooted. And most importantly, they could have been a lot less transformative of what America was trying to do in the world. And that would have been wrong."

And yet even after Bush's response to September 11, his liberation of fifty million innocents in Afghanistan and Iraq, his resuscitation of a moribund U.S. economy, the misunderestimaters persisted. They were typified by Richard Cohen of the *Washington Post,* who concluded a February 2004 column by describing the president as a "dope."

Secretary of State Colin Powell warned against such dismissiveness by the president's detractors.

"I'd advise them to get smart," Powell told me. "They keep grinding their teeth over his syntax or his not spending enough time on this or that. But he prevails. And they ought to look at his track record as opposed to these secondary features and characteristics, which don't reflect the man."

Powell said the president's penchant for encouraging low expectations "shows how wise he is. Because if you have something that people consider a weakness, you can use that weakness to your advantage—if it isn't really a weakness."

Even Bush referred to himself as "the master of low expectations."

"People tend to discount my ability to get things done, and that's exactly what I want," he told me. "I want people to underestimate.

"I don't know why people do that. Maybe it's because of the philosophy I believe in, and maybe it's where I'm from," he added. "In this town people discredit, in some ways, my philosophy, which I understand. On the other hand, the best way to bring credit to the philosophy is to set big goals and achieve big things for the country."

Bush recalled a discussion he held with Japanese Prime Minister Junichiro Koizumi in Tokyo about how to handle North Korean dictator Kim Jong-Il.

"And during the course of the conversation, I'm reflecting: What if America had blown the peace with Japan?" Bush told me. "I would not have been sitting with the Japanese prime minister, talking about a common problem."

This epiphany occurred in October 2003, during America's long, bloody struggle to restore order in postwar Iraq. "And it dawned on me that at some point in time, when this goes well—and there will be agonizing moments, and there will be tough moments to get to where we need to get—some American president fifty years from now will be sitting down with an Iraqi leader, worrying about how to deal with a common threat," Bush marveled. "Not only how to deal with it, but how to strategize and how to work in common for peace."

Rice put it this way: "It is a hallmark of this president that he does not intend to leave the world the way he found it. He intends to be bold in doing things, even if they're hard."

As I neared the end of my talks with Bush, I reminded him of his words on Ellis Island on the first anniversary of September 11: "I believe there is a reason that history has matched this nation with this time." Now I wondered whether history had also matched this time with this presidency.

"You're asking me to gauge my position in history," he protested. "But you and I aren't going to be around to see the effects of some of the big decisions I've made."

He added: "I view myself right now as planting seeds of freedom. If I set big goals, like I will continue to do, I'll never see the true history that this administration will have made."

It was a polite way of explaining that my question was unanswerable.

"This is an historic time," the president allowed. "I mean, this is an opportunity to act in motion a series of events that will make future presidents more able to deal with the security of this country."

Mindful that he wouldn't be setting events into motion much longer unless he won a second term, Bush prepared to bet everything on his strongest suit of all.

"I'm not afraid to lead," he said. "I'll make tough decisions and I'll stick with them—that's my nature.

"I'm not here forever," he added. "I'm here for a short period of time. And I want to make a difference."

In the end, Bush figured the best way to make that difference was to continue battling tyrants like Saddam Hussein, political opponents like John Kerry, and liberal institutions like the American press. As for his legacy, the misunderestimated president was content to let future generations sort it out.

"What's important, Bill, in this job, is to stay steady in the midst of turbulence, and to stay focused even when there's fog," concluded George W. Bush. "And I believe what I've told you is going to be true, that they'll look back and say: This was a historic moment, when the United States of America, and others, helped start to change the world—in places where there needs to be change—by introducing the concept of freedom."

ACKNOWLEDGMENTS

People sometimes ask me how I can write books in a house with five teenage children. Truth be told, I don't know how I could do it without them. Brittany, Brooke, Ben, Billy, and Blair were unwaveringly supportive as I wrote *Misunderestimated.* So was my spectacular wife, Becky, who, as usual, kept the family on task with an abundance of love and good humor. I appreciate the support and flexibility of everyone at the *Washington Times,* especially publisher Douglas Joo, editor-in-chief Wes Pruden, managing editor Fran Coombs, national editor Ken Hanner, and fellow White House correspondents Joe Curl and Jim Lakely. A special thanks to Roger Ailes, Brit Hume, Kim Hume, and all my friends at Fox New Channel. Enormous credit goes to publisher Judith Regan for championing this book and editor Cal Morgan for guiding it to publication. Lastly, this project would not have been possible without the generous cooperation of President Bush and many members of his administration, especially Secretary of State Colin Powell, National Security Adviser Condoleezza Rice, political adviser Karl Rove, and White House Chief of Staff Andy Card.